The Prime Minister in a Shrinking World

The Prime Minister in a Shrinking World

RICHARD ROSE

Polity

Copyright © Richard Rose 2001

The right of Richard Rose to be identified as author of this work has been asserted in accordance with the Copyright, Designs and Patents Act 1988.

First published in 2001 by Polity Press in association with Blackwell Publishers Ltd

Editorial office:
Polity Press
65 Bridge Street
Cambridge CB2 1UR, UK

Marketing and production:
Blackwell Publishers Ltd
108 Cowley Road
Oxford OX4 1JF, UK

Published in the USA by
Blackwell Publishers Inc.
350 Main Street
Malden, MA 02148, USA

All rights reserved. Except for the quotation of short passages for the purposes of criticism and review, no part of this publication may be reproduced, stored in a retrieval system, or transmitted, in any form or by any means, electronic, mechanical, photocopying, recording or otherwise, without the prior permission of the publisher.

Except in the United States of America, this book is sold subject to the condition that it shall not, by way of trade or otherwise, be lent, re-sold, hired out, or otherwise circulated without the publisher's prior consent in any form of binding or cover other than that in which it is published and without a similar condition including this condition being imposed on the subsequent purchaser.

A catalogue record for this book is available from the British Library.

Library of Congress Cataloging-in-Publication Data
Rose, Richard, 1933–
 The prime minister in a shrinking world / Richard Rose.
  p. cm.
Includes bibliographical references and index.
 ISBN 0-7456-2729-3—ISBN 0-7456-2730-7 (pbk.)
 1. Great Britain—Politics and government—1945– 2. Executive power—Great Britain—History—20th century. 3. Prime ministers—Great Britain—History—20th century. 4. Great Britain—Foreign relations—1945– 5. World politics—1945– I. Title.
 DA566.7 .R58 2001
 328.41'0762—dc21

00-011286

Picture research by Heather Vickers.

Typeset in $10\frac{1}{2}$ on $12\frac{1}{2}$ pt Palatino by Graphicraft Limited, Hong Kong
Printed in Great Britain by TJ International, Padstow, Cornwall
This book is printed on acid-free paper.

Contents

List of Table, Boxes and Plates   vii
List of Figures   viii

Introduction: The Paradox of Power   1

From old-school to new-style Prime Minister. At the intersection of three shrinking worlds.

1 Looking After Number One at Number Ten   14

Managing political capital. Doing politics. Handling policies while keeping out of trouble.

2 Glendower in a Shrinking World   32

The cloistered world of Westminster. The world North of Watford. National policies are no longer national.

3 What Makes Downing Street Change?   53

Events – expected and unexpected. Long-term irreversible influences. Combinations of causes.

4 Becoming and Remaining Party Leader   69

A long apprenticeship. Fortuitous circumstances. Involuntary exits.

5 From Private to Public Government   86

Keeping politics private. Going public. Blair's permanent campaign. An emerging political-media complex?

6 Winning Elections   110

From old-school to new-style voters. Targeting voters.
A fickle electorate.

7 Managing Parliament and Party   130

The House is no longer a home. Whipping MPs.
From Butskellism to Blatcherism.

8 Managing Colleagues and Bastards   152

Why the Prime Minister needs other ministers. The glue of
patronage. Diminished collegiality and diminished responsibility.

9 Running – and Running After – the Economy   175

Planning the mixed economy. Trying to take hands off
the economy. The pound at sea in the international economy.

10 Managing Decline in a Shrinking World   197

Scaling down commitments. Insular politics goes European.
Turbulence in intermestic politics.

11 Tony Blair: A Populist Prime Minister   216

Managing populism. Blunting the cutting edge of policy.

12 What Comes After Blair?   233

No going back. Number Ten is not the White House.
Adapting to a shrinking world.

Appendix A: Prime Ministers since 1945   252
Appendix B: A Guide to Further Reading   259
Notes   261
Index   278

Table and Boxes

Box 2.1	The many mini-offices in Downing Street	40
Table 9.1	The economic misery index: inflation plus unemployment	184
Box 11.1	Tony Blair's approach to touchstone issues	226
Box 12.1	The Prime Minister and presidents compared	242

Plates

Margaret Thatcher inspects redecoration at Number Ten in the summer of 1989	36
The leaders of the Big Three at Potsdam in July, 1945	46
'Crisis? What Crisis?' The *Sun* headline, January 1979	57
The removal van at Number Ten on John Major's last day	81
Supermac (Vicky cartoon)	89
Clement Attlee campaigning with his wife at the 1950 election	117
'If you must have a Conservative Prime Minister, I'm your man'. Keith Waite cartoon of Jim Callaghan	146
Tony Blair presents his government's first annual report in the rose garden of Number Ten	173
Black Wednesday for the £, September 1992	194
Ted Heath signing Britain's Treaty of Accession to the European Community, January 1972	208
The White House	238
Number Ten Downing Street	238
The European Union summit	246

Figures

Int. 1	Time lines of prime ministers	2
1.1	Multiple facets of the Prime Minister's job	23
3.1	Many centuries of ministries in Whitehall	54
3.2	Changing social class of MPs	65
4.1	Apprenticeship of prime ministers	72
4.2	Election record of prime ministers	82
5.1	Prominence in election broadcasts	98
5.2	Prime Minister dominates colleagues in news	99
5.3	Media eminence of Blair's Downing Street	106
6.1	Highs, means and lows in approval of prime ministers	122
6.2	Old Labour core of 1997 New Labour vote	128
7.1	Participation in divisions in the Commons	134
7.2	Major speeches by Prime Minister in the Commons	136
7.3	Moving consensus in party manifestos	149
8.1	Growth in Prime Minister's patronage	159
9.1	Britain's economy in international perspective	189
9.2	Decline of the pound	191

Introduction

The Paradox of Power

> It is needful to keep the ancient show while we secretly interpolate the new reality.
>
> Walter Bagehot

> You have got to understand I am a man with a mission to transform and modernise the country.... I want modernisation to happen quicker, faster, better.
>
> Tony Blair[1]

My first visit to the House of Commons came when Winston Churchill was Prime Minister and Clement Attlee Leader of the Opposition. Bessie Braddock, a Merseyside MP, was worried about the threat to school children of chemical particles in the iced lollies of Liverpool. There was nothing New Labour about this brontosaurus of a battler. The Conservative minister responding, Dr Charles Hill, was equally remote from today's world. Instead of starting his career by selling management nostrums for McKinsey & Co., he had made his name as the Radio Doctor, offering practical remedies for constipation.

During the war the Commons had been bombed, but it was rebuilt in the same style as before, so that the ancient show could continue. The Mace on the table of the House was the primal symbol of power in British politics; it was fashioned after a medieval club used to batter chain mail into shape. The new reality is that you do not need to go to Westminster to see the House of Commons in action; television brings the show of Prime Minister's Question Time into the living room. For Tony Blair, such changes are not enough; he wants the tempo of modernization to quicken. Whether

Figure Int.1 Time lines of prime ministers

The old school

Churchill	B MP Min PM		
Attlee	B MPMin PM		
Eden	B MP Min PM		
Macmillan	B MP Min PM		
Douglas-Home	B MP Min PM		

A generation schooled in depression and war

Wilson	B MP-Min PM
Heath	B MPMin PM
Callaghan	B MPMin PM

New-style television generation

Thatcher	B MPMin PM
Major	B MP Min PM
Blair	B MP PM >

1875   1900   1925   1950   1975   2000

B Year of birth
MP First an MP
Min First a minister
PM Downing Street entrance

this is desirable or not depends on who decides the direction of change. While there is disagreement about which party leader should be Prime Minister, everyone at Westminster assumes that the hands on the Mace will be British. This book challenges that assumption.

The paradox of power is simply stated: *at Westminster, the Prime Minister's power has increased greatly, but in the world beyond Dover it has greatly diminished*. In the world of Westminster politics, leaders such as Margaret Thatcher and Tony Blair have made obsolete the Victorian dictum that the Prime Minister is first among equals. Today, he or she is first without equal. The Prime Minister announces public policies and decides who sits in the Cabinet and who is dismissed. However, in a shrinking world many important policies are subject to international as well as domestic influences. In Washington a cricket-loving Prime Minister is no match for a President who plays hard ball, and in the European Union he or she is only one among fifteen prime ministers.

1 From old-school to new-style Prime Minister

In the lore of the Constitution, the meaning of 'old' and 'new' are relative. Sir Robert Walpole was a 'new-style' politician when he became the first Prime Minister in the reign of King George I. But by the time of Queen Victoria, a new-style Prime Minister had emerged. On the title page of his book about *The Governance of Britain*, Harold Wilson placed a description of Sir Robert Peel's activities in Downing Street in the first half of the nineteenth century, written by Lord Rosebery, a late nineteenth-century Prime Minister. Wilson claimed that, because of the durable conventions of parliamentary government, 'these words are still true today'.[2] But a lot has happened in the 5,000 weeks since Rosebery wrote. In the 8,000 weeks since Peel was in office twenty-seven politicians have been Prime Minister.

Since the end of the Second World War in 1945, Britain has been governed by prime ministers whose lives have spanned three centuries (figure Introduction. 1). Winston Churchill and Clement Attlee had their roots in Victorian England. Among the eleven post-1945 occupants of Number Ten, Harold Wilson and Alec Douglas-Home were the only prime ministers whose lives fell wholly within the twentieth century, but Douglas-Home was heir to an earldom dating from 1608. The votes that Ted Heath casts in a twenty-first century House of Commons reflect his experience of the worst of Europe before 1945. As Bagehot emphasizes, many British institutions mix both old and new realities, and the same is true of prime ministers. None the less, the combination of qualities characterizing prime ministers of the old school such as Churchill and Attlee differs from that of new-style prime ministers such as Margaret Thatcher and Tony Blair.

Prime ministers of the *old school* entered Parliament between 1900 (Churchill) and 1931 (Douglas-Home). Their views reflected continuity with the past, for Churchill was born when Benjamin Disraeli was entering Downing Street in place of William Gladstone. When Churchill entered the House of Commons, Victoria was Queen, and the Prime Minister was the third Marquess of Salisbury, who had become a Member of Parliament in 1853. Clement Attlee was a Victorian too. A half-century after the event, he wrote that the news of Queen Victoria's death was 'a tremendous shock'.[3]

Old-school prime ministers saw government rooted in traditional Westminster institutions: Parliament, Cabinet and party. They were also committed to the belief that Westminster had a global role, having entered politics when a fifth of the globe was coloured red to mark the extent of the British Empire. Churchill took part in a cavalry charge in the Sudan in 1898. Churchill, Attlee, Eden and Macmillan all saw active service during the First World War, and were ministers in the Second World War. Attlee was exceptional in his knowledge of government beyond Westminster, having been a welfare worker in the East End of London before 1914 and Mayor of Stepney.

Old-school prime ministers spent much of their time thinking about the interaction between policy and politics, and well they might, since both share the same Greek root. In French and German there is no distinction between the English words for politics and policy. In discussions with MPs, politics often came first, while in Whitehall policy came first. The longer the governing party was in office, the less attention Number Ten gave to election campaigning. An old-school Prime Minister could go weeks without talking to leading officials in the party organization. In despair at being ignored by an old-style Prime Minister whose mind was on 'higher' things, party officials talked half seriously about organizing a campaign to politicize Downing Street! While the balance between politics and policy varied from one incumbent to another, old-school prime ministers knew there was a difference and paid attention to both tasks.

The *transition generation* of prime ministers – Harold Wilson, Ted Heath and Jim Callaghan – were schooled by world depression and the Second World War. Each was raised in a family where pennies had to be counted carefully. Wilson and Heath won scholarships to grammar school and Oxford; Callaghan went from school to a job as a civil service clerk. War launched new careers. Heath and Callaghan served in the forces and Wilson entered Whitehall as a temporary civil servant. The two future Labour leaders became MPs in 1945, and Heath in 1950. Recruits to the House of Commons in the early postwar era looked up to leaders of the old school. They received their first ministerial posts under leaders who had served under Campbell-Bannerman, Asquith, Baldwin or Ramsay MacDonald. All three saw Britain's place in the world depending on decisions taken at Westminster. But once in Downing Street, they learned that decisions made in other countries had a big impact on Britain. Wilson was a Cabinet minister, then Prime Minister, during two devaluations of the pound, and so was Callaghan.

In breaking with the politics and economic policies of predecessors, Margaret Thatcher was a *new-style* Prime Minister. She became Conservative Party leader by challenging old-school Conservative values and manners. In advocating controversial policies and in treating compromise and consensus as unthinkable words, Thatcher departed from old-school prime ministers of both parties. In the single-minded pursuit of her convictions, Thatcher ignored or broke conventions of Cabinet government. The economics she expounded was sometimes of the nineteenth-century Manchester School, but it had contemporary policy relevance; for example, the privatization of nationalized industries. Thatcher's faith in free market economics put her at odds with old-school Conservative prime ministers but her efforts to project Britain's influence globally made her talk like a Prime Minister of the old school. Sometimes she was successful in foreign affairs, as in the Falklands War, and sometimes unsuccessful, as in her attempt to roll back the influence of the European Commission on British affairs.

The new-style Prime Minister lives in a television age that can create celebrities overnight. John Major became old enough to vote after London had become swinging. The Beatles were already famous by the time Tony Blair learned the guitar, and he could not vote until 1974. By the time Major reached the House of Commons old-school leaders were gone, and when Tony Blair became an MP in 1983 he was confronted with a palpable reason to reject old-school politics, a vote-losing Labour relic of the 1930s, Michael Foot. Whereas the royal death that most affected Clement Attlee was that of Queen Victoria, the royal death most affecting Tony Blair has been that of Princess Diana. Blair owes his election as Labour leader to the fact that he does *not* look or talk like an old-school Labour Party politician.

For the new-style Prime Minister, the box that counts is the television set rather than the despatch box next to the Mace in the House of Commons. What is said on television matches or surpasses in importance what is said in Westminster. In Opposition, Tony Blair and his associates showed extraordinary concentration on the crucial question facing an Opposition leader: how do I win the next general election? After gaining the biggest parliamentary majority in well over half a century, the challenge is one of policy: what do I do in government? A leaked memo by Blair's polling consultant, Philip Gould, offers an answer: 'Unless you handle the media well, you cannot govern competently.' But in a shrinking world, this is but a half truth, as the fate of John Major illustrates. In his 1992 election campaign, John Major stroked the *Sun* with great success, but he forgot to stroke the German *Bundesbank*. A few months later the Prime Minister's political capital was destroyed when the German central bank refused its support and the pound crashed in the foreign exchange markets.

The overlap in the political careers of successive prime ministers emphasizes a measure of continuity between incumbents of Downing Street. John Major found, for better and for worse, that he could not escape the legacy that Margaret Thatcher had left 'his' government. Although Tony Blair has created a New Labour Party in his own image, he had to praise his predecessors at the centenary celebration of the old Labour Party, and problems of the national health service that he inherited are a legacy from Aneurin Bevan. Blair has sought to avoid being caught in controversies about Britain's role in Europe that did great damage to Thatcher and Major. However, he faces challenges in Europe that have divided both Labour and Conservative Cabinets for a quarter century, and cannot be papered over by pasting on the label 'rebranded'.

2 At the intersection of three shrinking worlds

The Prime Minister lives in three worlds – the cloistered world of Westminster, the everyday world in which most Britons live, and a world of international interdependence. The growing importance of the Prime Minister at Westminster has given much greater political prominence to whoever lives in Number Ten. The growth of education, health and social security programmes has increased Westminster's influence on British society. As distances have been shrinking in the past half century, the influence on Downing Street of the world beyond Dover has grown enormously. But this growing influence on how, and how well, Britons live makes the Prime Minister vulnerable. If the Prime Minister takes credit when a world economic boom increases British prosperity, he or she cannot avoid blame when there is a world recession.

Technological advance is the most obvious cause of the growing interdependence of the three worlds of Downing Street. The slowness of sea travel greatly limited the time an old-school Prime Minister could spend abroad and the infirmities of old-fashioned telephones limited conversations. Today, clear-as-a-bell conversations can be conducted with leaders anywhere on earth, and jet airplanes make day trips possible to other continents. Moreover, political changes make it necessary for the Prime Minister to spend a lot of time doing business with foreign leaders, for in a shrinking world a new-style Prime Minister can only advance British interests by dealing with governments east of Dover and west of Land's End.

The optimistic view of the Prime Minister as a Master of the Universe sees him or her cleverly exploiting connections between three worlds, using popularity with the electorate to gain influence at Westminster, or exploiting favourable trends in the international economy to gain a general election victory. A realist, fearing conflicts between these three worlds, tries to keep them separate; a defeat in a European Union negotiation session may be overshadowed in the British popular press by the carefully timed release of a piece of domestic good news. A pessimist fears that the three worlds are bound to collide, as they threatened to do in January 1974, when an abrupt rise in world oil prices and British miners striking in defiance of government policy led Ted Heath's closest adviser to warn that the Apocalypse was nigh.

The plan of the book

Looking after Number One is the first priority of the temporary tenant of Number Ten, and the subject of this book's first chapter. In the past half-century, only one Prime Minister has left office voluntarily. The Opposition party is not a threat to policy, for the winner-take-all character of parliamentary politics means that Opposition MPs, however loud they bark, lack the votes to have a bite. The prospect of an election is usually several years distant. The immediate threat to the political capital of the Prime Minister comes from front bench colleagues feigning support with what Margaret Thatcher aptly described, after being deposed from office, as 'treachery with a smile on its face'.[4]

In dealing with public policies the Prime Minister is confronted by the 'really real' world that starts north of Watford and extends to Washington, to Brussels and farther still. The Prime Minister can call on exporters to export more, workers to produce more, and foreigners to stop pursuing their un-British interests. In doing so, the Prime Minister faces Glendower's problem, a lack of the power to match words to deeds. When Shakespeare's Glendower boasted that he could call spirits from the deep, Hotspur pricked his illusion by asking: 'But will they come when you do call?' Chapter 2 explains why Downing Street is inevitably and increasingly influenced by what happens in the 'vasty deeps' beyond Westminster.

Changes in Downing Street are influenced more by the steady accumulation of influences from the past than by transitory events. At one moment in time, the situation of the Prime Minister reflects the unintended as well as intended consequences of choices by a multiplicity of predecessors. Events, both expected and unexpected, also have consequences as Tony Blair learned when petrol prices went up, fuel supplies dried up and his popularity went down in September 2000. A reversal in the world economy, a death, or an unexpected scandal can cause the best laid plans of mice and prime ministers to go astray. Each change of Prime Minister brings a new personality with fresh foibles that interest the media. Yet personal mannerisms that attract comment in the media cannot cause the economy to turn up when it is heading down. Chapter 3 emphasizes the irreversible effect of trends arising from the compounding of changes, such as television replacing newspapers as the chief means of political communication, and Germany and Japan replacing Britain as leading world economic powers. In less than the half century covered here, such long-term changes have transformed British politics and policy, and Downing Street with it.

To succeed, the Prime Minister must be good at both politics and policy – and at juggling both. For clarity in exposition, changes in five major political roles are examined a chapter at a time: party leadership, communication, electioneering, managing Parliament and managing Cabinet. Becoming and remaining party leader is frequently treated as the sole goal of MPs, but Harold Wilson is unique among MPs in being photographed in short trousers outside Number Ten at the age of eight and subsequently entering there as Prime Minister. In the days of old-school prime ministers, British government was public in the sense an Anglican church is a public building, but many of its debates were carried on virtually in private. The need to turn the right phrases and show the right face to camera are primary tasks of new-style prime ministers. Election campaigns have been hard fought for centuries, as William Hogarth's engravings and Charles Dickens and Anthony Trollope's writings attest. In recent decades the Prime Minister has become the central figure in elections and, with the rise of three-party competition, needs fewer votes to gain control of Number Ten.

An old-school Prime Minister gave first priority to winning the confidence of MPs in the House of Commons by attending debates and tending to the anxieties and egos of MPs. A new-style Prime Minister relies on television performances and favourable press coverage to keep MPs in line. In Whitehall the increasing prominence of the Prime Minister has led Downing Street to appear responsible for more and more policies, but prominence does not give the incumbent any more hours in the week to deal with problems, nor has it made colleagues any less ambitious, or ready to stir up trouble or dump the blame on others if that is to their advantage.

The growth of government outside Westminster has made public policy the harder half of the job of the Prime Minister. Since the days of Gladstone and Disraeli, there has been a vast explosion in government activities and in the number of public employees. The Prime Minister is a single person ranged against a great maze of public sector institutions. As one expert on the health service has remarked, 'If Florence Nightingale were carrying her lamp through the corridors of the NHS today, she would almost certainly be searching for the people in charge.'[5] A new-style Prime Minister hands responsibility for most of the work of government to departmental ministers. But the economy is too important politically to be ignored, or to be left entirely in the hands of the Chancellor of the Exchequer. Prime ministers from Attlee to Wilson believed that the economic theories of Maynard Keynes had given government the mathematical tools to run the economy. But chapter 9 shows that this is hardly the case. As Denis Healey ruefully concluded after five years as Chancellor of the Exchequer in the troubled 1970s, 'Running the economy is more like gardening than operating a computer.'[6] The new-style Prime Minister is often reduced to running after rather than running the economy.

In a shrinking world, domestic and international policies cannot easily be kept separate. Membership in the European Union and the increasing flow of money, goods and people across national boundaries has created a new category of 'intermestic' problems that combine domestic and international concerns. When the Prime Minister is asked 'What will you do about a foreign automobile company closing a factory in the Midlands to switch production to another country?' it makes sense to discuss the question with foreigners. Chapter 10 shows how national defence ceased to be a strictly national matter when the Attlee government became a founder member of the North Atlantic Treaty Organization (NATO), providing collective defence under American leadership. The rise of new powers in the world has challenged prime ministers to manage decline rather than dominate international events. The growing importance of institutions of the European Union is a challenge to the politics and policy of new-style prime ministers.

Tony Blair's neophilia is a consistent feature of his political rhetoric. A content analysis of his speeches between 1997 and 1999 found that the word 'new' occurred an average of twelve times a speech, more than almost any other word except 'we' and 'Britain'. The adjective is most often applied to 'New Labour' or 'New Deal' or 'new ways' of doing things.[7] Confronted with the argument that past traditions justify current customs, Blair's instinct is to crack the cake of custom. Whereas Margaret Thatcher's radicalism expressed a desire to go back to an imagined past, Tony Blair wants to create a new Britain.

In rejecting ancient realities and proclaiming faith in rapid change, Tony Blair promises a break with all his predecessors. But how can his Prime Ministership be characterized? Chapter 11 shows that his populist claim to be Prime Minister of all the people is impossible to achieve. Democratic politics is about the expression of conflicting opinions of how the country should be governed as well as who should govern. To conciliate opponents or borrow ideas from other parties is normal politics, but to deny that differences of opinion exist and claim to speak for all the people creates managed populism. Policymaking is about making choices; however, Blair's focus on consensual goals tends to blunt the cutting edge of policy. A commitment to promote 'education, education, education' does not stir up opposition; it raises the question: how will the Blair government achieve success when both Labour and Conservative predecessors have not? Blair's Third Way philosophy tells us what government should not do, but it fails to give guidance about which alternative should be chosen to achieve consensual goals.

What will happen after Tony Blair leaves Downing Street? In part, the answer depends on how long he remains there, and the circumstances of his departure. A Prime Minister who leaves with the admiration of colleagues and respect of opponents will be emulated, whereas one who departs after having stayed too long will cause a reaction against his or her practices. The concluding chapter emphasizes two certainties. The first certainty is that there is no going back to political leadership in the manner of the old school. Secondly, similarities in media attention do not bridge the ocean of difference between the constitutional checks and balances that constrain the White House and the absence of constraints on Downing Street. One big uncertainty remains: the future relationship of Downing Street with a shrinking world. For half a century, prime ministers have boasted of influence in three circles: Anglo-American relations, the Commonwealth and Europe. But British leadership in the Commonwealth and Anglo-American relations is now an ancient show. By the time Tony Blair leaves Downing Street, his decisions or non-decisions will make clear the new reality of Britain's relationship with Europe.

Where the author is coming from

My education in the world of Westminster was encouraged by the elder Weller, who explains in *The Pickwick Papers* that he took great pains with the education of his son, letting young Sammy run in the streets of London at a very young age. The London in which I started studying British politics was far more austere than Regency

London, but at least it was free of the detritus of dray horses and the exhaust of automobiles. I walked the streets from Tyburn to Monument, including the streets of SW1, where Lord North Street carried a particular caution, for it was named after an eighteenth-century politician who succeeded in being Prime Minister for twelve years, but was responsible for losing the American colonies.

This book is concerned with a pride of prime ministers and draws on a plurality of sources, unpublished as well as published. For my doctoral thesis on the 1945–51 Labour government I interviewed one former Prime Minister, Clement Attlee; two future prime ministers, Harold Wilson and Jim Callaghan; and many would be prime ministers, beginning with Herbert Morrison. Researching the Bow Group in 1960 was an introduction to Conservatives who have since graced the Cabinet and now sit in the House of Lords. First-hand experience with generations of politicians makes me respect the positive achievements of each Prime Minister, without being blind to their limitations. In the word-pictures that follow, I have tried to respond to Oliver Cromwell's injunction to his portrait painter, to show him truly, warts and all.

In writing about prime ministers over half a century, it is easy to go on for a thousand pages or more. This book takes a selective approach, focusing on the most significant changes in the position of the Prime Minister in a shrinking world. Because the book is about prime ministers rather than political scientists, footnotes have been kept to the minimum. Much information is readily accessible in multiple sources. Neither Margaret Thatcher's victory in the Falklands War nor Anthony Eden's defeat in the Suez War could be kept an official secret. The book makes copious use of quotations. I am particularly grateful to Tony Blair's Downing Street for offering extensive descriptions of its strategy, because what is said can often be revealing in unintended ways. Where quotations are from a unique printed source, there is a footnote. I have often drawn on private conversations and what I have witnessed. When this is the case, there is no footnote, thus avoiding frustrating readers by directing them to a note that simply says 'private information'.

Comparing old-school and new-style prime ministers involves a dialogue between past and present. I have learned much from people whose first-hand experience of British politics predated mine, especially Frank Barlow, who began as a clerk for the Parliamentary Labour Party in the late 1930s and ended up its secretary, and James Douglas, who joined the Conservative Research Department under R. A. Butler. Over the years I have also benefited from the shrewd reflections and reminiscences of journalists whose experience extended back to the 1920s, especially the late David Wood of *The Times*, the late James Margach of the *Sunday Times*, and Bill Deedes of the *Daily Telegraph*, a living embodiment of how the old can illuminate the new with durable truths about politics and human nature.

The immediate stimulus to write this book was a very small grant from the Whitehall programme of the Economic and Social Research Council. Fortunately, the programme director, R. A. W. Rhodes, was shrewd, good humoured and patient in putting up with the challenges posed by Tony Blair's claim to introduce unprecedented changes in Downing Street. June Burnham, Simon James, George W. Jones, John Thompson and Frank Vibert offered useful comments on the manuscript. John Thompson did more; he responded promptly and enthusiastically to the initial manuscript of the book and, with staff at Polity Press, saw it promptly through production.

Having grown up during the Second World War, I share the view of old-school prime ministers that policy as well as politics is important. Unlike most of my fellow members in the Reform Club, I have not lived in London for four decades. This has taught me to see how remote the concerns of Westminster appear from the 'underall' perspective of most British people. Throughout my professional life I have lived in a shrinking world. As an American with an English wife and bi-national children, the Anglo-American relationship has a special meaning to me. For more than a quarter century I have also studied and written about presidents and prime ministers on five continents. My first-hand research on the American presidency has made me reject the pretence that whoever is in the White House can be equated with whoever is in Downing Street. Sojourns in research institutes from Florence and Madrid to Vienna, Prague and Berlin have helped in 'seeing ourselves as others see us'.

The question that this book confronts is deceptively simple. A London cabbie once put it to Bertrand Russell. The famous philosopher was reduced to silence when asked, 'Tell me, my Lord, what's it all about?' If the Prime Minister were ever to be asked this question, the answer he or she should give is short and direct: policy *and* politics.

1

Looking After Number One at Number Ten

> All the President's policies are political. And the same is true for a Prime Minister.
>
> Richard E. Neustadt, author, *Presidential Power*

Every problem facing the Prime Minister is both personal and impersonal. The impersonal question is: what should government do? The personal question is: what effect will action have on my stock of political capital? The Prime Minister cannot keep responsibility for government policy separate from the need to manage a political career. It is reasonable to argue that what is good for the country – for example, economic prosperity – is also good for Downing Street. More debatable is the proposition that what's good for the Prime Minister is also good for the country.

Policy is both an end and a means of enhancing the Prime Minister's political capital. That is the meaning of Richard Neustadt's dictum: 'All a Prime Minister's policies are political.' While every Cabinet minister can contribute to policymaking, none has the same stakes in government, and some hope to benefit if their leader's failure creates a job opening. Only the Prime Minister can look after Number One. The loneliness of the job makes the temporary tenant of Downing Street a Marxist in Groucho's sense, 'Take care of me. I'm the only one I've got.'

While the Prime Minister is self-interested, he or she is not self-employed. When we speak about the Blair or the Major government, the Prime Minister's name is the adjective modifying what should formally be described as Her Majesty's Government. The post has existed independently of personalities for almost three centuries; an individual incumbent is only in Downing Street for a few years. The post confers impersonal rights and obligations. While in Downing Street, a politician as modest in demeanour as Clement Attlee can order the building of a British atomic bomb. Without office, a politician as strong in character as Margaret Thatcher can only fret and fume at the direction of government. Whoever holds the Mace is also subject to many constraints from elsewhere in the United Kingdom, and even more from a shrinking world.

There is no agreement about how the job of Prime Minister fits into government. The Constitution is silent about it; the office was in effect for almost two centuries before being given a passing mention in a 1917 Act of Parliament. An unwritten constitution imposes no constraints on the incumbent in Downing Street. To accuse new-style prime ministers such as Margaret Thatcher and Tony Blair of behaving unconstitutionally is to miss the point; they are not violating explicit rules or conventions but unaware of them. Civil servants and academics are left to pick up the pieces of shattered constitutional myths. As a former Head of the Civil Service said when asked to describe the Constitution, 'We make it up as we go along.'

The fundamental dilemma facing the Prime Minister is that the activities for which he or she is notionally accountable are vast, but the number of hours in the week available to deal with them are few. Old-school prime ministers dealt with this dilemma by practising Cabinet government. In mid-Victorian days, Walter Bagehot described the Cabinet as the 'hyphen which joins, the buckle which fastens, the legislative part of the state to the executive part'. It gave the Prime Minister significance as he chaired meetings of the Cabinet. By the end of the Victorian era, John Morley, a minister in Gladstone's Cabinet, described the Prime Minister as *primus inter pares* (first among equals), being 'the keystone of the Cabinet arch'.[1] Both the buckle and the arch metaphor emphasize the link between the Prime Minister's authority and that of Cabinet ministers.

The logic of Cabinet government offers the Prime Minister an opportunity to stand aside from the day-to-day responsibilities of the Chancellor of the Exchequer, the Foreign Secretary, the Home Secretary, the President of the Board of Trade and other departmental ministers. An old-school Prime Minister such as Clement Attlee found that he had more free time when Prime Minister than ever before in his political life, for he had Cabinet ministers who knew their departments and had sufficient political weight to discourage interference. Likewise, between 1951 and 1955 Winston

Churchill gave a free rein to most Cabinet ministers, not only because he was physically infirm but also because he believed that running departments was their job, not his.

New-style prime ministers are expected to take a much more active role in government than Churchill did. The Prime Minister is now the central point of political reference for Cabinet ministers, senior civil servants, MPs, the governing party and the media. This has led to claims that Prime Ministerial government has superseded parliamentary government or Cabinet government. R. H. S. Crossman vigorously argued before becoming a Cabinet minister under Harold Wilson that 'primary decisions' are made by the Prime Minister, and 'secondary decisions' by departmental ministers in consultation with the Cabinet. Any decision made by an individual minister was dismissed as 'not at all important'.[2] But such a classification is tautological. It makes whatever the Prime Minister does of primary importance, whether approving the appointment of a bishop or sending troops to an international hot spot. It relegates to the second division the Chancellor of the Exchequer's taxation decisions, or spending decisions made in consultation with other ministers. It ignores completely departmental decisions that can subsequently blow up in the face of the Prime Minister, such as the Ministry of Agriculture's hesitancy about acting on the risk of 'mad cow' disease spreading to humans for fear of the reaction of farmers, and of the Treasury, which would have to subsidize a cull of cattle.

In a shrinking world, it is fashionable to argue that Prime Ministerial government has been superseded by the rise of the British President. The primary justification is that the media now give the Prime Minister attention comparable to that accorded to the American President, and a successful election campaign confers popular legitimacy. However, likening Downing Street to the White House ignores the parliamentary basis of the Prime Minister's authority, which can be withdrawn at short notice, as Margaret Thatcher learned to her surprise. By contrast the President can survive an impeachment trial with less than half the votes of the Senate, as Bill Clinton did.[3] Even if Britain had a popularly elected President, while his or her influence in the world beyond Dover would be more than that of the President of Finland, it would be less than that of the President of the United States.

The growth of government makes the doctrine of Prime Ministerial government inappropriate, for the scale and heterogeneity of government responsibilities are too great for any one individual to comprehend. The clock limits what a Prime Minister can do in a week. Devoting more time to one issue reduces the time the Prime Minister has to keep in touch with other issues. The word 'touch' is critical, for it implies there is contact between the Prime Minister and Whitehall departments, but the contact may be superficial. The first thing that struck a departmental civil servant after starting work at Number Ten was, 'It's like skating over an enormous globe of thin ice.'

The complexity of contemporary government requires abandoning the neat metaphors of arch and pyramid in favour of the *maze*, a dense agglomeration of corridors (and some dead ends), where policymakers arrive at decisions.[4] Within the maze of Her Majesty's Government, the Prime Minister is not alone; there is a transient population of ministers, civil servants and policy advisers who handle central government policies and arbitrate conflict between different parts of the structure of British government. While Tony Blair has increased the number in the maze who depend solely on him, the Prime Minister and his staff are not the sole tenants of Downing Street. The Chancellor of the Exchequer is at Number 11, the Chief Whip at Number 12, and the Foreign Office looms large on the other side of Downing Street. The population of the maze changes when issues such as pensions or transport arise. Its floating population gives the maze an elastic quality that can be stretched to accommodate anyone or anything. Within the maze, the new-style Prime Minister is like the Minotaur, a beast that can swallow anyone or anything at hand. But if the Prime Minister tries to swallow too much at one time, then political indigestion or worse will result, for many of the problems in the maze of British government are indigestible or even insoluble.

1 *Managing political capital*

Once a politician reaches the top of the greasy pole of politics, a new vista is open. There is no point in trying to rise higher; the Prime Minister simply wants to stay put. However, this is more easily said than done. To stay on top the Prime Minister needs to maintain personal political capital, that is, his or her reputation for being on the winning side when problems arise. Downing Street is well positioned to be associated with success, for the Prime Minister has many ways of monitoring issues without making a commitment until the outcome is clear. When there is good news, the Prime Minister can try to extract the maximum of credit. For example, Tony Blair did not cause the Millennium, but he showed great determination in exploiting it. If the news is bad, the Prime Minister can leave it to others in the maze to respond; for example, when more money had to be pumped into the Millennium Dome project when it failed to attract visitors.

Power is shown when the Prime Minister gets the government to act differently from the way it would have if he or she had not become involved. Harold Wilson's efforts to promote an industrial relations act illustrate the distinction between maintaining political capital and exercising power. When Wilson's attempt to legislate on industrial relations provoked strong opposition from the trade union wing of the Labour Party and the Cabinet, the Prime Minister accepted defeat. Wilson's political capital was 'sufficient for him to remain in office but insufficient for him to remain in office and have his way'.[5]

Westminster is a world in which the reputations of current and prospective prime ministers are continuously being bought or sold short. Because political capital is an intangible, there are uncertainties about how much or how little political capital the Prime Minister has at any one moment. Opinion polls can quantify the Prime Minister's standing with the general public, but this is not the same as the standing of the Prime Minister in Westminster or the world beyond Dover. Margaret Thatcher's career illustrates this point. For most of her time in office, Thatcher's political capital was very high in Westminster. However, in public opinion polls Thatcher's approval rating was almost always below 50 per cent.

Investing political capital

Political capital is not a jewel that can be kept in a treasure chest. Like other forms of capital, its value alters according to how it is invested. Any attempt to hoard rather than use political capital would be an abdication from governing. The uncertainties of political life are such that it is better to speak of the Prime Minister risking political capital rather than investing it. Like money, political capital can be used in different ways. It can be invested in collective leadership, advocating policies agreed within the governing party and reconciling differences between ministers in order to reach a collective decision. Alternatively, a Prime Minister can invest political capital in the advocacy of his or her own distinctive views. The former strategy reduces risk by ensuring a substantial backing within the governing party, but it also reduces the Prime Minister's impact. The latter strategy increases individual impact, but runs greater risks.

When Clement Attlee formed the 1945 Labour government, the Labour Party was his primary source of political capital. Attlee was happy to share in Labour's victory but did not claim to be its cause: 'I have neither the personality nor the distinction to tempt me to think that I should have any value apart from the Party which I serve.'[6] Attlee saw himself as the custodian of the values and interests of the Labour Party. The government's policy agenda was not his personal choice; it consisted of commitments adopted by the Labour Party between the wars and by the wartime coalition government. The government's welfare state legislation was unchallenged because there was broad inter-party consensus, and the government's nationalization policies were not challenged within the governing party. As long as government policies were viewed positively by Labour adherents, Attlee's political capital was high. In foreign policy there was controversy, as the Labour government's alignment with the United States did not match the principles of a socialist foreign policy to which leftwingers were committed. However, Attlee did not need to invest his own political capital in rejecting criticisms; he let his Foreign Secretary, Ernest Bevin, steamroller critics.

Both Harold Wilson and Jim Callaghan followed Attlee in seeking to promote their political capital through collective leadership of the Labour Party. Wilson was fond of describing his role in government as being like a team captain, whose job is not to score all the team's goal but to make sure that all the players on the team kick the ball towards the correct goal, and not foul each other. Wilson entered Downing Street with a lower stock of collective capital than Clement Attlee and a higher stock of personal capital. The 1964 Labour manifesto sought to paper over differences of opinions within the Labour Party, using Wilson's rhetorical association of socialism and science. In office, Wilson maintained the government's collective capital by preventing a split in a Cabinet including senior ministers as diverse in outlooks as Tony Benn, Denis Healey and Roy Jenkins, but he did so only at a cost to his personal political capital. When Jim Callaghan became Prime Minister in 1976, the Labour government had even less collective capital, for its working majority in the Commons had been lost and it was visibly heading for the economic rocks. Callaghan invested all his political capital in an effort to keep the Labour Party together and to prevent a defeat in the Commons by maintaining the support of third parties. By the end of the Parliament his capital was exhausted and the Callaghan government fell on a Commons vote of no confidence.

The record of John Major is a reminder that collective leadership requires cooperative Cabinet colleagues as well as a non-assertive Prime Minister. While Major managed to maintain enough political capital to survive in office for more than six years, he did so in spite of being unable to achieve a consensus. Thatcherite MPs felt that Major was too soft on Europe, and all Conservative MPs were nervous about the threat of Tony Blair's New Labour Party at the polls. In an unprecedented move, Major resigned as party leader in 1995 and stood for re-election, asking MPs to back him or sack him. MPs did neither. Major won enough votes to remain in Downing Street but his political capital remained weak. None the less, he survived far longer than Alec Douglas-Home, who entered Downing Street with neither personal nor collective capital and lasted less than two years as party leader.

Harold Macmillan pursued a mixed strategy in investing political capital. On many issues, he was content to promote collective one-nation policies that had been agreed under R. A. Butler's leadership when the Conservatives were in Opposition from 1945 to 1951. This was congenial, since Macmillan shared these views; it was also prudent, because Butler was his chief potential rival. From time to time Macmillan took personal risks as well, maintaining Keynesian economic policies in the face of the collective resignation of three Treasury ministers in 1958; cautioning white colonial leaders that a 'wind of change' was going to alter the course of government in Africa; creating new public–private economic development institutions; and applying to join the European Community only a few years after it was founded without Britain as a member.

Hagiographies praise politicians who invest all their political capital in pursuit of a grand goal, but overlook that all can be lost if the venture goes wrong. Anthony Eden invested all his political capital in seizing the Suez Canal from the Egyptians, keeping preparations for the war secret from the Cabinet. When the Suez intervention collapsed, Eden's political career was over. Ted Heath offers a positive example of running high personal risks, which he did in promoting British entry to the European Community, notwithstanding divisions within the governing party. When a bill about entry was put to the Commons in autumn 1971, there were 85 divisions in which one or more Conservative MPs voted against entry. In the most critical vote, division within the governing party meant that 'the instances of near heart failure in the Whips Office that evening were very high'.[7]

On becoming party leader, Margaret Thatcher rejected the idea of collective leadership, for she believed that the legacy of her predecessors was little more than socialism tied up in blue ribbons. Converting Conservatives to her market-oriented convictions was her priority, and Thatcher was prepared to risk conflict to achieve this goal, proclaiming: 'The Old Testament prophets did not say: "Brothers, I want a consensus." They said, "This is my faith. This is what I passionately believe. If you believe it too, then come with me."'[8] In her first years in Downing Street Thatcher was cautious in the use of political capital, for she had not yet mobilized sufficient support among Conservatives for her personal convictions. Victory in the Falklands War boosted her support. Henceforth, Thatcher was ready to take risks that sometimes were spectacularly successful, as in facing up to a strike by coal miners in 1984, and sometimes spectacularly unsuccessful, as in the introduction of the poll tax to finance local government.

In Opposition, Tony Blair was a venture capitalist, taking personal initiatives to turn the old Labour Party from a socialist Opposition into a party that was electable. The party organization was rewired so that Blair would not be subject to the constraints of collective leadership that had made life difficult for Harold Wilson, Jim Callaghan and their successors. New rules have given Blair great scope for personal initiative. In office, however, Blair has for the most part been averse to taking personal policy initiatives. His endorsement of market forces, keeping taxes down and being tough on public expenditure is a legacy from Conservative predecessors. Major constitutional reforms, such as devolution to Scotland and Wales, were a legacy from the old Labour Party.

Meeting expectations

The political capital of the Prime Minister depends on doing what 'significant others' expect, including Cabinet colleagues, MPs in the governing party, the media and, finally, the electorate. But what is the Prime Minister expected to do? Formally, the Prime Minister's only obligation is stated in the Privy Councillor's oath: to maintain the good government of the Crown. So vague are the formal terms of reference of the job that H. H. Asquith argued, 'The office of the Prime Minister is what its holder chooses and is able to make it.'[9] But Asquith's claim is a half truth. As he learned to his cost, being forced from Downing Street when he failed to meet parliament's expectations of leadership in the First World War.

The expectations that the Prime Minister must meet are formed long before he or she arrives in Downing Street. Some are more than a century old, such as appointing, reshuffling and dismissing Cabinet ministers. Others are specific to individuals; for example, Anthony Eden was expected to succeed in foreign affairs, to which he had devoted his entire political career, and Harold Wilson was expected to manage the economy successfully because he was an economist. Party activists expect the Prime Minister to fulfil commitments in the party's election manifesto. Cabinet ministers expect the Prime Minister to support departmental initiatives that will advance their own political careers. The media urge activity, or at least photo-opportunities that appear as news. Expectations also vary with context; the same politician behaves differently when answering Parliamentary Questions and in a television interview with David Frost.

The Prime Minister must wear many 'hats', for he or she is expected to undertake many roles. In the late 1940s a Cabinet Office memorandum identified a dozen different roles of an old-school Prime Minister, ranging from hiring and firing ministers and chairing the Cabinet to attending audiences with the monarch and appointing bishops. Peter Hennessy has identified thirty-one different roles for a new-style Prime Minister, and this number was arrived at without including such roles as dealing with the media, with the Chief Whip, with the governing party, and with the electorate![10] But the longer the list of expectations, the greater the need for priorities; that is why the following chapters focus on six major roles affecting policy and politics (figure 1.1).

Although the Prime Minister has many hats, he or she has only one head, which is at risk if expectations are not met. To maintain his or her political capital, the Prime Minister must juggle many roles simultaneously. What Richard Neustadt writes about presidents is true of prime ministers too:

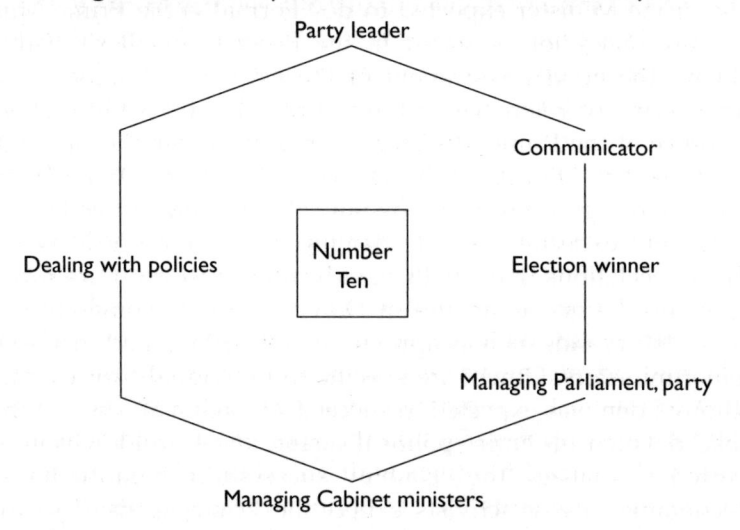

Figure 1.1 Multiple facets of the Prime Minister's job

- Party leader
- Communicator
- Election winner
- Managing Parliament, party
- Managing Cabinet ministers
- Dealing with policies
- Number Ten

From outside, or from below, a President is many men or one man wearing many hats or playing many roles. The President himself plays every role, wears every hat at once. Whatever he may do in one role is by definition done in all, and has effects on all. When he attempts to make his wishes manifest, his own will felt, he is one man, not many.[11]

While there are times when the Prime Minister must turn his or her back on policy or on politics, to remain at Number Ten, he or she must always keep in mind the demands of both politics and policy.

2 Doing politics

The roles with the first priority are political, starting with becoming and remaining party leader. Whereas a pop musician or actress has an agent to manage a career, the Prime Minister has no one but himself or herself. The route to the top involves a lengthy apprenticeship in party politics, learning how to meet the expectations of party members who control nomination for a safe parliamentary seat. Prime ministers of the old school started their political careers young and took more than a quarter of a century to rise to the top. The critical final step to the top is least predictable, for vacancies in party leadership often occur at unexpected times, and the expectations of the selectorate making the choice of party leader are often influenced by fortuitous events. At a given moment, the winner may be an MP who meets the expectations of the party rank-and-file (for example, Neil Kinnock), an MP who appeals outside the party's core constituency (for example, Tony Blair), or simply the only Cabinet minister at hand who can stop someone else (John Major's chief asset when running against Michael Heseltine).

The Prime Minister is expected to communicate through both public and private media. An old-school Prime Minister was expected to establish a reputation first among the political elite of Westminster by appearances on the floor of the Commons and in private and informal meetings with MPs there. His reputation was then diffused outwards by the opinion-forming press. Coverage of politics by the BBC was expected to impress (or anaesthetize) listeners rather than interest or entertain them. The new-style Prime Minister is expected to go public, projecting his or her personality and thoughts through electronic media. Tony Blair has opened his arms to the media; the intent of the embrace is to manage publicity. Concurrently, communication with MPs at Westminster has been greatly reduced. When Blair undertook a 'meet the Scots' tour while facing awkward questions in Parliament, he explained:

> I'm not trying to bypass the national media, but it's important that on the key issues of the day we find ways of communicating directly with the public, not simply with the Westminster village.[12]

The expectation of being an election winner directly influences the Prime Minister's political capital. In the era of the old-school Prime Minister, most voters were expected to have a lifetime loyalty to a party, based on Us vs. Them divisions in British society. The Prime Minister could expect to receive the continuing support of a large bloc of committed voters. Between 1950 and 1959 the vote for the Prime Minister's party fluctuated an average of only 1.6 per cent from one election to another. New-style prime ministers cannot expect voters to remain loyal for a lifetime, as their predecessors did. Social changes have encouraged those who reject old social divisions to support the Liberal Democrats or Nationalists.

The two parties competing for Downing Street together can now win only three-quarters of the popular vote. New-style prime ministers have launched appeals that have broken the mould of the past. Margaret Thatcher had a personal manifesto that combined pro-market values derived from old-fashioned liberalism and tough views on defending the national interest. Tony Blair campaigned for Downing Street by telling Labour Party activists not to expect him to govern like his predecessors but, as he said in the 1997 New Labour manifesto, to 'move on and move forward' from Labour's past.

In the days of old-school prime ministers, MPs in the governing party expected their Prime Minister to show loyalty to established party principles, interests and symbols. Incumbents of Number Ten had spent so many decades in the party that they knew what the party expected of its leader. When Harold Wilson led the Labour Party, he showed his respect for time-honoured symbols by opposing the removal of its traditional commitment to nationalization in Clause IV of the party constitution. Leaders of the old school were standard bearers, emphasizing themes common to many members of their party rather than proclaiming their personal beliefs. New-style prime ministers pay less attention to Parliament and to party; they see their authority as deriving from the electorate. Margaret Thatcher expected to use every platform available to her as a 'bully pulpit' from which to expound her convictions. With control of the New Labour organization in his hands and a much enlarged staff in Number Ten, Tony Blair expects MPs and party workers to do what he expects, whether or not he meets the expectations of veteran Labour supporters.

When it comes to appointing ministers, new-style prime ministers are expected to make much more liberal use of patronage to meet the big increase in the number of MPs hungering for a government post. The more MPs who hold government posts, the greater the 'payroll' vote for the Prime Minister, and the more secure he or she is against challenges. A Prime Minister of the old school treated ministers as colleagues, and was expected to discuss issues in Cabinet so ministers backed decisions that threatened conflict within the governing party. A new-style Prime Minister sees Cabinet meetings as a waste of time. The Prime Minister chooses whom to consult and who is kept out of the loop by fixing the membership of a Cabinet committee or holding informal discussions at Number Ten with select ministers. Cabinet members who are not shown the respect that they expect their position to merit can retaliate by becoming disloyal colleagues.

3   Handling policies while keeping out of trouble

The more policies in which the Prime Minister is involved, the greater his or her potential influence and the greater the potential number of successes. Yet the greater the number of issues receiving attention at Number Ten, the greater the number that can explode in the Prime Minister's face, depleting Downing Street's stock of political capital. If the first rule of the Prime Minister is to do what you must, keeping out of trouble is the second rule. In the words of a veteran Downing Street official, 'It is very dangerous for a Prime Minister to pick up the ball and run with it himself because in the end there is no one he can pass it to.'[13]

Prime ministers of the old school were well aware of the political advantages of distancing themselves from the daily affairs of Whitehall departments. Clement Attlee picked up *The Times* each day to do the crossword puzzle. In his final tour at Downing Street, an ageing Winston Churchill could take weeks privately recuperating from a partially disabling stroke. Harold Macmillan had time to re-read Jane Austen and Trollope, and was able to leave Downing Street for more than a month in January 1960 to make a political tour of Africa. Ted Heath played the piano to unwind, and when the weather permitted, jealously kept weekends free for sailing.

Changes in political expectations within the world of Westminster leave a new-style Prime Minister with little time to relax. Membership in the European Union has added to these claims. It has increased the amount of time devoted to foreign travel and meeting foreign visitors to London, and the number of intermestic issues that are pushed up to Number Ten, because anything involving the influence of Brussels on things British is potentially explosive.

To survive the daily routine of life in Downing Street, the Prime Minister must be 'both lark and owl. The Prime Minister's early mornings are disturbed by telephone calls about urgent political or government business. Yet he is often still at the Commons or at a State banquet until midnight. On return to his bed he may have boxes of official papers to read and remember. It is a pounding, physical and nervously stressful regime.'[14] Sleep can be interrupted by an urgent telephone call from a national leader on another continent; weekends disturbed by unwelcome stories in the Sunday papers; and holidays interrupted by crises that the Prime Minister will not trust to a political deputy or a civil servant. Margaret Thatcher revelled in being both a lark and an owl, ready to discuss issues of public policy at any time of her waking day.

The tyranny of the clock forces every Prime Minister, whether old-school or new-style, to practise management by exception. If the press focused on all the aspects of British government that the Prime Minister did not touch, it would no longer be producing a daily paper but a daily encyclopedia. There are not enough hours in the day, days in the week, or weeks in the year for the Prime Minister to keep an eye on all the major concerns of government. The staff at Number Ten is continuously filtering issues to avoid entangling the Prime Minister in matters that are not thought worth his or her attention. To keep the Prime Minister out of trouble, a variety of stratagems can be used to deflect problems away from Downing Street. If the Prime Minister does keep in touch with an issue, there are many ways of doing so while avoiding premature commitment of political capital. The Prime Minister's diary is arrived at by a process of exclusion and inclusion.

Keeping out of trouble

The simplest way for the Prime Minister to deal with a policy issue is to ignore it, and *non-involvement* is Downing Street's most frequent response to problems facing government. A new Prime Minister inherits from predecessors hundreds of policies adopted up to half a century or more in the past. Most of these commitments are administered routinely, and to the satisfaction of citizens; for example, the fire service. Downing Street can leave policies alone as long as they are operating routinely and generating satisfaction rather than demands for action. When minor complaints arise, these can be dealt with by the relevant Cabinet minister. The same is true of major problems that concern minor matters that are not central to the Prime Minister's own political capital, such as the great bulk of the concerns of the Welsh Office or of International Development.

Unwelcome problems that force their way to Downing Street's attention can sometimes be *deflected* to other bodies. This is a favoured tactic in foreign policy, for the Prime Minister can make a statement asking an offending foreign government to stop doing whatever it is that offends British MPs, or ask an international body to act. When a nationalist Iranian government nationalized the Anglo-Iranian Oil Company in 1951, the Attlee government took the case to the International Court of Justice in The Hague. Even though there was no expectation that the Court would enforce any judgment it made, doing so provided an answer to the question the Opposition raised: what is the government doing about the seizure of British property? When attacked for inaction by the Opposition leader, Winston Churchill, it enabled Attlee to accuse Churchill of war-mongering, and led the *Daily Mirror* to ask in a dramatic election day cover story: 'Whose finger do you want on the trigger?'[15]

Letting an issue *stew or simmer* buys time for Downing Street while others in Whitehall grapple with the problem and explore whether there is or is not a consensus in favour of a particular course of action. Having an issue investigated elsewhere in government allows the Prime Minister to keep options open and avoids committing political capital. As described by a Downing Street aide:

> The Prime Minister, curiously enough, was never keen on making decisions on matters that did not demand immediate action. Unless one had to be made, he liked to discuss the pros and cons at length, and would then adjourn the meeting for further thought, particularly if the decision was likely to be one which went against the grain.

This quotation could come from a story about the second Queen's Speech of Tony Blair's government, headlined, 'Blair kicks contention into the long grass' In fact, it is a description of how Winston Churchill handled many domestic issues.[16]

Old-school prime ministers encouraged lengthy deliberations inside and outside Whitehall on grounds of both politics and policy. Royal Commissions and departmental committees composed of the 'great and the good' were a favoured device for deliberation. Downing Street could use its control of each committee's terms of reference and membership as a means to ensure that their recommendations would not be politically awkward. Their deliberations offered a chance to gauge sentiments for and against alternative recommendations, and gave time to identify difficulties in the design and administration of a policy before a bill was put to the Commons. If the committee's members agreed a recommendation, the Prime Minister could endorse it safe in the knowledge of widespread support. If a committee split, the Prime Minister could use this as reason for avoiding action. From Clement Attlee's arrival at Downing Street until the arrival of Margaret Thatcher, there was a growing number of Royal Commissions and Committees in which issues were stewing.

Handling policies

New-style prime ministers face more pressures to act and expect to act across a wide range of policies. Margaret Thatcher rejected the compromises inherent in committee consultations; she believed that compromise produced worse policy. Nor did she consider it necessary to get the advice of the great and the good on matters central to her convictions. Under Thatcher, the number of Royal Commissions and government committees was less than half that of the Heath–Wilson years, and fell to the lowest in more than half a century.[17] Free market principles that Thatcher could pull out of her handbag identified what ought to be done, and outside consultants could be paid to advise how to implement privatization policies. When committees were appointed, they were used to deflect awkward issues away from Downing Street; for example, on the Brixton disorders of 1981 or on crowd safety at football grounds. Like Margaret Thatcher, Tony Blair has a desire for action, or at least, the appearance of action. Because he entered office without Thatcher's ideological goals and convictions, Blair has consulted widely in a search for practical means of achieving consensual goals, setting up almost three hundred task forces to review issues. The quantity of task forces results in the Prime Minister having no time for the great majority of them.

The simplest way for the Prime Minister to handle an issue without commitment is to *show concern*. For example, Jim Callaghan sought to stimulate a public debate about education that would lead to an improvement in educational standards by a speech at Ruskin College, Oxford, in 1976. The speech generated discussion leading to the publication of a government Green Paper, but it did not lead to government action. In his memoirs a decade later,

Callaghan lamented, 'More needs to be done, and I regret the slowness of change.'[18] Tony Blair often shows concern when events are in the news, and his leaked memos are full of requests to Downing Street staff to find ways of being seen to 'empathise with public concern' and be tough on claims to political asylum and on crime.[19] Showing concern can gain the Prime Minister a headline without committing the government to new legislation or additional public expenditure.

The Prime Minister can *request a departmental minister* to prepare a proposal that could be put to Parliament. Turning a Downing Street statement of intent or a party manifesto commitment into legislation is a lengthy process involving discussion and negotiation between departmental civil servants, affected interests and the minister. Major policy issues of concern to the Prime Minister are likely to have consequences for several departments and therefore require inter-departmental negotiations, a process aptly described as running the Whitehall obstacle course. The Prime Minister can create a Cabinet committee to consider the matter and appoint a favoured non-departmental minister to chair it in his or her interest. In the Blair government Lords Irvine and Falconer, long-standing friends of the Prime Minister, often served this purpose, knocking heads together to reach agreement (compare the words of a White House official assigned this task, 'Every President needs a bastard; I'm the President's bastard.'). Cabinet committees can include political appointees from Number Ten and civil servants from the Cabinet Office to monitor (or, critics would say, 'spy on') deliberations and make sure that whatever is agreed is acceptable to the Prime Minister. While departments are trying to agree a proposal, the Prime Minister can ponder what departmental ministers ignore: how each policy option affects the political capital of Downing Street.

Urgent events – a British diplomat is kidnapped, the pound sinks, or the media wants to know what the government will do after a bad rail crash – can *force the Prime Minister to act*. Downing Street can push responsible departmental officials and ministers to produce proposals, urgent meetings can be held with the Prime Minister probing their suggestions, revised alternatives considered and a decision arrived at in a matter of days or hours. If urgency is caused by bad news – for example, an IRA bomb in central London – whatever the Prime Minister decides is likely to be a 'second best' or 'lesser evil' alternative.

The decisions that most influence the Prime Minister's political capital usually arise from *wicked issues* involving conflicts between politically popular competing goals; for example, spending more money to promote the health services and lowering income tax, or protecting the green belt while building more new homes. Public policy theorists can analyse inter-departmental conflicts in impersonal terms and prescribe trade-offs between competing goods. But choices in Whitehall are often intensely personal conflicts between the egos of ministers. For a departmental minister, the right policy is 'my' policy, as their political fortunes rise and fall with the outcome of inter-departmental disputes. In such circumstances, the Prime Minister must balance politics and policy. In the run up to a general election, the Chancellor of the Exchequer can give priority to defeating inflation, while the Prime Minister gives priority to defeating the Opposition. Intermestic issues involve balancing international pressures against domestic pressures, and the priorities of one department against another. As a senior civil servant once explained to me:

> One should not think of policymaking as the outcome of a rational process. Imagine instead a group of politicians standing around in a circle, each throwing stones at a large lump of dough in the centre. The shape that the dough ultimately assumes is not the result of a central plan or decision but of the blows that randomly strike it. And in some cases the stones are not aimed at the dough, but at other Cabinet ministers.

2

Glendower in a Shrinking World

> Glendower: I can call spirits from the vasty deep.
> Hotspur: Why so can I, or so can any man. But will they come when you do call for them?
> Shakespeare, *Henry IV, Part 1*

> There are two kinds of countries: those that are small and know it and those that are small and don't.
> A Belgian Prime Minister

What you see depends on *where* you look. When major problems arise, the Prime Minister must look different ways at once. It is necessary to see how an issue will play in Birmingham or Preston as well as in the Palace of Westminster and the media headquarters of central London. A large number of problems facing a new-style Prime Minister are intermestic, requiring him or her to look at how decisions taken in Downing Street will play in Brussels or Washington as well as in Westminster and Worcester.

In the introverted world of Westminster, there is no Glendower problem. After serving in the Cabinets of eight postwar prime ministers, politicians as far apart ideologically as Tony Benn and Lord Hailsham have concluded that the Prime Minister is becoming 'unconstitutional' or an 'elective dictatorship'. Like a banyan tree, Margaret Thatcher put all other members of her Cabinet in the shade. A modern-day Glendower can use bleepers and pagers to call forth support from the depths of the back benches of the House of Commons. Computers at New Labour's Millbank headquarters monitor MPs' statements to make sure they stay on message when called. The Prime Minister's powers of patronage commit careerist ministers to be wary of opposing Downing Street, for fear that their careers will sink in the deep. A senior Whitehall official of Tony Blair declares, 'The Prime Minister is not *pares* [on equal footing with Cabinet colleagues]. He is way above that. Like Caesar, he bestrides the world like a colossus.'[1]

However, if attention is turned to the world North of Watford, the Prime Minister's capacity to summon spirits is much less. When Prime Minister Harold Macmillan proclaimed that exporting is fun, British manufacturers laughed at rather than with him. When Harold Wilson offered beer and sandwiches to trade union leaders in efforts to talk them into exercising wage restraint, the 'solemn and binding' agreements entered into there came unstuck on the shop floor of factories. In Scotland and Wales, some voters challenge the claim of any Westminster MP to be Prime Minister of Great Britain. In Northern Ireland rejection is expressed with bombs and bullets as well as votes. The record of prime ministers in the fifteen general elections called since 1945 is 'Glendower 8, Hotspur 7', for the Prime Minister has been rejected almost as often as winning.

Hotspur's scepticism is even more justified when the Prime Minister steps onto the international stage. The Prime Minister expects to play a big part in international affairs, not the minor part assigned a leader of a small country. Although the camera does not lie when showing the Prime Minister talking with leaders of other nations, it can mislead. A carefully staged photo of Tony Blair at the White House makes Britain appear important – but it does not show what the President does after his visitor has left. A statement in the House of Commons about a conflict on another continent is merely an aspiration. In a shrinking world, much that influences the domestic welfare of Britons is decided in other countries and continents by Japanese and Germans speaking languages that Britons do not understand. Foreign exchange markets in Tokyo trade the British pound up or down while people in London are asleep. When John Major cried defiance in defence of the pound on 'Black Wednesday', 1992, his call failed to raise dollars, Deutsche Marks or yen from the vasty deep. When policy on the euro is made at meetings of the European Central Bank in Frankfurt, Britain is not there.

What you see depends on *when* you look at British politics. Conventionally, prime ministers are differentiated by their party label, but from the perspective of half a century, the bigger differences are between prime ministers of the old school and new-style leaders.

When Winston Churchill led Britain to victory in the Second World War, there was no Glendower problem. Churchill gave the lion's roar and the British people responded victoriously.

When the world shrinks, power shifts. Europe is a prime example of this. Its development from a Community of six countries to a Union of fifteen has brought the new-style Prime Minister into regular contact with leaders of other governments from the Baltic to the Aegean. The integration of more and more countries in the European Union (EU) has also created a new centre of power in Brussels, the home of the European Commission. Like it or not, each new-style Prime Minister inherits treaty obligations to respond to directives from Brussels. In the European Union, the Prime Minister cannot announce authoritatively 'This is our policy'. In fields within the scope of Brussels, such as agricultural prices and weights and measures, policies cannot be decided in Westminster but only by bargaining among fifteen national governments. For all the respect that Europeans have for the genius of Shakespeare, histrionics in the style of Glendower lose allies rather than gain them. Negotiations are better captioned by the title of an existentialist play by Jean-Paul Sartre, *Huis Clos* (No Exit), for, in the words of a Downing Street negotiator, 'We are condemned to achieve a successful outcome.'

A new-style Prime Minister who seeks to emulate Glendower risks proving Hotspur right, when spirits refuse to respond. While English is the language of international decisionmaking, the great majority speaking it are neither English nor Scots. They are heads of governments in places as far apart as Berlin and Tokyo. Politicians who speak English or American as their second, third or fourth language do not do so because of a love for Shakespeare. They do so because English is now the language of money and power.

1   The cloistered world of Westminster

In Westminster the Prime Minister is at the centre of a very small and very introverted world. An old-school Private Secretary to Harold Wilson and Jim Callaghan placed the Prime Minister at the centre of overlapping circles showing power being shared with Whitehall, the House of Commons, and the governing party. All of these institutions are still in place, but the world of Westminster has shrunk. In Tony Blair's Downing Street there is less sharing of power. Blair's world is represented not by overlapping circles in which ideas and influence are shared but by concentric circles with a very small number of people very much on the inside. The distinction is important. A Prime Minister who deals with overlapping groups of senior civil servants, MPs and ministers receives diverse points of view about the problems of the United Kingdom. However, when the Prime Minister confines serious discussions to an inner circle, this reduces the diversity of opinions available and increases jealousies and friction between those in different circles.

Blair's innermost circle has included the Prime Minister's Press Secretary, Alastair Campbell, and his Chief of Staff, Jonathan Powell; the Prime Minister's chief strategist, Peter Mandelson; the Head of the Policy Unit of political advisers, David Miliband; and the Head of the Private Office of civil servants, Jeremy Heywood.[2] Only one of these persons is an MP. In the second circle are Gordon Brown, a former (and potentially future) rival as well as Chancellor of the Exchequer; and two long-time personal friends, the Lord Chancellor, Lord Irvine, and a junior minister at the Cabinet Office, Lord Falconer. The third circle adds one person, the Deputy Prime Minister, John Prescott, and the fourth circle adds two more, the Foreign Secretary and the Home Secretary. The outermost circle contains three-quarters of the Cabinet along with a residual category labelled 'everyone else'. The number of people assigned to the magic circles of the new-style Prime Minister vary, but only between a handful and a few dozen. While the names change according to their favour with the Prime Minister and the situation, the logic of 'inner' and 'outer' circles of access and influence remains. This was not always so.

The old school: more from less

The Prime Minister works from home with the staff that can be crammed into an eighteenth-century town house. In the words of Douglas Hurd, a former political secretary to Ted Heath, 'Number Ten Downing Street is a house, not an office, and that is its most important characteristic.'[3] As long as this is the case, there is a limit to the number of people who can work directly for the Prime Minister. Because Number Ten is a house, everyone who works there,

36 *Glendower in a Shrinking World*

Number Ten is a home as well as an office. Margaret Thatcher inspects redecoration in the summer of 1989.
Photo: Peter Jordan/Network.

from the telephonists who locate stray Cabinet ministers or heads of foreign governments to the most senior civil servants, is on close terms with everyone else.

In the nineteenth century the few people who assisted the Prime Minister were a motley mixture of political appointees, friends and relatives. Before the invention of the typewriter and carbon paper, Lord Palmerston pressed his wife into service to copy confidential correspondence. In Lloyd George's time, the war was not the only cause of emergency. He brought many ad hoc appointees into Downing Street to provide assistance, including his mistress, Frances Stevenson, who was classified as his personal secretary. The established civil service gradually took over the staffing of Downing Street. In the First World War the Cabinet Office developed to keep minutes of committee meetings and prepare and circulate documents throughout Whitehall.

Clement Attlee set the pattern for a generation of old-school prime ministers who believed in 'do-it-yourself' leadership. On entering office in 1945 he had only three private secretaries plus a handful of supporting civil servants. The highest ranking civil servant, the Secretary of the Cabinet, was not Attlee's personal adviser, but a very formidable civil servant, Sir Edward Bridges. Bridges was also Permanent Secretary of the Treasury and Head of the Home Civil Service. When Attlee wanted to take a decision, he read the papers that his civil servants placed before him. After four decades in the Labour Party, twenty-three years in the House of Commons, and five years as deputy Prime Minister under Churchill, Attlee was confident that he knew enough about politics and policy to decide what to do with the information at hand, sending papers back with handwritten queries or with instructions for action.

Attlee was unusual in not having cronies at Downing Street; he relaxed in such solitary pursuits as watching cricket. Most occupants of Number Ten have wanted friends at hand to provide a break from the strain and risks of the job. Churchill's cronies were friends from his days as a campaigner against appeasement in the 1930s or from wartime government. Harold Macmillan relaxed with individuals such as John Wyndham, an eccentric who was not a career politician. Ted Heath relaxed more readily at the piano than with other people. Margaret Thatcher has repeatedly paid tribute to the role of her husband in helping her bear the strains of office. *Private Eye*'s depiction in its 'Dear Bill' column of Denis Thatcher as a saloon-bar buffoon saved him from being cast as an evil Rasputin.

Attlee's practice of being his own chief of staff continued at Number Ten for a generation. The household consisted almost exclusively of high-flying civil servants providing expert technical knowledge and links between Downing Street and the Foreign Office, the Treasury, and other ministries and institutions with which the Prime Minister had to deal as head of Her Majesty's Government. By comparison with the 'chocolate soldiers' subsequently appointed as political special advisers,[4] civil servants have been 'plain vanilla' staff. However, to describe civil servants in Number Ten as non-political is to accuse them of failing in their job. Since all the Prime Minister's concerns are political, officials advising on economic affairs, foreign affairs, home affairs and parliamentary affairs require just as much political *nous* as party political appointees. A civil servant at Number Ten can be described as a 'government party man, who offers his best services to the party in power, to the government of any party'.[5] The relationship between the Prime Minister and his or her civil servants is a fair exchange, in which civil servants serve their political head with loyalty and discretion in return for sharing the status, excitement and influence found there.

Political appointees serving at the pleasure of the Prime Minister have been a regular feature of Number Ten since Harold Wilson brought with him in 1964 Marcia Williams (now Lady Falkender), his political secretary in Opposition. Her arrival was fiercely resisted by the civil service hierarchy, and her personal suspicion of civil servants as anti-Labour added to the resistance. None the less, her attachment to Wilson was strong, and she served there as long as Wilson was Prime Minister. In addition, Thomas Balogh, an unorthodox Oxford economist and long-term associate of Wilson, was given a peerage and installed in the Cabinet Office with two assistants. When Wilson's choice as press secretary turned out to be more a civil servant than a publicist, Gerald Kaufman, later an MP, was brought in from the *Daily Mirror* and paid from party funds to improve press coverage.

When Ted Heath entered Downing Street in 1970, he brought in Douglas Hurd as his political secretary. As an ex-diplomat, Hurd found it easier to get on with civil servants than had Marcia Williams. Heath also established the Central Policy Review Staff (CPRS) to examine long-term strategic issues cutting across conventional Whitehall departmental boundaries and prepare reports for the Cabinet. A non-party man, the scientist Victor Rothschild, was named head of a small staff recruited on grounds of expertise rather than partisan commitment. The assumptions underlying the CPRS were flawed. There was limited demand for long-term thinking from Cabinet ministers overloaded with briefs and often blown off course by unexpected events. Nor did Cabinet ministers welcome bright young graduates prowling around their departments asking awkward questions and reporting answers back to Downing Street. The CPRS was abolished by Margaret Thatcher, who wanted assistance in designing policies to put her convictions into practice rather than questions and comments about matters distant from her concerns.

When Harold Wilson returned to Downing Street in 1974, he invited Bernard (now Lord) Donoughue to head a Policy Unit at Number Ten. The decision was very much spur of the moment, and Donoughue, an academic and long-time Labour supporter, was left to devise his own terms of reference. The Unit monitored departmental actions of concern to Downing Street and wrote memoranda about issues for the Prime Minister. Policy Unit staff were recruited from a variety of backgrounds, political apparatchiks, academics, journalists and pressure groups. Each staffer was given the task of shadowing one or more ministries, and attending some departmental or inter-departmental meetings on behalf of Downing

Street. When civil servants and departmental ministers found that some Policy Unit staff carried influence in Downing Street, they consulted and squared them before sending memoranda to the Prime Minister on which the Unit's staff would comment. After momentary uncertainty, the Policy Unit was maintained by Jim Callaghan, and it has continued under successive prime ministers since.[6]

The institutionalization of the Policy Unit has meant that the Prime Minister now has both civil servants and party political staff on call. However, until 1997 responsibilities of the two groups were kept distinct. Civil servants in Number Ten did not want to be seen to be doing what they considered party political work, and were backed up by the Head of the Cabinet Office and of the civil service. At times the distinction between government and party work was difficult to define, but civil servants found many ways to insist that a line should be maintained. In the late 1960s civil servants kept a watchful eye on photocopying by Labour Party appointees, and protested if it appeared to be about electioneering rather than government business. While Douglas Hurd, an ex-Foreign Office official, was allowed free office space in Number Ten, Central Office was billed for Hurd's travel on government planes at first class fare rather than at the marginal cost of occupying a spare seat.

Margaret Thatcher wanted civil servants to abandon scepticism and adopt her committed, 'businesslike' approach to public policy. She was able to use her long tenure of Downing Street to alter the ethos of civil servants who came in contact with her. Thatcher also brought businessmen to work on projects intended to improve efficiency and cut costs of government. John Major showed his confidence in the civil service by drawing all his press secretaries from their ranks. The Prime Minister did not need to appoint a chief of staff. As long as there were few political appointees working in Downing Street, it was very clear who spoke for the Prime Minister: each did so himself or herself!

More staff and more friction

In Opposition Tony Blair had created an 'organizational weapon' to transform the Labour Party, and he brought to Whitehall a command-and-control strategy for Whitehall. Before the 1997 election, Peter Mandelson and Roger Liddle wrote that Blair had to take personal control of the central government machine, and required more political advice than could be provided by the small team of plain vanilla civil servants. They endorsed increasing the number of political appointees, and then some. The central theme in Blair's approach to Number Ten is that political advice from 'chocolate soldiers' should ripple through all the activities of Number Ten – and flavour the actions of civil servants elsewhere in Whitehall too.

The Blair revolution has more than trebled the political staff working in Downing Street; it could hardly be otherwise when John Major recorded only eight political appointees. The total number of staff, including civil servants, has risen to 150, but many working there provide support services, such as monitoring events at night and weekends, since in a shrinking world Downing Street must be open for business every hour of the night and every day of the week. Number Ten's staff are dispersed among a multitude of mini-units (box 2.1). The largest units, concerned with Press and with Policy, have no more than fifteen people; the smallest has only one. But size is not everything.

Box 2.1 The many mini-offices in Downing Street

> Private Office: Chief of Staff, Jonathan Powell. Political appointee with temporary civil service status.
> Principal Private Secretary: Jeremy Heywood, and private secretaries for economic affairs, foreign affairs, parliamentary affairs and home affairs. Civil servants.
> Diary Secretary: Kate Garvey. Political appointee.
> Special Assistant for Presentation and Planning: Anji Hunter. Political appointee.
> Secretary for Appointments: William Chapman. Civil servant.
> Policy Unit: Head, David Miliband. Political appointee.
> Political Secretary: Sally Morgan. Political appointee.
> Parliamentary Private Secretary: Bruce Grocott MP.
> Chief Press Secretary: Alastair Campbell. Political appointee with temporary civil service status.
> Strategic Communications Unit: Alun Evans.
> Executive Secretary: Pat Dixon. Civil servant.
> Parliamentary Clerk: Clive Barbour. Civil servant.

Source: Derived by the author from *The 34th Civil Service Yearbook, 2000*. London: Stationery Office, 2000, p. 281. Order of precedence as listed there.

Consistent with his manifesto commitment to leverage the influence of government, Blair has leveraged the influence of political appointees through an Order in Council giving two of his senior political advisers, Alastair Campbell and Jonathan Powell, the status of temporary civil servants with authority over career civil servants and also authorizing them to act 'in a political context'. Powell was previously a Foreign Office diplomat, making him *au fait* with Mandarin manners, and his brother, Charles Powell, served Margaret Thatcher. The shift from Thatcher to Blair is reflected in Charles Powell acting as a singular *éminence grise*, whereas Jonathan Powell is positioned at the top of a bureaucratic network with tentacles extending throughout Whitehall. Campbell brings to his work a tabloid journalist's toughness in pushing people to get a story, whatever the costs.

A small group of advisers meets in Downing Street each Monday morning in an effort to set the political agenda for the week. It consists exclusively of political appointees except for the civil servant serving as Principal Private Secretary and Philip Gould, who has no formal position in government, reporting on what the public is thinking, drawing on focus group discussions with small numbers of voters. The increased importance of party appointees has stimulated Opposition MPs to attack Blair for 'politicizing' the Prime Ministership. It has also encouraged Conservatives to note the precedents Blair has established, for use as and when they find themselves back in Downing Street.

A small group in a Georgian house lacks the collective mass to move the whole of Whitehall. Downing Street staff total but 0.001 per cent of all civil servants, and are distant from large Whitehall departments. For example, Downing Street has only three people to monitor education and health, whereas there are dozens of policy-relevant civil servants in each department. Furthermore, responsibility for delivering education is dispersed to more than a hundred local authorities, tens of thousands of schools and hundreds of thousands of teachers. The national health service is provided by a fragmented staff of more than a million. When the Prime Minister announces intentions to promote education or health, he risks being in the position of Glendower, calling to the vasty deeps of public sector agencies and employees.

To apply pressure to Whitehall departments, Tony Blair has leveraged his influence by making Sir Richard Wilson, the Head of the Cabinet Office and Head of the Civil Service, very much part of his team. The Cabinet Office is far larger than Number Ten; its officials are very able civil servants; and it routinely monitors all Whitehall departments and provides the secretariat for interdepartmental committees. A new Performance and Innovation Unit has been established to monitor programmes cutting across departmental boundaries. The Cabinet Office also has sufficient staff to monitor links between domestic Whitehall departments and the European Commission, an important task in a world of increasingly intermestic politics. Blair has described the takeover of the Cabinet Office as creating 'the corporate headquarters of the civil service in order to meet the corporate objectives of the government as a whole, rather than just the objectives of individual departments'. A Blair aide has said the same thing more directly: 'The Cabinet Secretary should be our Chief Whip in Whitehall.'[7]

Tony Blair's willingness to delegate his authority to staff has encouraged people in Whitehall to believe that 'everyone important in it (that is, Number Ten) *is* the Prime Minister'.[8] This is a constitutional novelty in the extreme, for even Tony Benn and Lord Hailsham have not accused previous 'dictators' in Downing Street of maintaining a squad of 'mini-dictators' there.

The expansion of political staff in Downing Street has created friction, as there are now many people who can throw their weight around there – and sometimes elbow or knee each other. In Tony Blair's first three years in office, some of the biggest battles have not been with the Opposition but 'spin doctor wars'. A press story revealing Peter Mandelson's 'loan' from a Cabinet minister, Geoffrey Robinson, was followed up by stories in which Mandelson's enemy, Charlie Whelan, Press Secretary to Gordon Brown, was accused of promoting the story and forced to resign along with Mandelson. Back bench MPs have voiced resentment about the tight control that the Prime Minister seeks to exercise over what MPs say and do, as compared to his inability to stop political appointees from conducting quarrels in public. The chair of the Parliamentary Labour Party, Clive Soley, has warned Blair that the government's practice of 'counter-briefing and spinning against each other' should stop.[9] However, it has not stopped. A veteran Labour minister, Clare Short, has observed, 'You know the entourages are much worse than the people themselves. They are at war for their prince.'[10]

2   The world North of Watford

Prime ministers of the old school took for granted the sovereignty of the Westminster Parliament over all parts of the United Kingdom from inner London to the Celtic periphery. Little attention was paid to distinctive features of public administration in Scotland, Wales and Northern Ireland. The First Lord of the Admiralty had more prestige than the Secretary for Scotland, and the Foreign Office was far more important than departments looking after English local government. The Prime Minister appointed ministers to deal with the Dominions, the Colonies and even Europe before naming a Cabinet minister to deal with Wales or Northern Ireland.

As long as politicians in all parts of the United Kingdom looked to Westminster for leadership, the Prime Minister did not make a special call for support from the 'vasty deeps' of the Clyde or Lough Neagh. Measures that met positive response in London were endorsed throughout the United Kingdom. The Conservative and Labour parties competed for votes without 'interference' by nationalist parties. Until 1964 the Conservatives could win more votes in Scotland than Labour; Unionist MPs from Northern Ireland formed part of the Conservative Party at Westminster; and the problems of Wales, Aneurin Bevan argued, were far beyond the resources of Tredegar District Council or of any institution based in Cardiff to resolve. Only by seizing the power and resources of Westminster could the economic problems of Wales be put right.

From the perspective of Westminster, the North of England began wherever industry was found North of Watford. The long economic boom after 1945 brought prosperity to industrialists and industrial workers. For decades, the chief problems they presented to Downing Street were highly visible strikes, or the hidden costs of manufacturers buying off workers with inflationary pay rises. When traditional industries such as cotton and shipbuilding went into decline, Conservative as well as Labour prime ministers were ready to offer subsidies, until this practice was 'handbagged' by Margaret Thatcher and then ruled as unfair by the European Union. North/South differences have affected voting behaviour, but not challenged the sovereignty of Parliament.

Harold Wilson was the first Prime Minister since Lloyd George to be confronted with challenges from within the United Kingdom to the authority of Her Majesty's Government. The first pricks came when Plaid Cymru won an unexpected by-election victory in Wales in 1966 and the Scottish National Party did likewise in the following year. Wilson adopted the standard delaying tactic of appointing a Royal Commission to sit on the problem. It obligingly took more than four years to report, and when it did so its members were so divided that Downing Street could ignore their recommendations. But the problem returned in 1974, when Wilson found that his tenure in Downing Street depended on the support of Scottish and Welsh Nationalist MPs. Legislation was twice put to Parliament to establish devolved elected assemblies in Scotland and Wales. However, the Welsh electorate rejected the plans in a popular referendum, and in Scotland plans failed to win sufficient votes to be put into effect. In protest, the Nationalists succeeded in bringing down the government of Wilson's successor, Jim Callaghan.

Civil rights marches began in Northern Ireland in 1968, demanding 'one person, one vote, one value'. Wilson's initial response was to offer sympathy, and avoid being drawn into the dispute. But when Protestants and Catholics began killing each other in August 1969, British troops were sent to restore order. By losing the 1970 election, Wilson avoided worse. Ted Heath's government stirred the troubles there by introducing internment and presiding over Bloody Sunday in Londonderry in January 1972. Civil disorder continued for more than a decade thereafter, occasionally claiming victims at Westminster. Thatcher became the first Prime Minister since Lloyd George to acknowledge that Westminster was no longer sovereign throughout the United Kingdom by signing the Anglo-Irish Agreement with the Irish Taoiseach in 1985. It recognized the joint interests of two sovereign states in Northern Ireland. By the time Tony Blair reached Downing Street, sovereignty was further diluted by bringing in the American President. After more than a decade of talk about talks, in 1998 a Good Friday Agreement was signed in Belfast. It acknowledged the power of guns in Ulster to influence policies at Westminster.

When Tony Blair entered Downing Street he brought with him a Labour Party commitment to establish elected assemblies in Scotland and Wales. Scotland and Wales each now has its own First Minister or First Secretary; the titles have been carefully chosen to discourage equating their posts with that of the Prime Minister of the United Kingdom. For the most part, the policies devolved have never concerned Downing Street, such as Scottish schools or Welsh housing, and Westminster Acts of Parliament limit the formal powers of the devolved bodies. During a 1997 election visit to Scotland, Tony Blair proclaimed, 'Sovereignty rests with me as an English MP, and that is the way it will stay.'[11] However, the creation of separately elected assemblies requires the Prime Minister to call votes from the vasty deep to make his will effective there. The Welsh Assembly has shown that it is prepared to dismiss Downing Street's choice as First Secretary, Alun Michael, for a leader of its own choice, Rhodri Morgan. If and when the Scottish National Party ever takes control of the Scottish Executive, it will demand separate and independent prime ministers for Scotland and England.

When Tony Blair called for London to have a popularly elected mayor, he assumed that Londoners, and especially the London Labour Party, would respond as he wished. But instead, the Thames yielded up the Cockney equivalent of the Loch Ness monster, Ken Livingstone, as an independent Mayor of London. Livingstone's enormous margin of victory gives him the legitimacy to pursue Blair-baiting inside and outside Westminster. Margaret Thatcher had an even worse experience with local government. The poll tax assumed that local authorities and citizens would respond to her call, backed up by an Act of Parliament, to change the system of local government finance. In the event, her chosen instrument, the poll tax, turned out to be a textbook example of *Failure in British Government*.[12]

Wherever one now looks in the United Kingdom there is evidence that the power that the Prime Minister wields within Westminster is not always suitable for export to other parts of the United Kingdom. When the Prime Minister attempts to act like Glendower, elected leaders there need not come to heel.

3 National policies are no longer national

When the Prime Minister speaks for Britain abroad, he or she can claim to represent the national interest, and not just the interest of the governing party. But when the Prime Minister deals with leaders of other countries, their task is to represent their own national interests. In a shrinking world, the Prime Minister cannot ignore other countries, for foreign policy is no longer foreign; it affects domestic policy too. When dealing with intermestic policies, the Prime Minister risks a call for action that is cheered in the House of Commons being shot down in foreign capitals.

Hotspur proved correct

Old-school prime ministers still believed that Downing Street had the power to summon indomitable spirits from the deeps; the response of the British people to Winston Churchill's wartime call was taken as proof of that. British participation in the Big Three meeting with President Truman and Josef Stalin at Potsdam in July 1945 reflected Britain's hard-won status. It also made clear the Prime Minister's democratic accountability, for Winston Churchill represented Britain for the first half of the meeting, but was replaced by Clement Attlee immediately the general election result was announced.

The leaders of the Big Three – Winston Churchill, President Harry Truman and Josef Stalin – meeting at Potsdam in July, 1945.
Photo: Popperfoto.

The Attlee government thought in terms of a *national* economic policy. It inherited unprecedented wartime powers over domestic policy, including the control of capital, imports and exports, the direction of labour and food rationing. It extended its control by nationalizing the Bank of England, coal mines, the railways, electricity and gas. However, nationalization of major industries still left the British economy vulnerable to international pressure. Britain was heavily in debt due to borrowing from abroad to finance the war effort.

The Treasury, encouraged by Keynes, was supremely confident that the White House would offer financial support. The spirit of the British delegation seeking American assistance was expressed in its rhyme:

> In Washington Lord Halifax [the British ambassador]
> Once whispered to Lord Keynes,
> 'It's true *they* have the money bags,
> But we have all the brains.'

The assumption was as ill judged as Keynes's use in negotiations of an elaborate ballet metaphor contrasting the good fairy of hope with the wicked fairy of doubt. The US Secretary of the Treasury, Fred Vinson, reacted by turning to a colleague and commenting, 'I don't mind being called malicious, but I *do* mind being called a fairy.'[13]

The end of the war triggered the end of lend-lease aid from the United States. A $3.75-billion loan was finally negotiated with the United States on terms dictated by sceptical Members of Congress. When the terms were put to the House of Commons, Churchill led the Conservatives in abstaining from support, and almost a hundred MPs, including a young Labour backbencher, Jim Callaghan, voted against the loan on the grounds that its terms could not be met.

The influence of Britain internationally was reduced because it lacked the domestic resources to aid postwar reconstruction. When Britain could no longer afford to give aid to Greece and Turkey in 1947, the United States stepped in. Following after this, the Marshall Plan offered economic assistance to European countries to reconstruct their war-ravaged economies. The founding of NATO (the North Atlantic Treaty Organization) in 1949 meant that there was no longer the prospect of Britain standing alone to resist aggression in

Europe. It also meant that the leader of the English-speaking world no longer spoke with an English accent but with the Missouri twang of Harry Truman.

The voices of colonial leaders demanding independence could not be ignored, when they could call on far more supporters than Westminster could mobilize against them. In the Indian subcontinent the Attlee government met demands for independence on terms laid down by Hindu and Muslim leaders rather than by Downing Street. In the face of insurgency against British authority in Palestine, Britain again withdrew. After the Egyptian government nationalized the Suez Canal in 1956, Anthony Eden correctly calculated that Britain, in league with France and Israel, had the military force to seize the Canal. But Eden failed to appreciate the interdependence of politics, money and military force, for after the White House refused to support the pound under heavy pressure in the foreign exchange market, Eden withdrew from the war, and shortly afterwards from Downing Street.

Changing terms of interdependence

Because intermestic politics is about the interdependence of power and money, the influence of the Prime Minister in the world beyond Dover has been progressively reduced by the changing international significance of the British economy. At the same time, the past half-century has seen a big increase in the influence of the international economy on what happens within Britain. Harold Wilson's ministerial career demonstrates the shift in the terms of trade of the British political economy. At the start, he shared the confidence of old-school prime ministers in the power of British government over the national economy. In 1956, Wilson ridiculed 'all the little gnomes of Zurich and the other financial centres about whom we keep hearing'.[14] As Prime Minister in 1967, Wilson was forced to accept that the gnomes towered over him. The pound was devalued, and his government went cap in hand for a loan to the International Monetary Fund (IMF). By 1976 Wilson could foresee that international economic pressures were again threatening his government's domestic policies, and left a sinking ship of state just in time to avoid responsibility for another IMF loan.

The power of the 'inter' as against the 'mestic' side of Britain's economy has impacted on prime ministers of all parties. Ted Heath's attempt to fight inflation by limiting public sector wage demands was blown up when oil-producing countries imposed a massive increase in oil prices and British coal miners struck for a big wage increase, leaving Heath looking like a frustrated Glendower when he called the 'Who governs?' election of February 1974. Jim Callaghan initially believed that the British government could control the British economy, but by the time of his second IMF loan, he was sadder but wiser. Margaret Thatcher thought that the monetarist theories of Milton Friedman, a Nobel laureate from the University of Chicago, would protect her government from the turbulence of international money markets, only to find during her time in Downing Street that the markets took the pound for a roller coaster ride, as it went up to $2.41, and plunged to $1.05 four years later. Yet new-style prime ministers continue to answer to the electorate for what happens to the British branch of an open, international economy.

Britain's entry into the European Community in 1973 has increased the extent of intermestic policymaking. European Union countries, rather than the United States or the Commonwealth, are now Britain's biggest trading partner. The hands of all ministers, including the Prime Minister, are bound by laws and regulations of the European Commission. Ironically, the successful campaign of Margaret Thatcher to promote the Single European Market has given Brussels a justification for promulgating more regulations as common rules for a common market. The deepening and broadening of the European Union reduces the number of issues reaching Downing Street that are exclusively British.

The 'mad cow disease' saga is a textbook example of how a domestic issue becomes an intermestic issue as a consequence of belonging to the European Union. The existence of BSE (bovine spongiform encephalopathy) was known to Department of Agriculture scientists in 1986, and the Ministry took steps to deal with it, but the risk of humans becoming fatally infected remained. When the Prime Minister, John Major, was first informed of the problem in March 1996, he faced a normal domestic policy problem of balancing a possible risk to health against the certain complaints of farmers and food stock suppliers against stringent safeguards against the disease. Major decided against a major ban on beef products that would be 'very costly to the taxpayer and to the beef industry' and lead to a 'huge national panic', but he did approve public health restrictions.[15] News of the British decision triggered an immediate response from European countries, which led to the European Union Commission banning the export of British beef to its member states. The Brussels ruling caught the Prime Minister in a crossfire. On the domestic front he was under attack for not moving faster to protect public health, while on the international front he was criticized for not forcing Brussels to repeal its ban and encourage more French and German consumers to keep on buying British beef.

The special relationship between the US and Britain by which old-school prime ministers put great store is no longer so special, because the United States became the global power while Britain's role was shrinking. The phone number for Downing Street is only one among dozens of numbers that the White House telephonists store, along with those for leaders scattered from Tokyo and Beijing to Moscow and Berlin. The United States and Britain work together in the NATO alliance, but this does not make the two equally important. The United States is the hegemon – that is, the dominant power – in any alliance of which it is a part, as the Gulf War and the war in Kosovo illustrate. Decisions about whether, when and how to use NATO weapons are taken in the White House rather than around an international conference table. The Prime Minister's position in discussions with the President is like the Queen's position in discussions with Downing Street: it is possible to inquire, advise, encourage or caution. But as a non-voting participant in Washington politics, the Prime Minister lacks real influence.

In intermestic policies, the world that matters most is the world beyond Dover. The economic activities that most affect Britain are calculated in dollars, yen and euros as well as (or instead of) pounds. Peace depends on what happens in the Middle East, in the Balkans and along the Irish border as much as or more than on what is decided in Downing Street. The Prime Minister attends the annual world summit meeting of the G-7 countries, but so too do the leaders of the United States, Germany, Japan, France, Italy and Canada, and sometimes the Russian leader too.

The inability of a Prime Minister to summon British forces strong enough to rule waves of foreign currency speculation is due not to faults in Downing Street, but to the success of other countries. In the lifetime of Tony Blair, Germany has achieved a gross domestic product double that of Britain, and the American economy has become six times larger. New economies and new democracies have been created around the world; Japan now has a gross domestic product more than three times that of Britain. Differences in economic growth rates have resulted in the British standard of living falling to the bottom quarter of countries in the European Union. While the national health service is a cherished British icon, after half a century of its existence the life expectancy of British men and women is now in the bottom half of countries in the European Union. When Tony Blair came under attack because of problems in the health service, he did not fall back on the old refrain, 'Britain is best.' Instead, he announced a policy of raising public spending on health to the level of that in the average European Union country.

Interdependence is neither good nor bad in itself; it is simply a fact of life. Britain benefits when the world economy booms, and faces recession when it slackens. At work, Britons must compete with high wage, high skill workers in Germany and with low wage, low skill workers in third world countries. As consumers, Britons enjoy electronic goods from the Far East, a choice of food from many continents and an assurance of sunshine when taking holidays abroad. A military alliance with the United States was vital in winning two world wars; it has also brought Britain into war on the far side of Albania. In discussions of intermestic and international issues, the Prime Minister has a voice, but it is far from the only voice.

The spirit of Glendower still permeates Westminster. When debating the economy, many MPs talk as if Downing Street could call up prosperity from the vasty deep of the international economy. Margaret Thatcher embodied the ambivalence of Downing Street towards Europe. Politically, she sought to make the English Channel a 'moat defensive' against Europe, while endorsing the Channel Tunnel, which has created the most tangible link between Westminster and France since 1558, when Calais was under the English Crown. The Mother of Parliaments can take cues from tabloid newspaper editors, and discuss such issues as: whose face do you want on your money – that of the Queen or of a dead foreigner such as Ludwig van Beethoven or Leonardo da Vinci?

Within the world of Westminster, Tony Blair has been quick to act. From his first day at Number Ten, he has accelerated the accumulation of power there, bringing in more political appointees and giving them more power over civil servants and ministers than did any predecessor. North of Watford he has presided over devolution to Wales and Scotland and actively promoted a new power-sharing executive in Northern Ireland. If these measures succeed as intended, the Prime Minister will be able to avoid such humdrum domestic issues as Scottish housing, the organization of Welsh schools, or the routing of parades in Ulster, and have more time to deal with intermestic issues.

Intermestic issues involve the intersection of conflicting domestic and international pressures. The good news is that this gives the Prime Minister a choice of policies, but the bad news is that the choice is often between the horns of a dilemma. Nowhere is this more evident than when the Prime Minister contemplates the gain in international influence in joining the European Monetary Union and the domestic political attacks that doing so would invite from opponents seeing it as undermining British sovereignty. To date, Tony Blair has avoided this dilemma by letting the issue simmer and stew.

In dealing with intermestic issues, there is always an inclination to put domestic considerations before international concerns. But doing so risks what a former Downing Street adviser has called 'that besetting weakness of British foreign policy, the expectation that foreign governments would, or should, feel and reason as we do'.[16] Dealing with intermestic issues requires more than calling votes from the 'vasty deeps' of the Thames. When domestic policies also involve the European Union, it is necessary as well to call on support from along the Tiber and the Tagus, the Seine and the Spree. When economic pressures bear down on the Prime Minister, calls go out to the Rhine and the Potomac too. Leaders there have their own political stakes to think about, and are accountable to un-British electorates. In a shrinking world, the oft-quoted maxim of an American Congressman – 'All politics is local' – has become a half truth. Because the Prime Minister stands where domestic and international pressures intersect, a more accurate maxim is, 'All politics is intermestic.'

3

What Makes Downing Street Change?

[Of Winston Churchill] There was a layer of seventeenth century, a layer of eighteenth century, a layer of nineteenth century and possibly even a layer of twentieth century. You were never sure which layer would be uppermost.

Clement Attlee[1]

A week in politics is a long time.

Harold Wilson

Shortly after Tony Blair became Prime Minister, he astonished a meeting of European social democratic leaders with the cry 'New, New, New: everything is new.'[2] Blair's impatience with the past and enthusiasm for the future contrasts sharply with the respect for tradition of old-school prime ministers, regardless of party. More than that, Blair's hymn to novelty implies that the past is as dead as yesterday's newspapers, that Britain can be 'rebranded' as readily as a tabloid editor can put a new headline on a story. Although Harold Wilson was a generation older than Blair, he too saw the political climate change in a week. Within a week, there are days when the Prime Minister must turn up in the Commons to answer questions; there are days when events provide good news, and days when they offer bad news. Some days there is no news, except what the Press Secretary creates for the media.

Constitutional historians disagree flatly with the emphasis on novelty in Downing Street. They argue that what is important about British government is what is unchanging. A major innovation, such as the creation of the office of the Prime Minister, is expected to happen only once in a quarter of a millennium. An academic

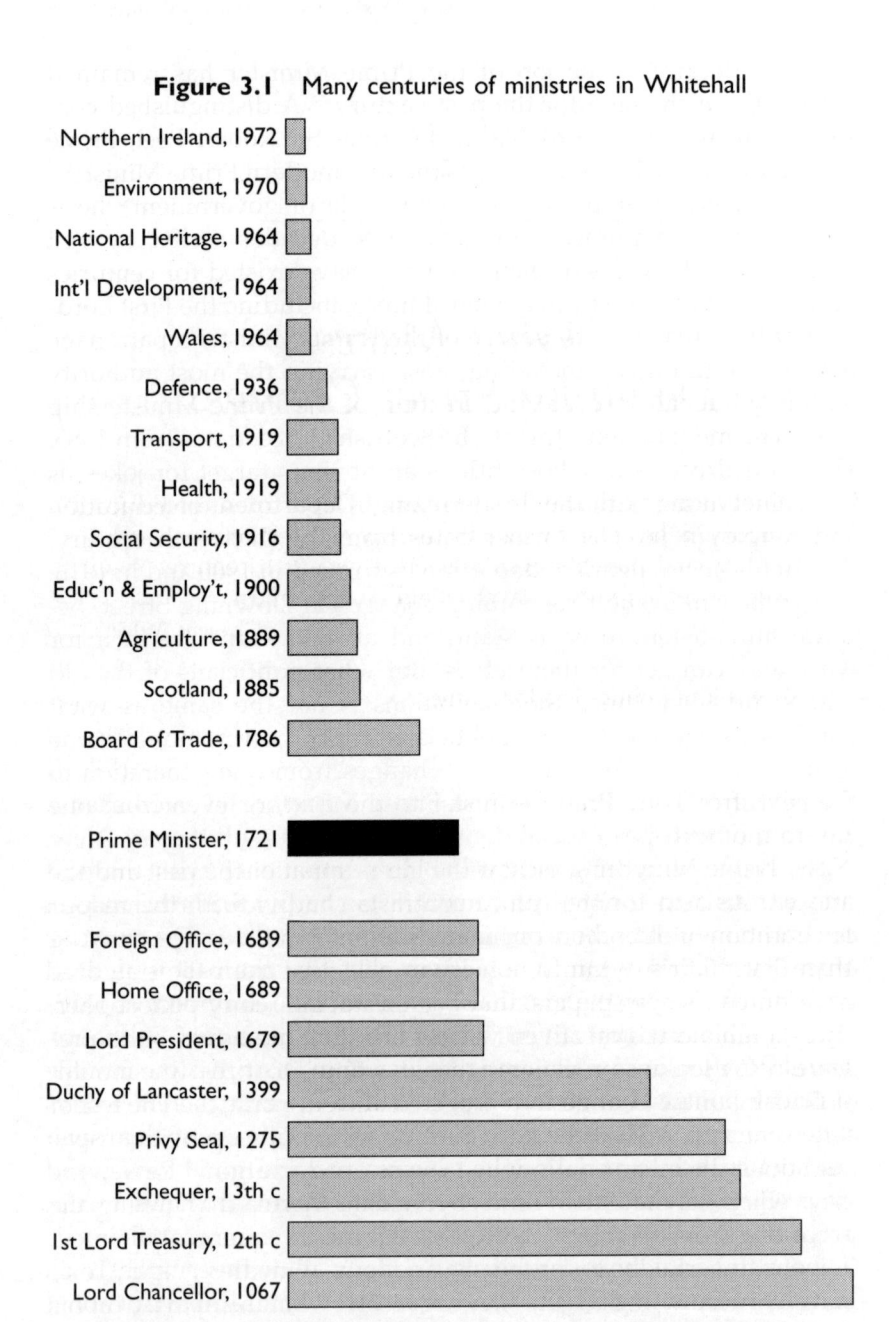

Figure 3.1 Many centuries of ministries in Whitehall

- Northern Ireland, 1972
- Environment, 1970
- National Heritage, 1964
- Int'l Development, 1964
- Wales, 1964
- Defence, 1936
- Transport, 1919
- Health, 1919
- Social Security, 1916
- Educ'n & Employ't, 1900
- Agriculture, 1889
- Scotland, 1885
- Board of Trade, 1786
- Prime Minister, 1721
- Foreign Office, 1689
- Home Office, 1689
- Lord President, 1679
- Duchy of Lancaster, 1399
- Privy Seal, 1275
- Exchequer, 13th c
- 1st Lord Treasury, 12th c
- Lord Chancellor, 1067

Notes: Defence combines Lord Admiral, 1540; War, 1794; Air, 1917. The office of First Lord of the Treasury and Prime Minister are held by the same person. The Foreign Office and Home Office are dated from the creation of the Northern Department and the Southern Department.

textbook declares, 'The job of the Prime Minister has remained essentially unchanged for the past century.'[3] A distinguished constitutional historian, Lord Blake, describes Sir Robert Peel, Prime Minister in the 1830s and 1840s, as the first modern Prime Minister.[4]

When Tony Blair promises a 'new style of government', he is actually using a phrase promoted three decades earlier by Ted Heath, and the offices of their ministers have existed for centuries (figure 3.1). Five date from medieval times, including the First Lordship of the Treasury, the source of the Prime Minister's patronage powers. Eight offices, including those carrying the most authority within Whitehall, predate the creation of the Prime Ministership itself. The median department, the Scottish Office, dates from 1885. The Lord Privy Seal, whose title is an obvious target for jokes, is in Cabinet along with the 'modernizing' Department of Education and Employment. The former dates from the thirteenth century; the later is an amalgam of departments formed in 1900 and in 1916.

A cynic can argue that nothing changes in Downing Street, because human nature is constant, and all politicians are in it for what they can get for themselves. But what politicians of the old school did to advance their ambitions is not the same as what Blairites do. Moreover, what politicians want – power, money, fame or the sense of a job well done – changes from one generation to the next, from one Prime Minister to the next, or even from one day to the next.

The Prime Minister stands at the intersection of the past and the present. As Attlee noted of Churchill, an individual's behaviour can combine influences from four different centuries. On entering office, every Prime Minister receives a legacy from the outgoing government. It was the maxim of an aristocratic Tory philosopher, Lord Hugh Cecil, that 'Even when I changed, it should be to preserve.'[5] Roy Jenkins proclaimed that he wanted to 'break the mould' of British politics, but he too respected ancient realities. 'The test of statesmanship will not be how many trees it pulls up by the roots, but how it fits into a continuous process of adaptation.'[6] Reviewing the problems of the 1964 Wilson government, Reginald Maudling, the preceding Conservative Chancellor of the Exchequer, commented, 'Labour inherited our problems and our remedies',[7] and Tony Blair has admitted that 'the hand of history' weighs heavily on his shoulder when it is the Red Hand of Ulster.[8]

The pattern of change in Downing Street differs with the angle of vision. A journalist sensitive to the idiosyncratic features of daily events can make the Prime Minister appear to be on a *random walk*, a statistical term for a sequence of activities without any predictable pattern. Colloquially, it means that life in Number Ten is just one damned thing after another, and one Prime Minister after another. In so far as the *economic cycle* or *electoral swings* are of primary importance, changes will be frequent but there will be no progress, for a cycle follows a pendulum pattern, going back and forth as boom and bust follow each other in the economy and Tweedledum replaces Tweedledee in Downing Street. From the perspective of the gallery of time, *irreversible structural changes* barely visible during one Prime Minister's term of office gradually create discontinuities between old-school and new-style prime ministers. For example, television needed years to break down the barriers between the media and the Prime Minister, but once it succeeded in doing so there was no return to the world of pre-television politics in Westminster.

1   Events – *expected and unexpected*

In the course of half a century, the job of the Prime Minister is altered by many influences – events, personalities, cycles in the economy and majority parties, and irreversible structural changes in the three worlds of the Prime Minister.

Events – expected and unexpected

When Harold Macmillan was asked to identify the most troublesome feature of his job, he replied, 'Events, my dear boy, events.' The Prime Minister spends much of the week reacting to events that come in many sizes, shapes and forms. An event can require immediate attention and merit a media headline, but have no long-term consequences. Most headline stories are ephemeral. Few journalists or voters can remember the Belcher affair or what led Christopher Mayhew to resign his ministerial post. Among a thousand or more so-called crises, only a few have a long-term impact. When public sector strikes broke out early in 1979, Jim Callaghan sought to deny that they were symptoms of crisis and chaos. But the headline writers of the *Sun* thought differently, and so did the voters, when Callaghan went to the polls in May.

What Makes Downing Street Change? 57

On returning from a Caribbean meeting in January, 1979, Prime Minister Jim Callaghan was asked about the mounting chaos in the country. He replied, 'I don't think that other people in the world would share the view that there is mounting chaos.' The *Sun* turned his words into the above headline.

Courtesy of John Frost Historical Newspapers.

Regular and predictable events such as the annual Queen's Speech to Parliament can be prepared well in advance, if the Prime Minister is so minded. Committees can sift issues for months, departmental civil servants and parliamentary draughtsmen can prepare bills, and Downing Street can decide they are worth an investment of legislative time and political capital. On entering Downing Street in 1997, Tony Blair was set to become the first English leader since King Ethelred the Unready (reign: 978–1006) to have his rule span two millennia, and to do so with far greater media resources than Ethelred had.

Unexpected events are the bane of civil servants but offer opportunities to politicians. Harold Macmillan entered Downing Street because of the vacancy created by Anthony Eden's collapse during the Suez War. Macmillan's tenure entered its final phase when a junior minister, John Profumo, was caught in a scandal with a prostitute. Downing Street's reaction to the accidental death of Princess Diana is a classic example of exploiting an event that was both ambiguous and unexpected. Blair's staff had made no secret of their scorn for royalty; while a journalist, Press Secretary Alastair Campbell had described royals as 'thick', and Princess Diana as 'vacuous, shallow, silly and egomaniacal'.[9] Yet following her unexpected death, Downing Street launched Princess Diana as 'the people's princess' – and the Prime Minister stepped into the limelight to express popular grief.

A crisis can require an immediate decision in conditions of high uncertainty. The Argentine invasion of the Falkland Islands required the Prime Minister to act on short notice. Thatcher chose a military response in a setting unfavourable to the deployment of Britain's military forces. The outcome was victory, but the Chiefs of Staff could not guarantee this when the decision to attack was made.

An event that bursts unannounced can be described as an 'I told you so' event if it is caused by difficulties that experts saw coming. Margaret Thatcher, for example, could not see that having her own economic adviser at Downing Street, Alan Walters, was bound to provoke trouble with her Chancellor of the Exchequer, Nigel Lawson, because of their different views about economic policy. Nor could Tony Blair see that taking a million pounds for the Labour Party from Formula One motor racing promoter Bernard Ecclestone could raise suspicions of cash for influence. Others could see trouble ahead – and events proved them correct.

There are also 'I hope not events', that is, difficulties that the Prime Minister can foresee but hopes do not explode while he or she is in office. While Harold Wilson was responsible for sending troops to Northern Ireland in 1969, he was not caught in the outbreak of civil war, for that occurred after Wilson had become Leader of the Opposition. The Prime Minister of the day faces many demands to deal with events that have not, or at least have not yet, happened. They are hypothetical threats, such as the risk of flooding or a bridge collapsing if more money is not spent on maintenance. If it takes twenty years for bridge deterioration to lead to a collapse, then the Prime Minister responsible for cutting expenditure on bridge maintenance will be well away from the scene as and when the collapse happens.

Many crisis choices are choices at a crossroads, for once the Prime Minister starts going down one fork in the road, there is no going back. When civil rights demonstrations were followed by mass rioting and killings in Northern Ireland, in 1969 Harold Wilson sent British troops to restore order. The presence of troops in Northern Ireland meant that Downing Street could no longer turn a blind eye to its divisions. The subsequent three decades and more have been marked by an accumulation of developments, some reflecting divisions from generations and centuries past, that were neither planned nor desired when the Prime Minister first sent troops there.

Individual personalities

The most visible change occurs at Number Ten when one tenant moves out and another moves in. Civil servants who have served a number of prime ministers can talk for hours about differences in the personalities of the ten men and one woman who have lived there since 1945. Clement Attlee would never use one word when none would do, whereas Harold Wilson could be garrulous to a fault. Harold Macmillan had a shy, introverted temperament, whereas Tony Blair is ready to chat with people as if he were a vicar welcoming parishioners to an ecumenical sing-along service.

Irritatingly for feminists, Margaret Thatcher is the best example of the Great Man (*sic*) theory of the Prime Ministership. Everyone who came in contact with Thatcher during her eleven years in Downing Street felt the full effect of a very forceful personality. Thatcher was a non-conformist and propagated a novel political programme of her own. When under attack at the 1980 Conservative Party conference, she declared, 'You turn if you want to; the lady's not for turning.' Instead of being pragmatic, she was ideological; instead of being emollient, she was combative; and instead of being willing to compromise, she was insistent. In short, she differed both from old-school personalities and from John Major and Tony Blair. The most striking feature of Margaret Thatcher is how *atypical* a Prime Minister she was. Even though Earl Grey gave his name to a tea and Gladstone to a travelling bag, none of her predecessors succeeded, as she did, in giving their name to an -ism, 'Thatcherism'.

Personality theories imply that the Prime Minister of the day can choose to do whatever he or she wants; they also imply that each incumbent will behave differently in keeping with his or her distinctive personality. A pseudo-sociological gloss can be added by describing the Prime Minister as a 'charismatic' figure. However, in the original sense a charismatic political leader is a person who destroys institutions and seeks to rule by personality alone.[10] In European history charismatic figures loom large, such as Adolf Hitler, Charles de Gaulle and Boris Yeltsin, exceptional personages who succeeded in very un-British circumstances. British political institutions are very resistant to charismatic personalities; see the fate of Enoch Powell, whose charismatic visions failed to transform first England and then Northern Ireland. Prime ministers are the opposite of charismatic; they do not want to destroy the institutions of Westminster, because these institutions give them power. Within a more or less fixed set of expectations, prime ministers differ in style, that is, how they go about the job.

An emphasis on individual personality implies constancy in the behaviour of a particular Prime Minister. Yet the two individuals who have served two different terms as Prime Minister since 1940 – Winston Churchill and Harold Wilson – behaved very differently in each term, as personal and political circumstances altered. During the Second World War Winston Churchill was the model of an active maker of policies. When he returned to office in 1951, his old staff brought out from their filing cabinets labels they had preserved from wartime saying ACTION THIS DAY. They remained there for three and a half years, and were never used.[11] When Harold Wilson first entered Downing Street in 1964 he did so after a campaign in which his youth and abilities were promoted as making him a 'Kennedyesque' leader. When he returned in 1974, Wilson was worn out and ageing prematurely, with neither the energy nor the inclination to deal with novel problems facing the country. Wilson governed with a lax hand and spent his final months anticipating early retirement. During a single term of office, a Prime Minister's political capital also fluctuates. It is high on entering, but sooner or later it falls and, even if it subsequently recovers, the ups and downs of events make prime ministers appear more or less successful during their term of office (cf. chapter 6).

Memoirs or biographies about the life of a Prime Minister usually explain achievements and failures in the context of the times, and not as the will of a single individual. Memoirs detail the efforts of the Prime Minister to deal with the problems thrown up by events and circumstances; Cabinet ministers with different ideas and priorities; constructive and obstructive groups in Parliament; perturbations in the economy; and the actions of foreign governments and leaders. Whatever the result, each chapter usually concludes that the Prime Minister did the best he or she could do. If the outcome is palpably unsatisfactory, it is blamed on circumstances that no Prime Minister could master.

The political business cycle

Although Marxists are now very rare at Westminster, there is a great deal of economic determinism in the analysis of what makes a Prime Minister's political capital go up and down. The simplest answer is that of Bill Clinton's 1992 campaign staff: 'It's the economy, stupid.' The theory is popular in Tony Blair's Downing Street. However, if the statement were a law of politics, Blair would not have won the 1997 election, for when the election was held the Conservatives were presiding over an economy growing at double the rate of the previous decade.

The political business cycle is derived from the Keynesian theory of macroeconomic management, which shows how the government can in theory stimulate wage increases and consumption or restrain the economy if inflation appears the greater threat. By combining Marx and Keynes, the Prime Minister can promote an economic boom and confidently call a general election when the boom is at its peak. The bitter anti-inflation medicine that Keynes prescribed can be administered after the election, when the harm to the Prime Minister's political capital is minimal.[12]

The theory of the political business cycle is very attractive to the Prime Minister, but in practice it delivers fewer benefits than promised. Downing Street has often been unable to synchronize the ups and downs of the economy with the electoral calendar. Developments in the international economy are beyond the control of Downing Street, as was spectacularly illustrated by the Organization of Petroleum Exporting Countries (OPEC) oil cartel introducing a massive increase in oil prices months before Ted Heath was due to call a general election. Moreover, some election outcomes, such as Margaret Thatcher's repeated victories in the face of unprecedented high unemployment, do not fit theories about incumbent politicians losing elections when the economy makes the electorate feel bad.

Partisan differences?

To become Prime Minister, a politician must first appeal to a highly partisan electoral college that chooses the party leader. But he or she must also win the support of a far less partisan electorate. Partisans view electoral competition as occurring between adversaries with conflicting philosophies of governance. The return of a Labour leader to Downing Street should therefore result in big changes in how the Prime Minister behaves, and the return of a Conservative leader should do the same, and the alternation of party leaders should therefore produce cyclical changes in the behaviour of prime ministers. In place of bi-partisan categories of old-school and new-style prime ministers, theories of party government imply that John Major and Winston Churchill should have more in common with each other than Churchill and Attlee, and that Tony Blair should resemble Clement Attlee (or, leftwing critics would aver, Ramsay MacDonald) more than Margaret Thatcher.

The Conservative and Labour parties formed expectations of old-school leaders in radically different circumstances. Conservatives saw their leader as the Prime Minister or as a potential Prime Minister not beholden to the party organization. By contrast, the leader of the old Parliamentary Labour Party was expected to advocate the policies of the party conference, which met annually and was dominated by trade unions rather than by MPs, a practice that Robert T. McKenzie attacked as unconstitutional.[13] Party leaders raised in the old school were accustomed to stressing differences between parties. In a 1945 election broadcast, Winston Churchill warned the electorate that the Socialist (that is, Labour) Party 'is inescapably interwoven with totalitarianism' and would require 'a Gestapo' to introduce its policies. Clement Attlee responded by thanking Churchill for making clear to the electorate 'the difference between Winston Churchill the great leader in war of a united nation, and Mr. Churchill, the party leader of the Conservatives'. Attlee eschewed violent language, but his then party chairman,

Harold Laski, claimed that a Labour Prime Minister would be an agent of a Labour Party organization committed to policies very different from those of a Conservative-dominated wartime coalition.[14]

Because each election produces a loser as well as a winner, the Opposition leader is under pressure to understand, and even mimic, the winner. Cumulatively, this has led to big changes in the Conservative and Labour parties, especially how they behave in government. The contrasts between the parties drawn by Churchill and Laski have become irrelevant. New-style party leaders seek the support of much the same group of middle-of-the-road voters, and this encourages them to appear similar. The idea of dying in the last ditch in protest against what the median voter wants does not appeal to party leaders who want to live in Downing Street. Instead of emphasizing differences in party policy, new-style leaders often emphasize differences in personal competence. The contrast that Tony Blair sought to draw between himself and John Major was not in terms of policy but of who was better in leading towards consensual goals.

Continuities between prime ministers are greatest when Downing Street changes hands but the party in control of the House of Commons remains the same. While Jim Callaghan or John Major did not agree with everything their immediate predecessor had done in office, neither could repudiate collective responsibility for actions to which they had assented in Cabinet. Before offering fresh ideas, a new Prime Minister must deal with the legacy of his or her immediate successor. The longer the governing party is in office, the more its choices are likely to reflect pressures of Whitehall and the world beyond Britain. As John Patten, a former Oxford don and Cabinet minister, has remarked, 'It is hard enough work to govern; to think anew while governing is desperately difficult.'[15]

2 Long-term irreversible influences

Journalism deals with the events of the week, the day, or the hour and a political biography focuses on a few years spent by one politician in Downing Street. From such perspectives it is impossible to see long-term structural changes affecting the work of the Prime Minister. Yet to ignore long-term change risks being stranded on the shores of time. French historians refer to the *longue durée*, a lengthy span of time within which many small changes accumulate with the force of inertia. The gradual forward movement of political inertia is often ignored. By definition, it is not newsworthy, because it merely repeats what has happened previously. But as Aristotle long ago noted, it is sophistical to argue 'If each is little, then all are little.' The cumulative inertia of small, even imperceptible changes cannot be ignored when they force structural changes in politics and public policy, and these changes are irreversible.

Long-term changes cannot be dated to a single day's headline or a particular Prime Minister's time in office, because they require many decades to be realized. The end of Empire that started under Clement Attlee was only completed after Tony Blair entered office with the handing over of Hong Kong to Communist China in 1997. Even when a significant event can be dated, such as Britain's entry to the European Community on 1 January 1973, this is only part of the story. The debate about Britain's links with Europe began in the 1945–51 Attlee government and it has continued under ten prime ministers since.

The longer the time-span, the greater the likelihood that the gradual accumulation of unnoticed changes will produce a large, irreversible change in the structure of politics and public policy. The turnover of generations is an example of irreversible long-term change. In postwar Britain this has radically altered the recruitment of Members of Parliament, the pool from which Prime Ministers are drawn. Even though party labels remain the same, the roots of a party's MPs have altered (figure 3.2). A half century ago the Labour Party still reflected its original aim of promoting the representation of manual workers in the House of Commons. At that time, 37 per cent of Labour MPs had started life as manual workers, including 35 coal miners. Today, a party founded for workers by hand and brain is represented almost entirely by brainworkers; lecturers and teachers are twice as numerous in the Parliamentary Labour Party as are manual workers. A Labour Prime Minister who wants support cannot appeal for loyalty on traditional grounds understood by trade unionists.

In the Conservative Party, inter-generational change has eroded the historic divide between the gentry and aristocrats as against the middle classes. In 1960 an intelligent, ambitious Conservative seeking a seat in the House of Commons explained to me the social stratification of the party at that time: there were those born in a great house (such as Winston Churchill, the grandson of a duke);

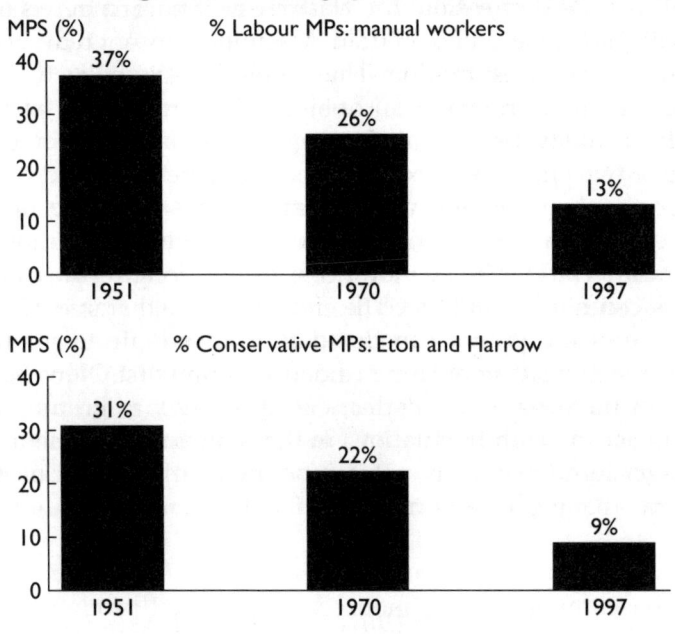

Figure 3.2 Changing social class of MPs

% Labour MPs: manual workers
- 1951: 37%
- 1970: 26%
- 1997: 13%

% Conservative MPs: Eton and Harrow
- 1951: 31%
- 1970: 22%
- 1997: 9%

Source: Derived from David Butler et al., *The British General Election*. London: Macmillan. For 1951, pp. 39, 41; 1970, pp. 302–3; 1997, pp. 204–5.

those who married into the aristocracy (Harold Macmillan, who married a duke's daughter); and people like himself, who were simply working their way, because they were 'first generation public school'.[16] Safe Conservative seats showed a preference for people with a good family pedigree. In the 1950s almost a third of Conservative MPs had attended Eton or Harrow. In the 1959 general election campaign Harold Macmillan joked, 'There were three Old Etonians in Mr. Attlee's Cabinet. I have six. Things have been twice as good under the Conservatives.'[17] It was not until the Thatcher years that the Conservative Party became unequivocally middle-class. Today, the number of Conservative MPs from Eton and Harrow is less than half what it was when Ted Heath became Prime Minister and less than a third that in Churchill's day. There are now twice as many Conservative MPs who have started out as journalists or Conservative apparatchiks as there are Etonians and Harrovians.

Irreversible structural change does not mean the end of history. The shifting definition of 'prosperity' in electoral politics illustrates this. For the first decade after 1945, prosperity meant the absence of a 1930s-style depression, for wartime rationing lingered on. At the 1959 general election Harold Macmillan took credit for the growth of mass consumption. The goods that symbolized this – a small car, a tiny refrigerator and a small black-and-white television set – have today been overtaken by goods that did not exist a decade or two ago. There are debates about whether too few homes have personal computers and too many homes have two cars.

The career of the pound in the international economy illustrates how short-term events, economic cycles and long-term structural changes combine to influence the fortunes of the Prime Minister. The value of the pound can fluctuate from minute to minute in response to transitory events in London, Frankfurt, New York or Tokyo. In the course of a Parliament, it is likely to go up and go down in accord with fluctuations in the economic cycle. However, the longer-term pattern is not a random walk or a cycle; it is a structural change, a trend down.

3 Combinations of causes

For clarity in exposition, causes of change can be categorized separately. But in the world in which the Prime Minister works, different causes often register their effect simultaneously, creating competing claims for attention. Within the space of a few days in July 2000, Tony Blair had suffered the embarrassing leak of private memos; an attack from a one-time Labour fundraiser for being a control freak; a negative reaction to a proposal for spot fines of lager louts; his 16-year-old son being arrested as drunk and incapacitated; and in a Freudian slip, telling the House of Commons, 'Let's concentrate on spin, not substance.' Twice in the month the press headlined 'Blair's worst week'. A content analysis found that twenty-five of the Prime Minister's 114 weeks since the general election had been headlined as his worst.[18] Almost once a month the Prime Minister can expect that events will make his or her tasks go from good to bad, to worse or even to the worst so far.

The circumstances facing an individual Prime Minister combine events, the contingencies of economic and political cycles and the current effect of continuing long-term changes. The Heraclitus principle – you can never step in the same river twice – means that even when the Prime Minister is the same, differences in circumstances produce different outcomes. Although Winston Churchill was a leading figure in the House of Commons in the 1930s, he was, in the words of Harold Macmillan, 'what the English call unstable – by which they mean anybody who has that touch of genius which is inconvenient in normal times'.[19] Churchill was kept out of a government pursuing peace at home and appeasement abroad, because of his forceful personality and erratic judgement. But Stanley Baldwin privately recognized that if circumstances altered, Churchill's talents would be needed in government. He wrote to a friend, 'If there is going to be a war – and no one can say that there is not – we must keep him fresh to be our war Prime Minister.'[20] When war came, Churchill entered Downing Street. Five years later, when peace returned, the electorate voted Churchill out of office. Changing circumstances account for both his entry to and his exit from Downing Street.

When the Prime Minister executes a reversal of policy, this does not put the clock back to where things were before, for circumstances meanwhile have changed. The vagaries of British relationships with Europe illustrate this. Three prime ministers – Harold Macmillan, Harold Wilson and Ted Heath – each sought to negotiate British membership in the European Community. None did so in circumstances as favourable as those offered Clement Attlee and Anthony Eden when European institutions were initially mooted in the 1950s and British influence was still very high. Similarly, when European governments discussed establishing the European Monetary Union, Britain could have participated in discussions as an equal partner, but this was not acceptable in domestic British politics. However, as and when Tony Blair seeks British entry to the European Monetary Union, the starting point will be different. The Prime Minister will be offered on a take it or leave it basis arrangements established in Britain's absence.

The combined effect of past government commitments determines the path of public policy when a new Prime Minister arrives in Downing Street. As long as established programmes continue routinely, the Prime Minister is free to concentrate on fresh events. However, the more the Prime Minister's policies are inherited from the past, the less impact the new incumbent has. Margaret Thatcher's inheritance dated back generations; a third of the laws had been on the statute books before the end of Queen Victoria's reign. Inherited legislation authorized hundreds of policies dealing with everything from maternity leave to cemeteries, and claiming many billions of pounds in public expenditure. By the time Thatcher left a decade later, some new laws had been introduced, some old laws repealed, and some of her own programmes repealed too; for example, measures unsuccessful in stemming the rise of unemployment. In total, 74 per cent of policies in effect when she left Downing Street had been there when she entered. Moreover, open-ended statutory entitlements to free health care, higher education and other public services doubled public expenditure. In her final year, 89 per cent of public spending was devoted to programmes that Margaret Thatcher had inherited from her predecessors rather than chosen herself.[21]

Tony Blair readily proclaims a desire to create a 'new' Britain. The word is invariably used with positive connotations; 'new ways' are contrasted with out-dated old ways that ought to be abandoned, whether legacies from past Labour or Conservative governments. When changes do not occur as quickly as desired, Blair becomes frustrated. His neophilia has blinded him to obstacles to change. To ignore obstacles is to risk policies written in the sands of rhetoric being washed away when the tide comes in.

4

Becoming and Remaining Party Leader

British politics is a team sport. In the 20th century, only three outsiders (Lloyd George, Winston Churchill and Margaret Thatcher) made it to the top. The rest of our 19 prime ministers over the past 100 years – from Arthur James Balfour to Tony Blair, at least until he got into No. 10 – had first proved themselves as team players.

Anthony Howard[1]

Baseball reporter to Lefty Gomez, leading member of world champion New York Yankees team: Lefty, you're not a good pitcher; you're just lucky.
Gomez: I'd rather be lucky than good.

Anyone ambitious for personal fame should take up golf or tennis, because success in these sports depends on what an individual does. By contrast, British politics is a team sport. In a team sport, there is competition between two opposing groups. Within each team, there is cooperation in trying to beat the opposition, and competition to be recognized as the team's star. Enoch Powell's failure shows that a British politician who makes himself a national figure by attacking his own team cannot rise to the top. When Powell put his name forward for the Conservative leadership in 1965, he received only fifteen of the 298 votes cast by fellow MPs. Powell would have been better off running for President of the United States or of a Latin America country, where personal followings count for more than party.

Becoming party leader requires luck, for the circumstances in which leaders are chosen are often unexpected, and the outcome fortuitous. Clement Attlee did not spend years plotting to become Labour leader, having had the good fortune to be one of forty-six

Labour MPs who retained their seats in the party's landslide defeat of 1931. A politician who becomes leader of the governing party is doubly fortunate, for this carries with it the post of Prime Minister. Since 1955, five Cabinet ministers have become Prime Minister as the choice of the governing party's selectorate rather than the electorate. But luck is only half the story. A successful athlete such as Lefty Gomez started training in youth to develop the skills for success in major league baseball, and an ambitious politician must start young to achieve success in major league politics.

Whereas an athlete can gain national recognition when young, it takes decades before an aspiring politician can get near the top at Westminster. The first step upwards is to secure nomination for a safe parliamentary seat. Once in the Commons, an ambitious MP faces the prospect of years on the back benches and then years as a shadow or a real Cabinet minister. The average Prime Minister enters Downing Street more than a quarter-century after becoming active in party politics.

A British party leader has a unique authority, for there is no other office in the Conservative or the Labour Party to match it. By contrast, in Washington the President must share power and influence with his party's leaders in Congress, and with leaders of the opposite party if they are the majority there. In many European countries, the Prime Minister shares power with the leader of the party in Parliament or its general secretary. Where there is a coalition government, the Prime Minister shares responsibilities with heads of other parties too.

A Prime Minister whose political capital stands high can discipline backbench MPs and intimidate Cabinet ministers with the threat, 'Back me or you will be sacked.' But the need for election victory places a Damoclean sword over the head of a party leader. Election defeat, or the threat of defeat, can cause the party's selectorate to plunge in the sword and secure a new and potentially more winning leader. Since 1945 more prime ministers have been pushed out of office by their onetime supporters than have left office voluntarily.

1 A long apprenticeship

A desire to become Prime Minister is an unrealistic ambition for anyone starting a career at Westminster. For every MP who aspires to this office, hundreds fall short. Of the thousands of politicians in the House of Commons in the past half century, 99.7 per cent have *not* become Prime Minister. In each generation, only a handful of MPs reach Downing Street. In the 1945 Parliament, there were only four future prime ministers – Winston Churchill, Anthony Eden, Harold Wilson and Jim Callaghan – and the 1964 Parliament had only three: Callaghan, Ted Heath and Margaret Thatcher. John Major was the only MP in the 1979 Parliament who subsequently became a Prime Minister.

A British politician's career invariably begins young. The idea of politics being in the blood applies not only to leaders from aristocratic families such as Winston Churchill and Alec Douglas-Home, but also to the daughter of a local government council member in Lincolnshire, Margaret Thatcher. Early entry into party politics also characterizes individuals without parental encouragement. Jim Callaghan and John Major canvassed for their respective parties well before they were old enough to vote. Both Harold Wilson and Margaret Thatcher stood as candidates for Parliament in the first election in which they could vote. While Harold Wilson was always interested in politics, his entry into politics was postponed by hesitation about whether to join the Liberal or Labour party.

An ambition to go into politics is realistic, for British political parties offer many openings for activists. Student politicians are often articulate; however, ministers expect student activists to change when they grow up. A young party member serves an apprenticeship learning about the nuts and bolts of electioneering and party organization. An apprentice is a follower not a leader. If a person is prepared to spend years gaining the political skills and contacts needed for adoption for a parliamentary seat, becoming an MP is a realistic goal.

Getting to Westminster

An appetite for politics is not enough: to get anywhere in British politics a young person must become a Member of Parliament. To become an MP requires canvassing constituency associations to gain the nomination for a safe or winnable seat. Going the rounds seeking support of constituency association members puts pressure on an aspiring politician to shape views in ways that are agreeable to party elders. Parties now offer ambitious young politicians posts as personal or political assistants to senior ministers or shadow

72 *Becoming and Remaining Party Leader*

ministers. In the current House of Commons, sixty MPs 'jump started' their careers through employment by a party organization or MP while searching for a winnable seat.

Prime ministers show their skill (and luck) by entering the House of Commons at a youthful age, often while still in their twenties. The median, Tony Blair, entered Parliament when he had just turned 30, and all eleven postwar Prime Ministers were below the age of 40 when first elected to the Commons (figure 4.1). By contrast, less than 2 per cent of the current House of Commons is below the age of 30 and five-sixths are over the age of 40.

While a new MP may enter Parliament hoping to change the world, the House of Commons is more likely to change the ambitious politician. New members of the House must learn its dis-

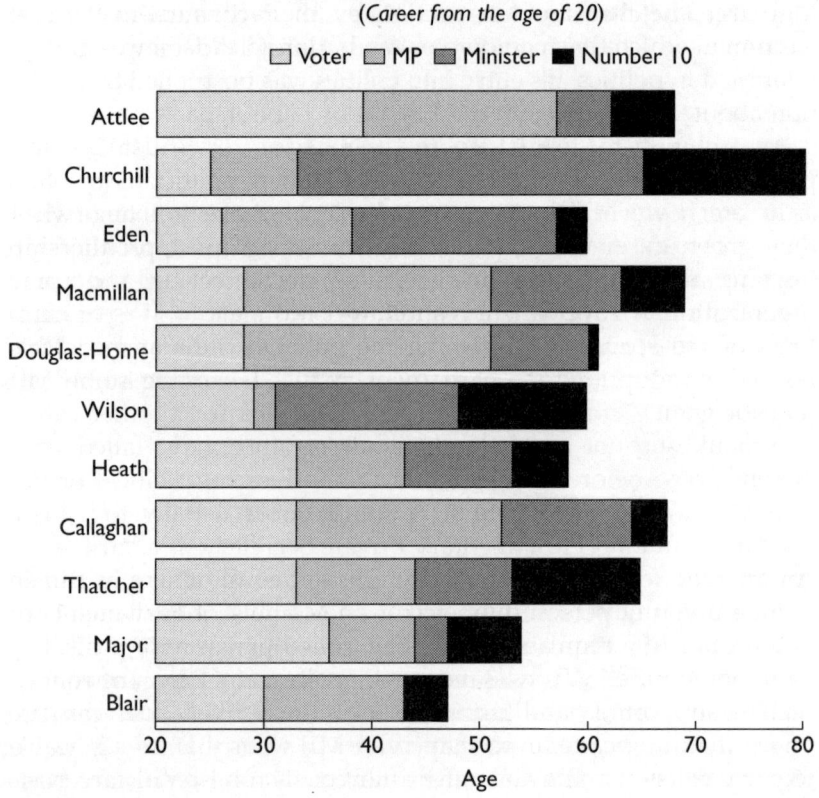

Figure 4.1 Apprenticeship of prime ministers

(Career from the age of 20)

tinctive ways in order to win the respect of senior colleagues who decide whether or not they are ministerial material. There are many informal and formal opportunities for judging character in the political hothouse of Westminster, and whips keep an eye out for which MPs are ministerial material and which are not. Most young MPs regard obsequiousness as the safe route to follow.

To have a ministerial career, an MP must secure repeated re-election. An MP averages twenty-five years in the House of Commons before becoming Prime Minister, and fewer than one in four MPs remain in the Commons that long. A general election defeat terminates or brutally interrupts a politician's career; only two of the eleven postwar prime ministers, Churchill and Macmillan, lost their seat at an election and fought their way back to the top. While the great majority of MPs secure re-election on their first bid, the vicissitudes of election swings, population movement and the periodic redrawing of constituency boundaries are recurring threats to an MP's career. Today recruits to the House of Commons also face the threat of deselection by their constituency if they aggrieve local party members or the national leadership.

Climbing the ladder

If an ambitious MP survives the hazards of re-election, he or she is odds on to receive at least a junior ministerial post, for there are more than 125 posts that must be filled, and the closed shop practices of British government restrict appointments to MPs or members of the House of Lords. The competition among more than 300 MPs in the governing party is reduced because some MPs do not want a ministerial job that would disrupt another career, are manifestly not up to the demands of office, have failed when given a post before, or disqualify themselves on political or personal grounds. An MP's first appointment is usually to a lowly post as an unpaid Parliamentary Private Secretary or a Parliamentary Under-Secretary. A majority of recipients of a government appointment never rise higher that one of these jobs, which carry less authority within a ministry than senior civil service posts. Less than one-third of MPs who receive a government appointment ever make the Cabinet, and rising up the ministerial ladder can take more than a decade, especially if an MP's party loses a series of general elections.[2] Jim Callaghan started his ministerial career as a

Parliamentary Secretary at the Ministry of Transport in 1947 and did not become a Cabinet minister until seventeen years later.

Long service as a Cabinet minister was normal for an old-school Prime Minister, including years at the Treasury, the Foreign Office and other major offices of state. Winston Churchill, Harold Macmillan and Jim Callaghan had each held three leading offices; Clement Attlee had been Deputy Prime Minister in the War Cabinet; Anthony Eden and Alec Douglas-Home had been Foreign Secretary; and Harold Wilson and Ted Heath had each been President of the Board of Trade. A different pattern is found among new-style prime ministers, for whom youth rather than experience appears an advantage. Although John Major had been minister at both the Treasury and Foreign Office, he had only served a total of three years in Cabinet before becoming Prime Minister. Tony Blair is the first Prime Minister without any experience as a minister since Ramsay MacDonald entered Downing Street in 1924, and if William Hague ever enters Number Ten he will bring with him only two years of experience as a Cabinet minister in a minor department.

Becoming a senior minister encourages ambitious politicians to start thinking not only about keeping their party in office but also about which office they hold. Continuing talk of Cabinet reshuffles and the 'up or out' mentality of Westminster encourages ministers to look out for opportunities. Because senior ministers are responsible for major government departments and answer to Parliament for major policies, the Chancellor can think of the budget as his rather than that of Number Ten, and view his career similarly. The Prime Minister recognizes that ambitious and awkward MPs may be less of a threat if kept in Cabinet rather than being sacked and free to criticize from the back benches.

The media often scrutinizes Cabinet reshuffles in an attempt to identify who will be the next or the next but one Prime Minister. However, such speculation is usually misguided, for most senior Cabinet positions are *not* stepping stones to Number Ten. Of the nineteen MPs who have been Chancellor of the Exchequer between 1945 and 1997, only three subsequently became Prime Minister. Of the eighteen Foreign Secretaries in the period, only five subsequently became Prime Minister, and only one of nineteen postwar Home Secretaries. Even though two Presidents of the Board of Trade subsequently became Prime Minister, twenty-seven did not. While eleven MPs in the past half century have reached the top, more have been frustrated just when their greatest ambition seemed near at hand. Few have been as philosophical as R. A. Butler, who was Chancellor of the Exchequer, Foreign Secretary, Home Secretary and Leader of the House of Commons, but twice missed opportunities to become Prime Minister: 'You don't have to be the Pope to be a success; you can be a perfectly good cardinal.'

2 Fortuitous circumstances

A staple part of conversation at Westminster is speculation about who will be a party's next leader and Prime Minister, but this talk is usually no more than idle gossip, for changes in party leadership are infrequent. Since Clement Attlee started his twenty-year career as leader in 1935, the Labour Party has averaged a change every eight years, and since 1940, the Conservative Party has averaged a change every seven.

The selection of a party leader is compressed into a few weeks or months, and greatly influenced by momentary considerations. The circumstances in which the choice occurs are often fortuitous and beyond the control of ambitious leadership candidates. This is especially the case when a vacancy is created by death. In January 1963, the 56-year-old Hugh Gaitskell was looking forward to becoming Prime Minister in the following year, as the Labour Opposition led a flagging Macmillan government by 13 per cent in the Gallup Poll. By the end of the month Gaitskell was dead, and the following year Harold Wilson became Labour's Prime Minister. In April 1994 the 55-year-old John Smith led the Labour Party, then 24 per cent ahead of the Conservatives in the Gallup Poll. Smith's death in early May caused the election of a new leader, giving Tony Blair the opportunity to become Prime Minister.

Selectorates

The choice of a leader is contested and contentious, and so are the rules for deciding the outcome. These rules differ between the Conservative and Labour parties, and each party has changed its rules in the postwar period. Three features are constant, two positive and one negative. Candidates for the leadership must be Members of Parliament and a very small number of people participate in the decision, but both parties reject the Liberal Party practice of electing the leader by a postal vote of members.

For its first eighty years, the Parliamentary Labour Party (PLP) was solely responsible for electing its leader by an absolute majority of votes. If this was not achieved on the first ballot, elimination ballots were held until this happened. In this way, MPs chose Clement Attlee over Herbert Morrison, Hugh Gaitskell over Aneurin Bevan, Harold Wilson over George Brown, and Jim Callaghan over Michael Foot. Since 1981 the Labour Party has chosen its leader through an electoral college of three 'estates', a system analogous to pre-revolutionary France or the Kingdom of Prussia. The winner requires a majority of the total vote of the three estates, that is, trade union, constituency parties and MPs, each voting separately. The trade union estate was initially given 40 per cent of the total vote, constituency parties 30 per cent and the PLP 30 per cent. At the 1993 party conference the division was modified; each estate was given a third of the total vote. To encourage more participation by individuals, constituency parties and trade unions are now required to send ballot papers to each registered party member, and to divide their votes according to the way their members divide, a reform promoted with the slogan OMOV (One Member One Vote).

The traditional Conservative method of choosing a leader had fewer participants and rules than the College of Cardinals use to elect a pope. Conservative elders who were not contenders for the office, such as leading party figures in the then hereditary House of Lords, consulted with each other and unspecified individuals and then 'anointed' the person to whom the Queen should offer the post of Prime Minister. In this way, Winston Churchill, Anthony Eden, Harold Macmillan and Alec Douglas-Home emerged as the party leader and simultaneously became Prime Minister. In 1957, the choice of Harold Macmillan rather than the more senior R. A. Butler surprised many Conservative MPs. In 1963, the retiring Prime Minister, Harold Macmillan, instructed the party elders to 'get the general opinion of ministers, MPs, peers and constituency parties' before making their recommendation to the Queen. The selection of Douglas-Home, then a member of the House of Lords, led Conservative ministers such as Iain Macleod to protest publicly about the Prime Minister being imposed by an unelected, aristocratic 'magic circle'.[3]

After losing the 1964 general election Douglas-Home sponsored a new procedure to elect the party leader by a ballot of MPs. To win on the first ballot the front-running candidate requires more than half the votes of all eligible MPs, and a lead of at least 15 per cent over the second place candidate. The 15 per cent rule is a vestige of the desire for a 'consensual' winner rather than one endorsed by a bare majority. There is provision for new candidates to enter the contest in the second round, allowing a stalking horse to stand in the first round to test the strength of the leader's support. If it is lukewarm, Cabinet ministers precluded by loyalty or patronage from a first round challenge can then enter the race. In the second round, an absolute majority of eligible MPs is required for victory, without the additional requirement of a 15 per cent lead. If no candidate receives an absolute majority, a third round run-off can be held, with the top two candidates in the second round the only names on the ballot. In response to pressures from the extra-parliamentary party, the Conservative system now encourages polls of the preferences of Conservative members of the House of Lords, Members of the European Parliament, chairs of parliamentary and European constituency associations and National Union officials, but they lack votes. In 1997 their views were published in advance of MPs voting. Extra-parliamentary Conservative groups consistently favoured Kenneth Clarke; the choice of Conservative MPs was William Hague.

The right face at the right time

The choice of leader is most important when a party is governing, for the winner becomes Prime Minister. Six postwar prime ministers have been fortunate in reaching Downing Street by winning an *intra*-party contest: Churchill, Eden, Macmillan, Douglas-Home, Callaghan and Major. In Opposition, an ambitious MP faces two hurdles, intra-party competition for the party leadership, and then inter-party competition at a general election. Attlee, Wilson, Heath, Thatcher and Blair each followed this longer, harder route to Downing Street.

There is no agreement in the selectorate about what constitutes a 'good' leader. The term can be defined by a candidate's views on policy, experience in the Commons, appeal to voters, or a combination of all of these attributes. Social status is a poor predictor of who becomes a party leader. While a majority of MPs are university graduates, Churchill, Callaghan and Major did not attend university.

Generalizations such as 'a party leader is a middle-class man' fail to explain why one particular middle-class male emerges above the mass of middle-class males who predominate in the Commons.

The performance of an outgoing leader can cause MPs to reverse their ideas of what a leader should be like. After eleven years of the intensely ideological leadership of Margaret Thatcher, Conservative MPs voted to replace her in 1990 with an emollient John Major. When Margaret Thatcher dismissively said of her successor, 'There is no such thing as Major-ism', she missed the point. Major's appeal was that he represented the absence of Thatcherism. After the Labour Party had been led to four successive election defeats by MPs whose appeal was primarily within the Labour movement, in 1994 the Labour Party selected Tony Blair as leader, because he did not look or talk like a Labour Party member.

The aura of Downing Street makes every Prime Minister appear to be the 'obvious' choice for the post. However, this is not the case when the race starts. A multiplicity of senior ministers always put their names forward, and MPs disagree about their first choice for the job. When Clement Attlee stood for the Labour leadership, he got only 42 per cent of the vote on the first round ballot and in 1963 Harold Wilson likewise fell short of a majority. When Wilson retired in 1976, six Labour ministers entered the initial ballot. Michael Foot led on the first round, although supported by only 29 per cent of MPs, and Jim Callaghan came second with a quarter of the votes. Both increased their support in the second ballot and Callaghan finally won a majority on the third ballot. Tony Blair is the only Labour Prime Minister who won the support of a majority of selectors on the first ballot, with a total of 57 per cent of the electoral college vote.

In the Conservative Party, the old system of anointment by elders often caused controversy. In 1940 Churchill became Prime Minister only because the Labour Party refused to enter a coalition under Neville Chamberlain, the Conservative Party leader, or Viscount Halifax, the preferred Conservative successor. Churchill did not become leader of the Conservative Party until the terminally ill Chamberlain resigned that post in September 1940. Had there been a ballot in 1963, it is doubtful whether Douglas-Home, then in the Lords, would have stood for the leadership and even less likely that he would have been elected. Anthony Eden was exceptional in being acclaimed Prime Minister without opposition, after years of being the heir apparent to Churchill.

Replacing anointment with election brought Conservative competition into the open. In the 1965 ballot, the first round margin between Ted Heath and Reginald Maudling was only 6 per cent, but Maudling stood down rather than face almost certain defeat on a second ballot. In 1975 a relatively junior former minister, Margaret Thatcher, won 49 per cent of the first round ballot and had a 4 per cent lead over Ted Heath. Heath dropped out and four ex-ministers entered the second ballot. When John Major fell just two votes short of an absolute majority in 1990, his two opponents conceded defeat rather than force another round of balloting. By contrast, when Major resigned in 1997, there was a cornucopia of candidates of differing political shapes and sizes. In the five-candidate initial ballot, Kenneth Clarke was the front runner, but took only 30 per cent of the vote; William Hague came second with a quarter of the vote. In the second round there were only three candidates and Clarke remained in the lead, albeit with less than two-fifths of the vote. To produce a majority, it was necessary to reduce the race to two candidates; an anti-Clarke coalition gave Hague 57 per cent of the vote.

Divisions in the first round ballot show that many leaders are initially seen as the 'second best' or 'lesser evil' choice. When Harold Wilson challenged Hugh Gaitskell for the leadership of the Labour Party in 1960, he received less than a third of the votes of PLP members. Before the Parliament ended, Gaitskell was dead and his supporters faced a fresh choice between Wilson, George Brown and Jim Callaghan. Although many Gaitskellites at that time loathed Wilson for his intrigues with the left, in the second round ballot most switched to Wilson as the lesser evil than George Brown, whose temperament and drinking were deemed to make him unfit for the job. When Wilson resigned in 1976 the votes that gave Jim Callaghan his majority came from MPs who had originally voted for Roy Jenkins, Denis Healey or Tony Crosland and disliked or distrusted Callaghan, but felt compelled to vote for him against what they considered the completely impossible alternative of Michael Foot as Prime Minister.

Like every Prime Minister, Margaret Thatcher was nervous about political allies becoming 'too' successful and being spoken of as her successor; she preferred to decapitate rather than groom potential successors. Therefore, when she withdrew from the leadership vote in 1990 her supporters were in disarray. In the second round, there were two 'wet' candidates unacceptable to Thatcher: Michael

Heseltine, who had precipitated the contest, and Douglas Hurd. Faced with the awkward political fact that you can't beat somebody with nobody, Thatcher backed John Major. At that time, Major was virtually unknown. In an August 1988 MORI poll, only 2 per cent could recognize a photograph of him, whereas more than half could recognize photographs of Michael Heseltine, Nigel Lawson and Cecil Parkinson.

A missing contender can have a decisive impact too. Margaret Thatcher benefited when, out of loyalty, senior ex-Cabinet colleagues such as William Whitelaw, the widely tipped successor, refrained from challenging Ted Heath when the ex-Prime Minister stood for re-election in 1975. Given a choice between a candidate who had twice led the party to defeat the year before and Thatcher, MPs placed Thatcher ahead of Heath, if only as the lesser evil. At this point, four ex-ministers entered the lists, including Whitelaw. But it was now too late. When the second round votes were counted, a majority of Conservative MPs endorsed Thatcher. Although John Major's resignation as Conservative leader in 1997 was widely anticipated, the absence from the Commons of Michael Portillo, a front-running candidate to succeed him, was not. Portillo lost a Commons seat which he had held with a 15,000 majority at the 1992 election. Portillo's absence opened up an opportunity that, after some hesitation, William Hague took.

Ruthlessness is also important in deciding who runs and wins in a race in which rewards are great and rules are few. Harold Macmillan explained his unexpected rise to the top by saying, 'When you get your chance, take it.'[4] The actions of Tony Blair and his supporters immediately following John Smith's unexpected death demonstrate that when great prizes are at stake, Blair can push forward in ways that leave bruises years later in relationships with the MP thrust aside, Gordon Brown. The absence of ruthless ambition is fatal. R. A. Butler's failure to become Prime Minister twice, in 1957 and again in 1963, is mute testimony to this. While Harold Wilson perennially worried about Roy Jenkins scheming to overthrow him, Wilson's concerns were exaggerated, for Jenkins lacked the inclination and talents that Wilson had shown in mobilizing support effectively against an existing party leader.

The conjunction of events that enables one MP to end up at the top while others fall short is so dominated by fortuitous circumstances and events that it resembles a random walk. In the words of Jo Grimond, onetime Liberal leader, 'The trick of being a good leader is to be on stage when the audience is ready to like your sort of performance.'[5]

3   Involuntary exits

Personality is often invoked to explain who gets to the very top of politics. Virtues are discovered in the Prime Minister of the day that had previously been unnoticed by family, friends and enemies. However, the virtues accounting for a politician's rise can hardly explain why the same individual usually leaves Downing Street involuntarily. As a Conservative MP remarked in 1990 following the unseating of a very determined Margaret Thatcher, 'The trouble with great leaders is that they don't know when to go.'

Among postwar prime ministers, Harold Wilson is alone in having left Downing Street voluntarily. The Labour Party was ahead of the Conservatives in the Gallup Poll, and Wilson's personal opinion poll rating was also higher than that of Margaret Thatcher. After thirty-six years on the line in wartime Whitehall and Westminster, Wilson realized that he had run out of political ideas and energy. He was addressing old and familiar problems with old and familiar solutions. He preferred gossiping and drinking with intimates

The removal van is a familiar visitor at Downing Street; above, it marks John Major's last day at Number Ten in 1997.
Photo: Mirror Syndication.

Figure 4.2 Election record of prime ministers

(Elections won as Prime Minister or Opposition Leader)

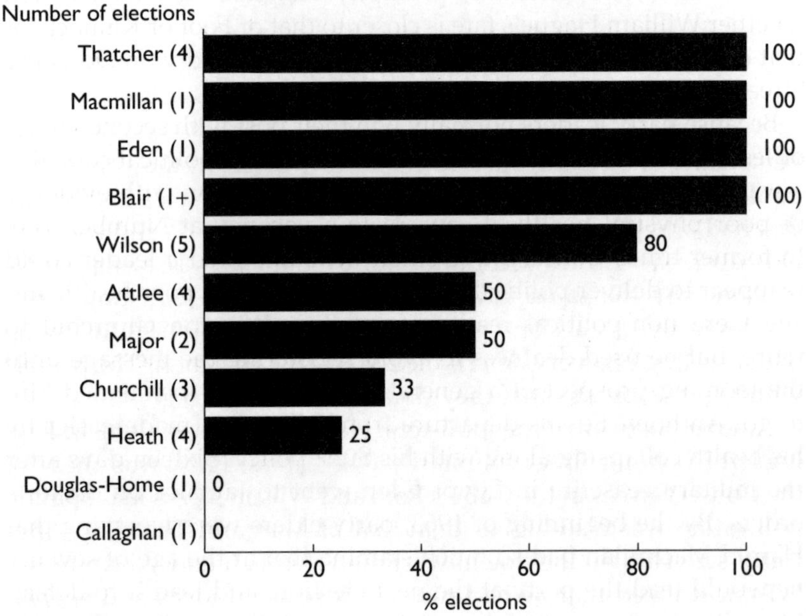

Leader (Number of elections)	% elections
Thatcher (4)	100
Macmillan (1)	100
Eden (1)	100
Blair (1+)	(100)
Wilson (5)	80
Attlee (4)	50
Major (2)	50
Churchill (3)	33
Heath (4)	25
Douglas-Home (1)	0
Callaghan (1)	0

at Downing Street to managing egos in the governing party. At the age of sixty, Wilson retired to an easier and more profitable life as an elder statesman.[6]

To gain or retain Downing Street, a leader must win an election; however, the record of prime ministers is variable (figure 4.2). Four Prime Ministers, including Tony Blair to date, have won every election they fought, while two failed to win the only election they fought from Downing Street. The median leaders – Clement Attlee and John Major – won and lost an equal number of elections. Of the seven prime ministers who led their party to defeat at the polls, John Major resigned the party leadership immediately; Alec Douglas-Home and Jim Callaghan resigned soon after their party digested defeat; and Ted Heath was promptly pushed out of office. Churchill, Wilson and Attlee had built up enough political capital while in office to remain as Leader in Opposition and the first two subsequently re-entered Number Ten. The increased emphasis given the leader's role as chief campaigner is reducing the tolerance of Opposition MPs to support a leader who leads them to defeat.

Michael Foot fought only one disastrous election as Labour leader and Neil Kinnock, when he failed to recover all of Labour's lost ground after two elections, promptly resigned. Events will tell whether William Hague's fate is closer to that of Foot or Kinnock, or that of Ted Heath, who was given two chances and won Downing Street on his second attempt.

Because party leaders normally win their post with second choice or lesser-evil votes, a fall in the Prime Minister's political capital is a warning of political mortality, and in conjunction with evidence of poor physical health, it can create a vacancy at Number Ten. In former times Conservative elders who anointed a leader could reappear to deliver political last rites. In the 1950s, poor health and age were non-political reasons for telling Winston Churchill to retire, but he used deafness to avoid registering the message until the looming prospect of a general election finally persuaded him to go. Anthony Eden's departure from office was made easier by his health collapsing along with his Suez policy. Sixteen days after the military ceasefire in Egypt Eden went to Jamaica on doctor's orders. By the beginning of 1963, party elders were worrying that Harold Macmillan had so much stamina that at the age of seventy he would lead the party at the next election, and lead it to defeat. Macmillan's unexpected hospitalization at the start of the 1963 Conservative Party conference convinced him to bow to pressures to retire.

Ideological disputes and personality differences can combine to fuel disputes about the leadership among rival MPs. The left–right differences that split the Labour Cabinet in 1951 were paralleled by bitter disputes between Aneurin Bevan, the leader of the left faction, and Hugh Gaitskell, whom he described as 'a desiccated calculating machine'. During Gaitskell's seven years as party leader his claim to the post was three times challenged by votes in the Parliamentary Labour Party. The economic policies of the 1974–9 Labour government produced massive disillusionment in Labour ranks, but the parliamentary position was so fragile that critical MPs did not want to cause their government to fall. In 1980 disillusioned Labour MPs elected Michael Foot as party leader, even though the 67-year-old nuclear disarmer was known to be electorally unpopular and had also been part of Callaghan's excoriated Cabinet. Foot's 1983 Labour Party election manifesto was far more leftwing than any Labour Prime Minister had ever endorsed; Gerald Kaufman described it as the 'longest political suicide note in history'. After Labour's crushing defeat, Neil Kinnock replaced Foot. Each general election defeat increased pressures from unions to make the party more 'electable'. After the 1992 Labour defeat, John Smith became the party's first centrist leader since Jim Callaghan; his unexpected death opened the way for Tony Blair to lead the party.

Disillusioned selectorates accounted for Margaret Thatcher's rise and for her fall. She gained the party's leadership in Opposition because Conservative MPs had lost confidence in Ted Heath. After a decade in office Conservative MPs were ready to think about her successor, but the idea of retirement was alien to a Prime Minister with enormous confidence in her convictions and her indispensability. However, a decade in office had caused a fatal disease: hardening of the political arteries. A friendly political journalist noted Thatcher had a 'sometimes driven, and yet desperately weary white-knuckle look of being too tired even to sleep, too knackered to loosen grip'.[7] After the Conservative Party fell 23 percentage points behind Labour in a spring 1990 Gallup Poll, Michael Heseltine, an ex-Cabinet minister on the back bench, challenged Thatcher. In a straight fight, Thatcher won more than half the votes cast but fell just short of the 15 per cent margin required for victory, because a majority of backbench MPs had refused to vote for her. When Cabinet ministers made clear to Thatcher that their support would not continue on a second ballot, she withdrew from the contest. The organizers of the challenge called it a 'peasants' revolt'; Thatcher described what happened as treachery by Cabinet colleagues.

Challenging a sitting Prime Minister is a risky political business. The most obvious risk to the challenger is that it does not succeed. A greater disincentive is that the Prime Minister is removed but the challenger does not gain Downing Street. Harold Wilson took comfort in knowing that while half a dozen Cabinet colleagues were intriguing against him, they were playing 'the game of musical daggers' in which the rule was 'never be left holding the dagger when the music stops'. Wilson then quoted one of Lord Beaverbrook's laws on conspiracy, 'The man who wields the dagger never wears the crown.'[8] Michael Heseltine is the latest in a line of senior ministers to learn this lesson the hard way.

While the prudence or cowardice of disillusioned colleagues offers the Prime Minister and leader of the Opposition a degree of security, both Tony Blair and William Hague have sought to make it more difficult to propose a vote of no confidence in the leader.

The Labour Party had moved in this direction after Tony Benn challenged Neil Kinnock in 1988, requiring 20 per cent of Labour MPs to sign a petition calling for a leadership ballot. The barriers for challenging a Labour Prime Minister are much higher. In addition to a petition from MPs, holding a ballot must also be endorsed by a two-thirds majority vote at the next annual party conference. After fortuitously being elected leader by Conservative MPs, William Hague balloted party members to endorse his selection and his vaguely stated principles of reform, 'unity, democracy, decentralization, involvement, integrity and openness'. Four-fifths of party members voted in favour. Revised rules for an electoral challenge require at least 15 per cent of MPs to request a vote of no confidence. If the no confidence vote among MPs is carried, the party leader must resign and not stand in the subsequent contest, which is ultimately decided by a one-person-one-vote ballot of all who have been party members for at least six months prior to the no confidence vote.

Rules determine procedures but circumstances and fortune determine outcomes. Every Prime Minister needs both skills and luck. However, sooner or later a sequence of unexpected or mishandled events and a threatened or actual electoral defeat will create disillusionment in the selectorate. However tall a Prime Minister stands at the pinnacle of success, like King Charles I, on leaving Westminster he or she is usually a head shorter.

5

From Private to Public Government

> I have come here to talk, not to talk with you and certainly not to enable you to spread the tale all over the place but just to enable me to see what are the conditions under which this thing they call TeeVee is going to make its way in the world. I am sorry, I must admit, to have to descend to this level, but we all have to keep pace with modern improvements.
>
> Winston Churchill, in an unscreened trial television broadcast[1]

> I explain. You boast. They spin.
>
> Anonymous

When the 1951 general election was announced, the BBC sent a television crew to Downing Street, so that when the Prime Minister came out an interviewer could put a microphone in front of him and ask, 'Mr Attlee, you've announced a general election. Is there anything you would like to say about the forthcoming general election?' The Prime Minister answered, 'No.' At least the journalist could claim he had interviewed the Prime Minister. This was not possible after Winston Churchill returned to Downing Street. Interviewers were kept away from the Prime Minister, his civil servant press secretary was not given an office in Number Ten and television was anathema.

When John Major went to Buckingham Palace in 1997 to tell the Queen the unsurprising news that an election was to occur, an ITN helicopter tracked his journey. The meeting was timed so that the Prime Minister could follow up his Palace visit with sound bites for television's *One O'Clock News* and radio's *World at One*. Whether the general public was better informed by what happened in 1951 or 1997 is moot. What is certain is that Downing Street today is keen to manage publicity rather than protect the Prime Minister's privacy.

Old-school prime ministers were accustomed to conducting public affairs in virtual privacy. In the eighteenth century, debates in Parliament had been secret, and it was not until 1909 that a verbatim account of debates began to be published. Affairs of state were discussed face to face within a restricted political class at Westminster. Affairs of prime ministers were also kept private; for example, Lloyd George having a mistress. The existence of Cabinet committees was an official secret, and senior civil servants were in a political purdah.

The press cooperated with Downing Street. *The Times* put classified advertisements on the front page, and the day's debate in Parliament, which had little influence on public policy, received more attention than the day's discussions in Downing Street. Newspaper owners wanted flattery from the Prime Minister, a reputation for influence or a peerage and sometimes all three. A party leader's private lunch with Lord Beaverbrook could decide what went in or what stayed out of the *Express*. When Winston Churchill had a stroke in 1953, an aide wrote by hand to three press lords – Beaverbrook, Camrose and Berry – asking them to keep the Prime Minister's illness out of the papers, and this was done.[2]

The shift from private to public government has been determined by politics not technology. Originally the British Broadcasting Corporation adopted a deferential approach to public affairs. It followed the press in not reporting the prospect of King Edward VIII abdicating to marry an American divorcee. The BBC also insulated itself from parliamentary politics, in 1944 deciding not to broadcast comments on any issue which might be debated in the next fourteen days. The Director-General, Sir William Haley, argued, 'Parliament is the only grand forum of the nation. Once a matter is under discussion there, it should not also be discussed in the ether.'[3] The rule was enforced until controversy in the Commons during the Suez War made it impossible to maintain.

Journalists have altered their values and behaviour. No longer are reporters willing to be valets, seeing prime ministers as they are in the flesh, but keeping observations private.[4] Nor do BBC interviewers act like a butler, changing into evening dress to read the evening news in dignified tones. Granted an interview by the

Foreign Secretary, Sir Anthony Eden, in 1951, the BBC interviewer, Lesley Mitchell, asked, 'I wonder if you'd allow me to put a few questions to you about foreign policy?' Ludovic Kennedy recalled Robin Day's reaction to that type of reporting, 'It made him want to throw up. We were determined to put an end to that sort of thing.'[5] Journalists began to create as well as disseminate news. Day used his barrister's skills to ask pointed political questions of the Prime Minister. The *Sunday Times* Insight Team and campaigning television stations such as Granada emulated American counterparts in uncovering scandals. Media superstars have come forward, seeing themselves as central to any story involving a politician. Broadcasters now use their control of the microphone to hector Cabinet ministers in a way that the Speaker of the House of Commons would not allow at Westminster.

Opposition leaders have welcomed the change for, lacking responsibilities of government, their politics is all talk. On becoming Opposition leader in 1963, Harold Wilson combined private meetings with business people in which disarming statements were made, and private briefings of journalists whose readers were Labour's target voters. On becoming Opposition leader, Tony Blair made campaigning through the media central to his political strategy, as if he were an American politician running for the presidency. This reflected advice from Dick Morris, one of President Clinton's campaign team, 'Every day is election day. The Lord created seven days, politicians should use them. Any leader whose poll ratings have fallen below 50 per cent is functionally out of office.'[6]

As the central personality in British government, the Prime Minister has no difficulty in getting attention, and cartoonists seek to create 'trade marks'; for example, Vicky turning Harold Macmillan into 'Supermac'. Old-school prime ministers managed their political capital through private discussions or giving deadpan explanations of their policies. New-style prime ministers want publicity, and now have staff to promote their views. Margaret Thatcher started the trend by licensing Bernard Ingham to voice what he thought she thought; this produced attention-getting phrases with Prime Ministerial deniability. Tony Blair has gone further, with Alastair Campbell as chief 'spin doctor'[7] in charge of round-the-clock efforts to put the best gloss possible on what the Prime Minister is doing.

When Prime Minister Harold Macmillan's ratings began soaring in the opinion polls, Vicky caricatured him as Supermac.
Photo: Centre for the Study of Cartoons and Caricature, Canterbury/© Atlantic Syndication.

1 Keeping politics private

News management is about power. In the United States, where the Constitution emphasizes government by 'We, the people', public policy and publicity go together. But in Whitehall, Her Majesty's Government has been cloaked in regal privacy. The Prime Minister and Cabinet colleagues swear the thirteenth-century Privy Councillor's oath that 'all matters committed and revealed unto you shall be treated secretly in council'. Decisions of Her Majesty's Government shall not be revealed 'until such time as, by the consent of His or Her Majesty or the Council, publication shall be made'. In Latin, publicity and public have the same root, but the Mandarin of English civil servants follows the European convention of regarding public business as official business. Officials decide what affairs of state may be made public and which should remain official secrets. The American doctrine of the public's right to know is trumped by the French invocation of *raison d'état*. In the words of a senior civil servant, 'It is no business of any official to allow the government to be embarrassed.'[8]

Controversies within government have historically been kept private. Clement Attlee reminded his ministers, 'The underlying principle is, of course, that the method adopted by ministers for discussion among themselves of questions of policy is essentially a domestic matter, and is no concern of Parliament or the public.'[9] Attlee believed that the public should only be told the results of Cabinet deliberations, and not the reasoning and arguments that led to decisions. A misleadingly entitled White Paper of Harold Wilson's government, *Information and the Public Interest*, declared, 'It does not follow, of course, that public consultation on tentative proposals is invariably the right course. It may result in slower decisions and slower action when prompt action is essential.'[10] Both quotations used the phrase 'of course' to shut off discussion of the rules being laid down.

Being economical with the truth

Downing Street has traditionally respected the value of information by keeping it scarce. During the Suez War the practice was carried to the extreme. Anthony Eden refused to tell the House of Commons whether or not the country was at war with Egypt.[11] Normal practice is to release information selectively and sometimes in ways that can be, and are intended to be, misleading. When Robert Armstrong, Secretary to the Cabinet under Margaret Thatcher, was accused of telling a lie in a case involving the security services, he replied, 'It is a misleading impression, not a lie. It was being economical with the truth.'[12]

Because knowledge is power, Downing Street wants to control information. The Official Secrets Act of 1911 gave it the power to do so, making it a criminal offence for civil servants to communicate any information obtained in the service of the Crown to unauthorized persons. The act was designed to protect the confidentiality and frankness of advice that civil servants give to ministers. It did so by making the deliberation of public policy private.

If taken literally, the Official Secrets Act would make it impossible to conduct modern government, since millions of public employees spending hundreds of billions of pounds need to know what they are doing and explain their actions to citizens. In practice, those with a 'need to know' can be informed of what government is doing. On that basis interest group leaders and journalists are regularly briefed by Downing Street. In oral evidence to the 1971 Franks Tribunal on Official Secrecy, Jim Callaghan explained, 'Leaking is what you do. Briefing is what I do.'

A classic device for disseminating information selectively is to release it in code, that is, circumlocutions and oblique references that can only be understood by those already in the know. When the Macmillan government wanted to promote tighter control of public expenditure in Whitehall, it invited Lord Plowden, a former civil servant, to carry out a private investigation. The introduction to the published report said:

> For these studies we co-opted the Permanent Secretaries of the departments with whose expenditures we are concerned or who had special experience of the general problems under review. In some cases we sought specialist advice from outside the civil service. We decided, however, not to take evidence from outside bodies; our review was primarily concerned with the inner working of the Treasury and the departments, and was necessarily confidential in character.

A classical philologist and former wartime civil servant translated the Plowden Report from Whitehall code into plain English, decoding the above paragraph thus: 'We proceeded on two principles; no dirty linen in public; outside critics are bores.'[13]

Within the closed world of Whitehall, information has always circulated by word of mouth. Being up to date on its informal 'bush telegraph' is a necessity for ministers and senior civil servants. News is sought about the mood of the Prime Minister and the policy predilections of those currently in favour in Number Ten. When Margaret Thatcher was Prime Minister, a question frequently asked was 'Is she in or out?' – that is, would she scrutinize a particular set of recommendations agreed by ministers and civil servants and possibly 'handbag' (that is, reject) them, or would their recommendations go through without scrutiny or question?

As long as communication in Whitehall was restricted, prime ministers saw no need for a press officer. When the intensely private Clement Attlee became Prime Minister in 1945, he accepted having Francis Williams, a wartime civil servant and former editor of the Labour-sponsored *Daily Herald*, to act as a buffer between himself and the press. Williams convinced Attlee of the value of installing a news ticker tape in Number Ten by pointing out that it would give the Prime Minister up-to-the-minute cricket scores. After Williams left in 1947, the post was filled by civil servants kept at a distance and valued for discreetness to the point of evasiveness. There was one exception, William Clark, a diplomatic correspondent employed by Anthony Eden when the Prime Minister ran into political difficulties. Clark resigned during the Suez War on a point of principle, refusing to give misleading information to the media. Clark's resignation was interpreted as justifying the press secretary's job being kept in the hands of civil servants.

The lobby code

The old school of prime ministers was complemented by an old school of lobby journalists who saw themselves not as public figures but as craftsmen. They had started work at the age of fourteen on provincial papers, prided themselves on the accuracy of their shorthand notes, and eventually arrived at the Palace of Westminster through their professional ability. They were shrewd observers of human nature, especially *Homo politicus*. In the words of one lobby correspondent, 'We are war reporters wanting to know who is winning a battle in Cabinet.' After a moment's reflection, he added, 'We are not so concerned with what the war is about.'

Lobby correspondents spent their working hours at the Palace of Westminster in daily contact with MPs. By being walled in the Palace of Westminster, a lobby journalist learned to anticipate how MPs react to events, including crises of confidence in the Prime Minister. Journalists kept their sources anonymous, disguising them by such phrases as 'It is said in Downing Street' or 'a source close to the Prime Minister'. Opinions of the Prime Minister could be expressed without committing him; only those who knew the code could identify the source. The lobby system gave its members the privilege of moving at will about the Palace of Westminster, but also imposed obligations. The third paragraph of notes on lobby practice stated:

> The work of a lobby journalist brings him into close daily touch with Ministers and Members of Parliament of all parties and imposes on him a very high standard of responsibility and discretion in making use of the special facilities given him for writing about political affairs.

The occupational hazard of the old-school lobby correspondent was that of dismissing as 'not worth reporting' information about ministers with whom they had worked and lived for many years. There was no mention in print of the bisexual Conservative MP who was believed to have fathered a child by a Prime Minister's wife. Nor did the lobby print anything when one of their own members fathered two children by one of Harold Wilson's aides in Number Ten.[14]

Enterprising lobby correspondents were among nature's sceptics. When given a self-interested briefing by Harold Wilson, David Wood of *The Times* considered, 'You may not believe what the person is saying, but if it is the Prime Minister, he has a right to have his views known.' If Wood did not believe the briefing, he prefaced the report with the political health warning, 'For what it may be worth, a highly placed Downing Street source says . . . .' James Margach, whose lobby career spanned every Prime Minister from Ramsay MacDonald to Jim Callaghan, continued to pursue news with professional scepticism after his retirement, going to the Public Records Office to compare official minutes of Cabinet meetings with his shorthand notebooks recording what ministers at the time had told him had happened.

The cultural ethos of the traditional BBC was respectful of the political economy of Downing Street. The BBC was (and is) a public corporation with a charter authorized by Act of Parliament; its principal source of revenue is a licence fee set by the government; and the Prime Minister controls the appointment of the BBC Board of Governors. The first Director General of the BBC, John Reith, a Scottish minister's son, saw the purpose of radio as informing, educating and uplifting the standards of the population. The Reithian BBC was often best at broadcasting events that were not news, major state occasions that could be planned far in advance, such as the coronation of Queen Elizabeth II. Reith promoted a priestly or 'sacerdotal' view of the BBC's role as linking the populace with matters of ultimate value. The Reithian ethic resulted in 'very few people at the top of the Corporation knowing or indeed caring what the audience made of the service it receives'.[15]

The Reithian BBC saw public interest and official interest as much the same, and expected the government of the day to decide what it was. The BBC treated election broadcasting 'as if it belonged solely to the political parties',[16] giving parties free political broadcasts that they controlled in their entirety. Its election coverage avoided hard choices by a policy of comprehensive omission. In the words of the 1950 Nuffield election study:

> The BBC kept as aloof from the election as if it had been occurring on another planet. Every programme was scrutinised in search of any item, jocular or serious, which might give aid or comfort to any of the contestants, and after February 3rd [the start of the election campaign] virtually all mention of election politics disappeared from the British air.[17]

A bizarre consequence was that when Winston Churchill called for talks with the Soviet Union about atomic weapons, the story was headlined around the world – except by the BBC and the Soviet Union.

From the perspective of the twenty-first century, the idea of keeping public business private appears incongruous, or a violation of democratic values enunciated by John Stuart Mill in the middle of the nineteenth century. But the idea has a perennial appeal to the Prime Minister, since it can keep mistakes out of the media limelight and give more attention to what Downing Street considers its successes. In the words of Bernard Ingham, a *Guardian* reporter turned civil servant turned Margaret Thatcher's press secretary:

> There is no freedom of information in this country; there's no public right to know. There's a commonsense idea of how to run a country and Britain is full of commonsense people.
>   Bugger the public's right to know. The game is the security of the state, not the public's right to know. Don't confuse public interest with media interest.[18]

2 Going public

The aim of the Prime Minister's Press Secretary has changed little through the years – to get good news into print and on the air, and to bury bad news out of sight – but the means of doing so have evolved over the decades. As long as old-school values prevailed, less staff was better, for people who are not there cannot generate unwanted headlines by intention or accident, and this gave the Prime Minister more time to deal privately with policies and politicians. In going public, the challenge to Downing Street is to control, or at least substantially influence, what the media highlights as news.

In Downing Street there has been a legal fiction dividing news into two categories: 'government' news from the Queen's First Minister, and 'party political' news about the leader of the governing party. Communicating about government was regarded as a proper duty of civil servants and paid for by public funds; party publicity was meant to be handled by political appointees paid from party funds. The distinction implies that the Prime Minister should have two press secretaries. But if confusion is not to result, only one individual can be the authoritative voice of the Prime Minister.

Between 1957 and 1997 a career civil servant was Number Ten's Press Secretary for all but three years. Recruits from the Foreign Office brought with them skills in being diplomatically, if not fully, informative. Other civil servants had previously worked for newspapers before transferring to the Government Information Service. Civil servants must have the knack of serving masters of different political parties with equal loyalty. Even the pugnacious press secretary of Margaret Thatcher, Bernard Ingham, had acted as an official spokesman for Barbara Castle and Tony Benn, and all three of Ingham's successors were civil servants. For civil servants, a tour of duty in Downing Street is a highlight, but not the end of a career. After their tour of duty in Downing Street, they expect to return to another civil service post in Whitehall.

Harold Wilson's arrival in Downing Street introduced a political complement to the civil service approach. Wilson named as his press secretary Trevor Lloyd-Hughes, political correspondent of the *Liverpool Daily Post*, which covered Wilson's Huyton constituency. The appointment turned out to be less helpful to the Prime

Minister's political capital than Wilson had expected, for Lloyd-Hughes saw his job as giving 'impartial, truthful, no-spin guidance'.[19] Gerald Kaufman, a Labour journalist (and subsequently MP), was appointed the Prime Minister's parliamentary press liaison officer. The distinction between 'government' and 'party political' roles was maintained, as Kaufman was paid from Labour Party funds. In 1969 Joe Haines replaced Lloyd-Hughes. Haines was a committed Labour Party member, being a local councillor and a *Daily Mirror* journalist. When Wilson lost the 1970 election, Haines left Downing Street with him; he returned temporarily for Wilson's second tour of office. Ted Heath and Jim Callaghan restored the practice of drawing the Press Secretary from the civil service.

In his first several years in Downing Street Wilson was on very good terms with the lobby; his interest in talking with journalists was a welcome change from the aloofness of his Conservative predecessors. However, in 1967 a relatively minor incident blew up about whether a story by defence correspondent Chapman Pincher had violated the D-notice system used to prevent publication of articles that could jeopardize national security. Wilson's hypersensitivity to the press prompted him to make an ill-judged response that soured his relations with the lobby. He used his Downing Street position to collect information about the alleged misdeeds of critical lobby correspondents and sought to intimidate them directly. On occasion, he approached proprietors in efforts to get reporters he deemed unfriendly, such as David Wood of *The Times* and Nora Beloff of the *Observer*, transferred from Westminster or fired. The proprietors ignored Wilson's diatribes.[20]

During Wilson's years in Downing Street television gradually gained recognition as the primary medium of political communication. The way in which television reported political news also changed, as the BBC's monopoly was ended by the introduction of independent commercial television. Lord Reith declared that admitting commercial television to Britain would be an unmitigated disaster, 'like dog-racing, smallpox and bubonic plague'. A Conservative minister argued that, given the choice, people would prefer the attractions of commercial television to the BBC just as a man would prefer a prostitute to his wife.[21]

Independent television pioneered a more open style of reporting news. Granada Television and Independent Television News broke with the BBC's refusal to cover by-elections in 1958. *World in Action* screened programmes that Whitehall sought to suppress. On *Weekend World* interviewers had time to let ministers speak first – and then point out contradictions in what they had said. For example, Brian Walden asked Margaret Thatcher whether her government was going to cut spending on health, education and social security policies. The Prime Minister vigorously recounted how much more her government was spending on these electorally popular programmes. After politely remarking that he thought the point of Thatcherism was to cut public spending, Walden asked: 'Mrs Thatcher, are you still a Thatcherite?' The Prime Minister was given twenty-five minutes of airtime in which to square the circle between ideology and practice.

Television's visual character has encouraged the personalization of news, and the Prime Minister, as the country's leading political personality, has gained most attention. Wilson welcomed television, since it enabled the Prime Minister to speak directly to a mass audience rather than through lobby journalists. Between 1964 and February 1974, broadcast references to the Prime Minister during elections more than doubled. By 1987 broadcast references had more than trebled (figure 5.1). Even though John Major was less of a personality than Margaret Thatcher, in 1992 he achieved even more broadcast coverage than she or any or her predecessors had at election time.

Licensing requirements compel television and radio to give balanced coverage to the parties during election campaigns, and this specially benefits the Leader of the Opposition. During the life of a Parliament, an Opposition leader cannot compete with the Prime Minister as a source of news, but whatever the opinion polls show, during an election he or she can. Even though Michael Foot was an inevitable loser in 1983, he received almost as much broadcast coverage as Margaret Thatcher, and in 1987 Neil Kinnock actually received more. Campaigning in opposition in 1997, Tony Blair came within 6 per cent of the coverage of John Major.

Ironically, attempts to hold American-style television debates between the Prime Minister and the Leader of the Opposition have been exploited by party leaders to control (that is, stifle) debate. If the Prime Minister is leading when an election campaign starts, he or she has no need to engage in a televised confrontation that makes the Opposition leader appear their equal. However, when trailing in the opinion polls, the opposite is the case. In 1979 Jim Callaghan offered to debate with the then Opposition leader, but

Figure 5.1 Prominence in election broadcasts

(Total mentions of Prime Minister in TV and radio news)

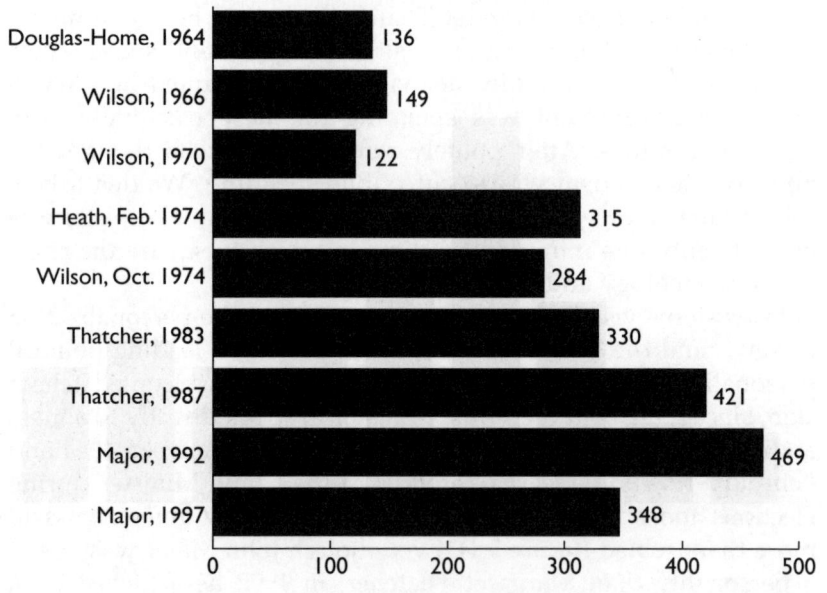

Douglas-Home, 1964	136
Wilson, 1966	149
Wilson, 1970	122
Heath, Feb. 1974	315
Wilson, Oct. 1974	284
Thatcher, 1983	330
Thatcher, 1987	421
Major, 1992	469
Major, 1997	348

Source: Compiled by the author from Nuffield election studies by D. E. Butler and others; 1979 omitted because the data is not comparable.

Margaret Thatcher refused for fear that the more experienced Callaghan would make her look bad. In 1997 Tony Blair avoided appearing in a studio with John Major, as the latter's decade of experience in government was likely to show up Blair as having only 'shadow' knowledge of government.

Centralized electioneering has increased the attention given the Prime Minister by comparison with Cabinet ministers. In the days of the Attlee government, the index of *The Times* shows that the Foreign Secretary, Ernest Bevin, and the Chancellor, Stafford Cripps, were referred to as often as the Prime Minister. Churchill and Eden were sometimes overshadowed in the press by their senior ministers too. However, after Harold Macmillan reached his stride, press references to the Prime Minister became more numerous than the combined total for the Chancellor, the Foreign Secretary and the Leader of the House of Commons.[22] Television has accentuated the trend (figure 5.2). In the 1964 and 1966 election campaigns, Alec

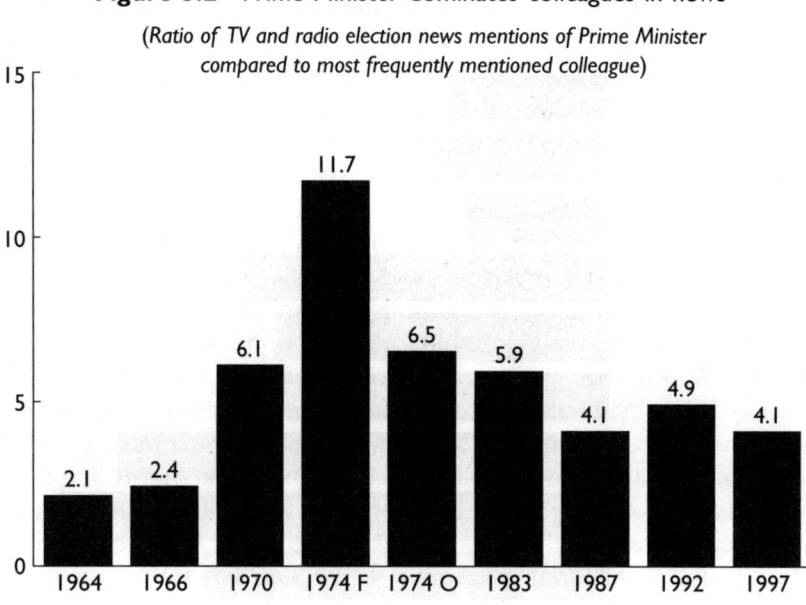

Figure 5.2 Prime Minister dominates colleagues in news
(*Ratio of TV and radio election news mentions of Prime Minister compared to most frequently mentioned colleague*)

Year	Ratio
1964	2.1
1966	2.4
1970	6.1
1974 F	11.7
1974 O	6.5
1983	5.9
1987	4.1
1992	4.9
1997	4.1

Source: As in figure 5.1.

Douglas-Home and Harold Wilson were each mentioned twice as often as any Cabinet colleague. By 1970, Wilson was mentioned six times as often as the Chancellor of the Exchequer, Roy Jenkins. In the exceptional circumstances of the February 1974 'Who Governs?' election, Edward Heath was named eleven times more often than any Cabinet colleague. Margaret Thatcher was undoubtedly the media star of her government. But the more publicity she attracted, the greater the danger that she might appear bossy and unsympathetic. However, when the party chairman, Norman Tebbit, appeared 'too prominent' during the 1987 campaign, this led to controversy in the campaign group and his departure from government.

Old-school politicians were reserved about discussing public issues publicly. However, Margaret Thatcher's faith in her political convictions and evangelical upbringing made her ready to preach her beliefs whenever the opportunity offered. Occasionally, she put her foot in it. In an interview with a women's magazine, Thatcher did not flannel on about problems of house-keeping at Number Ten. Instead, she gave a full-scale statement of her Victorian belief in individual responsibility, declaring, 'There is no such thing as society.'[23] At election time, Thatcher's obvious enjoyment of answering questions at daily Smith Square press conferences put her handlers on edge. Conservative publicists nervously awaited the end of each session, fearful that her enthusiasm might lead her to go 'over the top' with a politically suicidal statement of free market beliefs.

On becoming Prime Minister, an individual does not drop his or her established mannerisms, and a press secretary cannot determine what these are. When Alec Douglas-Home was Prime Minister, Conservative Central Office was in a quandary. It knew that his aristocratic mien was unsuitable for competing with a pipe-puffing Harold Wilson but, in the words of an official, 'Dammit all, the man is Prime Minister; we can't deny that.' Central Office spent large sums on posters and hoardings with Home's face. In 1997 John Major wanted to campaign as a normal bloke doing the best he could in Downing Street, but Central Office believed that being ordinary was out of fashion, and wanted to place him on an elevated 'Prime Ministerial' podium.[24] Tony Blair has given no problems to public relations staff for, if he had not won nomination to a safe Labour seat in County Durham in 1983, he could have become a television successor to David Frost or Michael Parkinson.

3   *Blair's permanent campaign*

The longer Labour remained in Opposition, the stronger the desire for election victory. Although the goal was uncontroversial, there were fundamental disagreements about how this could be done and who could do it. When John Smith succeeded to the Labour leadership after its loss of the 1992 election, he believed that 'one more heave' would return Labour to office, a belief made more credible by the immediate collapse of John Major's government. By contrast, Peter Mandelson, Alastair Campbell and Philip Gould believed that a revolution was needed in how the party campaigned and what its message was. The would be transformers of Labour had to seize power within the party as a precondition of their making headlines. John Smith's unexpected death and the succession of Tony Blair to Labour's leadership in 1994 opened the door to a revolution.

Seizing control of the agenda

Old-school prime ministers thought managing the agenda of politics meant managing the business of the House of Commons. Even after giving up the post of Leader of the House of Commons, the Prime Minister had frequent discussions with the Chief Whip, and what would go into the business of the Commons the following week. The Queen's speech to Parliament set the agenda for the year, announcing bills that would be presented during the session. The Prime Minister could look ahead a year by monitoring discussions in the Future Legislation Committee of the Cabinet, which sifted proposals from departmental ministers and determined which should be put to Parliament in the following session.

The idea of setting the agenda was first applied in British elections in the 1987 election. Peter Mandelson and Patricia Hewitt, who helped organize media coverage, wrote, 'Competition between rival agenda-setting is at the heart of election campaigning, and disciplined execution is essential in creating an image – a much-needed image in the case of the Labour Party – of a united party, fit to govern.'[25] John Major established a Co-ordination and Presentation Committee, which was meant to meet daily with Michael Heseltine in the chair and staffed by civil servants. Lacking media skills, political direction and a Prime Minister who knew how to exploit the media, it achieved nothing. Viewing the way the media undermined John Major's authority, coverage in which Alastair Campbell had both a hand and a boot,[26] Blair was determined to dominate rather than be overwhelmed by the media.

Tony Blair has been distinctive in making agenda setting a high priority of Number Ten, and in the thoroughness and professionalism with which this has been done. His campaign team operates with a frame of mind formed in Fleet Street not Downing Street. Managing the agenda of politics means managing what the media reports and how it interprets events. The media is targeted in the belief that influencing the public presentation of the Prime Minister positively influences the attitudes of both the electorate and those who work in Westminster. The strategy was framed by electioneering in Opposition. Blair's media team prefers being called 'control freaks' to being accused of professional incompetence.

As Chief Press Secretary, Alastair Campbell is the central figure in telling the world what the Prime Minister is thinking. Campbell holds a novel post, being both a political appointee and a civil servant; he can thus draw on inside knowledge as a civil servant of Her Majesty's Government, to 'set things in a party political context' as the Prime Minister requires.[27]

> Now, the Prime Minister gets hundreds and hundreds and hundreds of requests for interviews from around the world every single day. Journalists who want briefings have to be briefed. He has to have somebody who is doing that and who is organising that whom he can trust, who knows his mind, who knows what he thinks about the big issues of the day, and indeed about the small issues of the day, and who can brief at the drop of a hat, so that if anybody asks me a question, I can answer it.[28]

Years of working with Tony Blair in opposition have qualified Campbell to know his mind. Campbell is so close to Blair that he can sometimes take decisions in the Prime Minister's name without informing him and not notice that others know this. On one occasion, Blair looked blank when journalists asked him about a speech he was to make in a few hours. Campbell explained without apology, 'I haven't told you about that yet.'[29]

Campbell is most visible when taking the twice daily briefings of the press at Number Ten and at the Palace of Westminster, and can be publicly credited as the source of news, albeit by the quasi-anonymous title of the Prime Minister's Spokesman. Blair's regard for Campbell (and disregard for his own unique standing) is shown in his remark that Campbell has made press briefings the equivalent of 'Prime Minister's Questions twice a day'.[30] In briefing the media, Campbell applies skills developed in the 'no holds barred' school of tabloid journalism. In an initial briefing, he told the assembled journalists, 'Explain to me just why I should waste my time with a load of wankers like you, when you're not going to write anything I tell you anyway.'

A Cambridge graduate in modern languages, Campbell is capable of making very fine linguistic distinctions that show a Mandarin's skill at being economical with the truth. When asked whether the Prime Minister had phoned the Italian Prime Minister to intervene on behalf of a Rupert Murdoch project in Italy, Campbell told journalists, 'I can certainly say that it's balls that the Prime Minister intervened over some deal with Murdoch. That's C-R-A-P.' When questioned by a House of Commons Select Committee about his denial of Blair intervening on behalf of Murdoch, he carefully explained that Blair could not have 'intervened' when it was the Italian Prime Minister who telephoned Downing Street. Campbell covered himself against a transcript of the conversation leaking in Rome or London by adding the proviso that 'at no time have I said whether Mr. Blair and Mr. Prodi discussed Mr. Murdoch or not'.[31]

Campbell has a staff that is several times larger than that of his predecessors. It liaises with departmental information officers and he prepares a computerized grid that controls the flow of major statements from Whitehall departments, so that their press releases do not 'collide', stealing headlines from each other. After three years of daily briefing the media, Campbell found himself in a situation 'where combat was the only language that was really being spoken'.[32] He turned over daily briefings to other staff in order to concentrate on less visible but no less important activities within Whitehall and to prepare for the next general election, when he is authorized to take leave from his civil service job to work for the Labour Party.

Campbell is a senior member of Tony Blair's government. He has been more assiduous than his predecessors in seeking to enforce the Cabinet Office's *Code of Conduct and Guidance on Procedures for Ministers* requesting that all major interviews, media appearances, speeches and press releases be cleared with the Number Ten Press Office before any commitments are entered into. In addition, a daily summary of Downing Street's briefing of journalists is circulated to every department's press office so that they know the message they are meant to stay on for the next twenty-four hours.

When the Cabinet holds its short and infrequent meetings, Campbell is there. Cabinet discussion and minutes now give much more emphasis to presentational aspects of policy, including a regular briefing on the Grid, the Press Office schedule of events for media release in the week ahead. Even more important, Campbell is in Downing Street when the Cabinet is not there. For example, critical decisions about the war in Kosovo were taken in small groups in which Campbell was one of six persons present, along with the Chief of the Defence Staff, the Foreign Secretary, the Defence Secretary, the Downing Street Chief of Staff, and Blair. Campbell recognizes that as the Prime Minister's spokesman, he cannot speak against policies that offend his personal opinions; for example, about New Labour's tolerance of selective and fee-paying schools.

What I can do, if this or that policy is going through the system, is say, 'Look, you do realise that if you do this, this is what people are going to say about it.' Or I can point out that it is inconsistent with what we are trying to do in another area.[33]

Labour candidates who had welcomed electronic briefings when campaigning in 1997 now find that as MPs they are expected to carry pagers and bleepers, to receive centrally prepared bulletins intended to make sure they stay 'on message' by giving them the message of the day or the hour. The results can sometimes be ironic, as when an MP's bleeper goes off when he or she is talking to a journalist and the message is 'Be careful of journalists', or the bleeper bleeps when an MP is telling a BBC interviewer that there is no such thing as thought control within Tony Blair's New Labour party.[34]

A Freedom of Information Act has created a right to public access to some details about government, but the right is hedged with restrictions that allow many deliberations of government to be kept secret. In Opposition Tony Blair had been outspoken about opening up Whitehall, and a Cabinet Office White Paper was issued promising this. However, when the Home Office bill on the subject was published, the scope for keeping Whitehall secret was substantially expanded. Clauses 33 and 34 of the act state that a minister of the Crown or anyone authorized for this purpose by a minister may withhold information that may 'prejudice the effective conduct of public affairs' and information relating to 'the formulation or development of government policy'.

Campbell's Fleet Street training makes him scornful of those who wait for their morning paper to see what the papers have to say, including many old-school civil service information officers. When John Major's Press Secretary, Christopher Meyer, inquired about obtaining the late night editions of the next morning's papers so that he could brief the Prime Minister on the papers at 7 a.m., he was advised to make arrangements with his local news agent, as there was no official money or need for seeing papers early. Every department's chief information officer is now responsible for monitoring departmental news on an around-the-clock basis, a routine journalistic procedure but involving 'anti-social' hours for Whitehall civil servants. The object is to identify negative stories in the 10 p.m. editions of papers. In the next four hours rebuttals, countercharges or diversionary stories can be produced so that the 2 a.m.

edition, which cues the morning television and radio news, has a more favourable, or at least a less unfavourable, gloss on what the government is doing.

To make a revolution, one must get rid of people who hesitate to fall into line. Many senior civil servants in the Government Information Service have questioned the propriety of their office preparing and issuing what they see as party political material. Career civil information officers who have insisted on this point have formed a 'Tumbrel Club' (named after the cart carrying political prisoners to execution during the French revolution), open to all who have been unceremoniously wheeled out of Whitehall. In the first two years after Blair arrived in Downing Street, there was a wholesale turnover of top information staff in place before Blair arrived.[35] Every head that rolled gave Campbell the opportunity to appoint more pliable staff to serve the Blair revolution.

A practice initiated by Bernard Ingham – publicizing Downing Street's dissatisfaction with Cabinet colleagues – has been continued by Labour political appointees. Ingham dismissed a Foreign Secretary, Francis Pym, as a 'Mona Lott' figure, and described the leader of the House of Commons, John Biffen, as a 'semi-detached' member of the Cabinet. Downing Street has rubbished ministers and ex-ministers such as Mo Mowlam and David Clark. At a difficult time in the relationship between Tony Blair and the Chancellor, Gordon Brown, the media was briefed that Brown was 'psychologically flawed'. One dismissed minister, Frank Field, attacked Tony Blair's team for 'excesses and obscenities of behind-the-scenes briefings'.[36]

At times, the messenger, Alastair Campbell, has become the message. Old-style servants of the Prime Minister kept out of the public eye. Joe Haines, latterly Harold Wilson's Press Secretary, imposed a rule that any member of his staff whose photograph appeared in print forfeited a bottle of wine. Blair's staff are now as newsworthy as senior ministers, and with good political reason. An analysis of national newspaper coverage in the first full calendar year of the Blair administration found that Peter Mandelson and Alastair Campbell together had more media mentions than the Foreign Secretary, the Deputy Prime Minister or the Home Secretary (figure 5.3). The only Cabinet minister to score better was the Chancellor of the Exchequer. While publicity increases the political status of both Campbell and Mandelson, it also increases jealousy and enmities among Cabinet ministers ignored by both the Prime Minister and the media.

Figure 5.3 Media eminence of Blair's Downing Street
(*Total number of references in the press*)

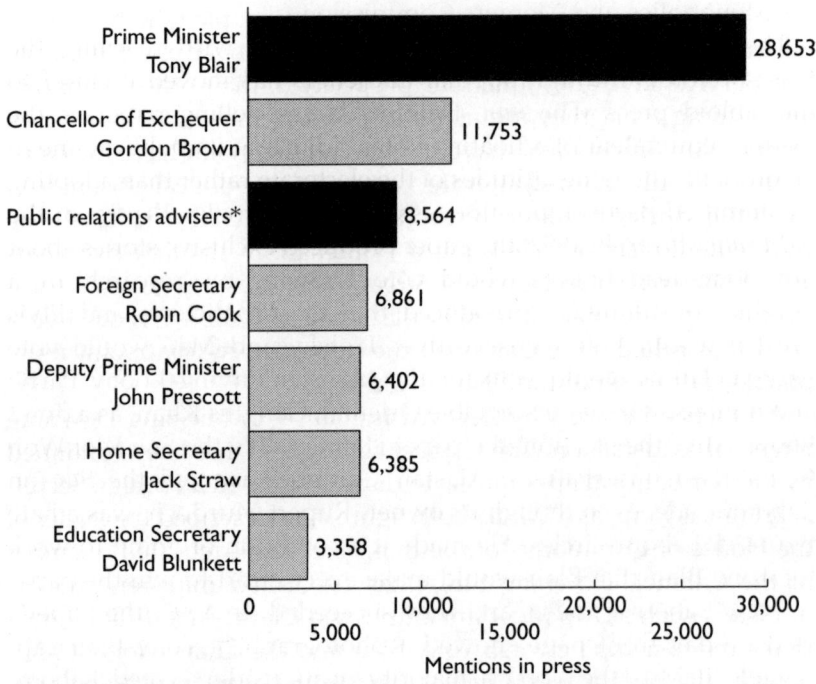

Person	Mentions in press
Prime Minister Tony Blair	28,653
Chancellor of Exchequer Gordon Brown	11,753
Public relations advisers*	8,564
Foreign Secretary Robin Cook	6,861
Deputy Prime Minister John Prescott	6,402
Home Secretary Jack Straw	6,385
Education Secretary David Blunkett	3,358

* Combines Peter Mandelson, Minister Without Portfolio, then President of Board of Trade, 6,323; Alastair Campbell, Press Secretary, 2,241.

Source: Computerized databases of national newspapers between 1 January and 23 December 1998, as reported in *The Times*, 30 December 1998: 'Tony Blair – Has He Got News for Us'.

4 An emerging political-media complex?

The Blair revolution in Downing Street has been paralleled by changes in the media. There are now more television channels and radio stations broadcasting news and views, some favourable to the Prime Minister and some unfavourable. Both the BBC and commercial television channels remain regulated by Acts of Parliament, and since broadcasters cannot anticipate which party will be governing when a licence review occurs, broadcasting executives look over their shoulders at both major parties. The national and international expansion of the media has created opportunities to build multinational media empires and made media barons anxious to maintain good relations with politicians who ultimately control the Monopolies and Mergers Commission.

The increased concern of Downing Street with reaching the mass of voters through popular audiences has moved it closer to the tabloid press. The *Sun*, Britain's largest-selling paper, is the media's equivalent of a floating voter, adjusting its political line in accord with changing attitudes of the electorate rather than adopting a committed partisan position, as did Beaverbrook's *Express* or the old *Daily Mirror*. In 1992, the paper produced exclusive stories about how long-dead figures would vote. Drawing on 'research' by a psychic consultant, it announced that Queen Victoria and Elvis Presley would vote Conservative; Trotsky and Mao would vote Labour; Hitler would vote for the Monster Raving Loony Party; and it put down that inscrutable Oriental, Genghis Khan, as a don't know. After the election, the paper claimed, 'It's the *Sun* Wot Won It' for the Conservatives. Alastair Campbell wanted the *Sun* on Labour's side, even though its owner, Rupert Murdoch, was a hate figure in Labour circles. He made it a condition of going to work for Tony Blair that Blair would make every effort to win the paper to New Labour's cause, and they succeeded. In 1997, the paper's election-day front page showed a photograph of Tony Blair captioned, 'It Must Be You'; a majority of its readers voted Labour. Tony Blair penned a handwritten note to the *Sun* thanking it for 'its magnificent support' which 'really did make the difference'.[37]

The media as players

While Downing Street's media goals have been constant for decades – favourable coverage or silence about the Prime Minister – there has been a sea change in journalistic values. Today, the media see themselves as players in the Westminster game. Most journalists and editors now believe that they, rather than Downing Street, ought to be the ultimate arbiters of what the public should know, because the media 'represent' readers and viewers better than MPs beholden to party whips and prime ministerial patronage. Given this outlook, journalists search out unofficial news about the government of the day in order to show that they are not taken in by spin doctors. The result may be a breathless exposé of what is 'really' happening behind the scenes, based on interviews with sources out of favour with Downing Street or on discovering information in the public domain hitherto only of interest to academic specialists. An alternative, specially suitable to the broadcast media, is an interviewer disdainfully looking down on the politician being interviewed and casting doubt on whether any politician can be trusted to tell the truth.[38] Alastair Campbell has adopted the pose of man more spinned against than spinning, complaining about 'the journalist as spin doctor', while admitting 'I did it myself as a political editor.'[39]

The media has an advantage over Downing Street: bad news about the Prime Minister is just as much a story as good news. Margaret Thatcher, John Major and Tony Blair have not yet offered targets on the scale of Richard Nixon or Bill Clinton. However, the pursuit of stories about sleazy activities of unknown Conservative backbench MPs while John Major was Prime Minister indicates that the attack mentality has grown in Britain and the behaviour of some New Labour ministers has fed it. Even without going on the attack, the media is randomly offered bad news about the government. For example, when Tony Blair badly miscalculated the nature of his audience when addressing the annual conference of the Women's Institute in June 2000, the sight of the Prime Minister getting a slow handclap was automatically headline news. The Prime Minister's surprised reaction was also news. One television commentator compared the look on his face to that of Nicolae Ceauşescu when he suddenly 'realised with incredulity that the plebs, hitherto so effectively manipulated, so utterly biddable, were barracking *him*'.[40]

When the media and Downing Street are at loggerheads, this creates a 'feeding frenzy' in which each side tries to demonstrate that the other is misleading the British people. The result is a series of allegations, rebuttals and re-rebuttals. The Blair media team have not only created a rebuttal unit but also developed 'pre-buttal' strategies designed to take the sting out of a bad news story before it breaks. For example, when the media started chewing over a leaked Downing Street memo in July 2000, Blair's staff 'accused' the Conservatives of denying that they had leaked the memo, a statement that was true in its content, yet so aggressively negative in its overtones as to make it sound as if the Conservatives were somehow to blame for the way Blair and his aides talk about policy and politics.

The increased concern of Downing Street with media coverage, combined with the growing self-importance of the media, is creating what former Conservative minister William Waldegrave has described as the 'political-media' complex. Messages and messengers are drawn together in a gigantic political echo chamber. David Butler, whose first-hand knowledge of elections covers two-thirds of a century, sees the Blair revolution as a 'landmark' in the development of the political-media complex:

> The media become more interested in the gimmicks than the substance. They discuss whether there should be leaders' debates more than what the debates should be about. They spend more time assessing the style of speeches and interviews than their content. Dramatic criticism can become more important than the drama itself. The words of the commentators get more column inches than the words of the politicians.[41]

In the 1997 election, stories about the campaign, the tactics of campaigners, opinion polls and media treatment were the subject of 70 per cent of front-page newspaper stories. Only 30 per cent of front-page stories were about policy.

While voters today see and hear far more of a new-style Prime Minister than of their old-school counterparts, there is far less opportunity for a two-way dialogue. In an old-style election meeting an audience was not a passive target; it could heckle or cheer the Prime Minister, or do both. Harold Macmillan, whose career spanned the era from private talk in country house weekends through street-corner meetings to televised campaigning, recalled: 'People of my age were brought up on the hustings. Now with television, it is like playing lawn tennis and there isn't anybody to hit the ball back from the other side of the net.'[42]

In so far as two-way communication occurs, it is between Downing Street and the media elite. Introverted dialogue encourages the isolation of both sides from the electorate. A BBC producer has reflected, 'We were in no position with our dispositions to understand what was moving voters. We were almost entirely focused on the press conferences, the leaders on the trail, reporting how a campaign was going as if it were primarily a media-party based affair.' There is a mismatch between news that the political-media complex offers voters and issues of popular concern.[43] For voters, the election campaign organized by the political-media complex is an exercise in failed political communication.

6

Winning Elections

> Something is required, simpler and more permanent, something which can be loved and trusted, and which can be recognized at successive elections as being the same thing that was loved and trusted before, and a party is such a thing.[1]
>
> Graham Wallas

> 'It's always best on these occasions to do what the mob do', said Mr Pickwick. 'But suppose there are two mobs?' suggested Mr Snodgrass. 'Shout with the largest', replied Mr Pickwick.
>
> Charles Dickens, *The Pickwick Papers*

A new-style politician such as Tony Blair claims to speak for all the people, but Mr Pickwick and his friends saw electioneering in old-school terms. He knew it was not practical politics to run after all the people at once; his recipe for success was consistent with that of a new-style politician wanting to reach or remain in Downing Street: shout with the largest mob.

For the Prime Minister of the day, an election is the political equivalent of Russian roulette. If the campaign succeeds, then power is held. But if it fails, then everything is lost. In Russian roulette there is only a one in six chance that the trigger fires a bullet. The odds on a Prime Minister losing a general election are much worse. In fifteen general elections since 1945, voters have seven times shot down the Prime Minister, while eight times allowing the incumbent to stay in office.

A Prime Minister of the old school campaigned as a party leader, emphasizing simple loyalties to trusted and familiar principles. A new-style Prime Minister campaigns as if his or her name were on every ballot as a candidate for Prime Minister. Even though the Liberals and other 'third' parties now poll a quarter of the popular vote, in a first-past-the-post electoral system only two parties have a realistic chance of gaining a majority in the House of Commons, and some theories of British democracy reduce popular rule to a choice between two party leaders.

Once in office, the Prime Minister must decide how to invest the political capital gained through election victory. If the Prime Minister was already in office, he or she is likely to have used up popular policies in the run up to the general election. A new Prime Minister often finds that the problems inherited are bigger than anticipated, and can take unpopular decisions straightaway, while there is time to blame them on the outgoing government. Even if the Prime Minister enjoys a 'honeymoon', sooner or later, domestic, international or intermestic issues will present Downing Street with problems where all choices are unpopular. At that point, the governing party's support slumps in opinion polls and by-elections, reminding the Prime Minister of electoral mortality.

In seeking re-election, an incumbent has a head start, having won the most seats at the previous election. In three postwar elections – 1955, October 1974, and 1983 – the governing party's vote has fallen and yet it has still had a majority in the Commons. An old-school Prime Minister could count on long-standing party loyalties mobilizing most supporters to vote the same at the next election as the last one. But because a small swing in votes can make all the difference between winning or losing a majority of seats, the Prime Minister cannot count on the next election simply being a repeat of the last. In 1951 the Attlee government had the misfortune of seeing its vote rise, yet not enough to retain its slim parliamentary majority.

The Leader of the Opposition party has much more time to campaign for votes and is also free of the burdens of governing. Harold Macmillan saw the advantages of this better than the conscientious Hugh Gaitskell, whom he criticized for 'going through all the motions of being a government when he isn't a government'. At a time when Labour was running even with the Macmillan government in the opinion polls, Macmillan argued, 'It is bad enough having to behave like a government when one is the government. The whole point of being in opposition is that one can have fun and lend colour to what one says and does.'[2] Since Harold Wilson succeeded Hugh Gaitskell, Opposition leaders have normally concentrated on running a full-time campaign against the government of the day.

1 From old-school to new-style voters

Even if the number of votes required to win re-election remains the same, the electorate is a moving target. Just as one cannot step in the same stream of water twice, so the turnover of generations means the Prime Minister cannot win two elections with the votes of exactly the same people, for older voters die and young people are added to the electoral register. The number of new recruits required is small in proportion to a party's total vote, but at the margin it can spell the difference between winning and losing a parliamentary majority.

Cumulatively, changes in the population produce a structural change in the electorate's political experience. At the time of the 1945 general election, a large majority of voters had been born into a pre-1914 society with big differences between classes. By 1974, very few voters could recall pre-1914 Britain; the median voter, born in 1934, was a child in wartime, and first voted when a mass consumption boom was starting. Today, death is rapidly removing from the electorate the small minority who voted for Churchill or Attlee in 1945. At the next general election, more than half the electorate will have cast their first vote after Margaret Thatcher entered Downing Street and Elvis Presley was dead.

Party loyalty before personality

Whereas a Prime Minister has only a few years in Downing Street, the average elector can vote for or against at least ten Prime Ministers at fifteen elections or more. If the personality of the Prime Minister were the only thing that influenced voters, we would expect big swings in voting every time a party changed its leader. But this does not happen. For a quarter-century between 1945 and 1970, under three different leaders the Labour vote fluctuated by only five percentage points, and it fluctuated by less than eight per cent for Conservatives under five different leaders in two decades from 1950.

Old-school prime ministers relied for their core support on persisting party loyalties. When a party changes its leader, voters do not look at the new leader with a fresh eye; people tend to judge politicians in the light of their long-term party identification. Pre-existing party loyalties encourage a Labour loyalist to judge a new Labour leader positively, and a loyal Conservative to be positive about a new Conservative leader. Party loyalties develop well before an individual is old enough to vote. Children in a middle-class home with Conservative-voting parents have tended to see themselves as Conservative supporters, and children in a working-class home with Labour-voting parents to support Labour. The Labour Party long weighed votes by the ton in constituencies where people would be prepared to vote for a pit pony decked in red, and a Conservative candidate once remarked, 'My mother is the sort of Tory who would vote for a baboon if you painted its bottom blue.' The Central Office official who told me this story added, 'People thought it was a bit raw; the chap should have left his mother out of it.'

In the past quarter-century political shocks have disrupted the link between family background and voting. The collapse of the Heath government in the face of the miners' strike in 1974, along with the unpopularity of the Labour alternative under Harold Wilson, gave the Liberal Party (and in Scotland and Wales, the Nationalists) a chance to become established as third parties. The leftward lurch of the Labour Party after the 1979 general election reduced its vote by a quarter in four years. The emergence of the Social Democratic Party offered voters from Labour homes the choice in 1983 of two parties led by politicians who had been colleagues in Jim Callaghan's Cabinet. Margaret Thatcher's conviction politics attracted some 'tough'-minded voters from Labour's ranks and repelled some 'tender'-minded Conservatives. Tony Blair has confused loyalties further. Voters dissatisfied with the party their parents supported can wash their hands of the choice between Thatcher and Foot or Blair and Hague by endorsing a 'half-way house' third party.

Demographic facts of life are not politically neutral. Conservatives have tended to live longer and vote in more elections than Labour voters, because they are more often middle-class. But Labour's working-class families have had higher birth rates than middle-class Conservatives. When these facts were published by David Butler and Donald Stokes a quarter-century ago,[3] a reviewer of their book drew the Orwellian policy prescription, 'Make babies for Labour.'

Great changes in social structure have also affected party loyalties. The model family of Butler and Stokes was one in which both parents had the same party, family ties were long-lasting, and social changes did not lead adults to re-evaluate what they had learned when young, because society as well as the party system was relatively stable. However, social change means that voters no longer live in the same world as their parents or grandparents. For a start, families are not the same as before. A young person's father may wear the earrings in the family, and parents who change partners as well as parties can confuse all kinds of loyalties.

The rise of a post-industrial economy has undermined leadership appeals to industrial workers and deferential pre-industrial Tories. The world of work has been transformed first by a great contraction of the number of male manual workers in heavy industries and a boom in middle-class jobs. Secondly, trade union membership has declined to less than a third of the labour force – and unions of public sector middle-class employees, such as school teachers, are now larger than industrial unions. Thirdly, the proportion of women in work has increased by more than half. Recognition of these facts gave impetus to the creation of the New Labour Party.

Independence of thought has been encouraged by a great expansion of education. In 1945 the median voter had left school at the age of 12 or 13. Today most voters have had almost twice as much education as voters in 1945. Educated voters can make political judgements based on knowledge independently of their social background.[4] For example, a half century ago many industrial workers could vote Labour because it favoured full employment and factory chimneys belching smoke (cf. the Lancashire saying, 'Where there's muck there's brass'). Their more educated offspring may today vote Liberal in hopes of protecting the environment from industrial pollution.

Life styles have been transformed too. Class-based differences in dress and speech that George Bernard Shaw described in *Pygmalion* were part of the everyday lives of Clement Attlee and Winston Churchill. Sentries in front of defence ministries in Whitehall were ordered to salute anyone wearing a bowler hat, lest they unintentionally snub an officer in civilian dress! Today, voters shop in classless chain stores and fashion outlets while Armani suits are de rigueur for Blairites, and Tory leaders put on baseball caps backwards. At the funeral of Princess Diana, more members of the audience were familiar with the singing of Elton John than with her brother's classical reference to Diana, the goddess of the hunt.

Changes in British society have produced a more volatile electorate, so that a new-style Prime Minister can no longer rely on traditional party loyalties to win an election. Nor can the leader of the Opposition rely on the swing of the pendulum to shift control of Downing Street between the parties. In 1964, 84 per cent described themselves as Conservative or Labour supporters; in 1997 76 per cent did so.[5] The strength of partisan commitment has declined even more. In 1964, the biggest group of voters, 44 per cent, said that they identified very strongly with their party, and the second largest group reported fairly strong ties. But by 1997, only 16 per cent said that they strongly identified with a political party and those only weakly attached to a party had risen from 18 per cent to 42 per cent of the electorate. Between 1992 and 1997, the Conservative Party lost a quarter of its vote, and Labour did the same between 1979 and 1983. There has been an even larger gross movement of electors from a major party to a third party or between voting and not voting; about one-third behave differently between one election and the next.[6]

In place of party loyalties

With the decline of votes delivered by the stork, new-style Prime Ministers must find other ways of mobilizing support. While novel in her policies, Margaret Thatcher was old-fashioned in seeking to mobilize support for her principles of free market economics and Victorian virtues. The Social Democratic Party stressed political principles too, mixing support for a market economy and publicly financed social benefits. However, many voters are indifferent to debates about policies and marginal voters can be repelled if party leaders sound 'too' political, talking all the time about distinctive party principles. Consensus goals, such as peace, prosperity and full employment, have a broad potential appeal to voters, for few people are in favour of war, depression and millions out of work. But the goals are indiscriminate; all parties can proclaim them, thus leaving no party with a competitive advantage.

Downing Street is happy to provide the media with information that calls attention to positive 'non-political' features of the Prime

Minister and his or her family, but it does not follow that what makes an appealing photo-opportunity also wins votes. A Prime Minister cannot divorce himself or herself from the record of his or her government by changing clothes, favourite foods or holiday venue. An attempt to turn a non-political event to party political advantage can also backfire, as Tony Blair learned when he sought to turn an invitation to address the Women's Institute into a sales presentation on behalf of New Labour.

The Prime Minister seeks a competitive edge by emphasizing his or her competence in achieving agreed goals, pointing to popular achievements of the government of the day. This was the logic behind Harold Macmillan's 'You've never had it so good' slogan. However, when the record is unsatisfactory – for example, the economic tailspin of the Heath government in 1974 or of the Callaghan government in 1979 – then the Opposition leader can point to government's failings and claim votes on the grounds of being better than 'that incompetent lot'. In a parliamentary system, the Prime Minister's popularity cannot be divorced from that of the party he or she leads or the record of the government as a whole.

2   *Targeting voters*

The Prime Ministership was almost two hundred years old before elections became democratic. The right to vote was not granted to all men and some women until 1918. The legacy of the past remained important among old-school Prime Ministers, who saw themselves as part of a governing class whose sophistication, experience and family qualified them to hold high office. The Prime Minister did not think it necessary to be continuously taking the popular pulse, attending instead to opinions at Westminster. Elections were accepted as necessary to decide which party and which member of the governing class became Prime Minister, but they were not seen as part of finding out how the mass of the population wanted to be governed. Deciding that was the responsibility of MPs in Westminster.

At election time, old-school party leaders made lengthy set-piece speeches to invited audiences of the party faithful. The speeches were taken down in shorthand by the attendant press and printed

At election time Prime Minister Clement Attlee went campaigning with an entourage of one, his wife, here shown driving him to deliver nomination papers at the 1950 election.
Photo: Popperfoto.

verbatim in many newspapers. Party leaders were ready to engage in controversy with each other, but as in debates at Westminster, it was controversy within the governing class. In 1945 the Conservatives did not present a party manifesto; Winston Churchill issued a patrician *Declaration of Policy to the Electorate* setting out his ideas about how the country should be governed. The Labour Party did have a party manifesto, produced by a combination of committees, caucuses and votes at the Labour Party Annual Conference. It stated what the party's leadership thought was best for the country. The parties had agents employed to get out the constituency vote at election time; the agents were servants of their constituency, and sometimes paid by the MP himself. Clement Attlee did not have a group of 'minders' to look after him; his wife drove him around the country to speak at engagements.

The transformation of electioneering began when innovators in both parties began introducing modern communication methods.

The new-style campaigners are primarily of two types: salesmen operating by gut instinct and experience, and clinically dispassionate strategists using sample surveys of voters to target specific groups of the electorate. The best-conducted election campaigns have usually involved a mixture of both.

After Suez, the unpopularity of the Conservative government made it evident that something needed to be done to gain electoral support for the government. Atypically for a Prime Minister, Harold Macmillan had been in trade. Working in the family publishing firm taught Macmillan the need to publish books that people would buy. The Old Etonian head of the party organization, Lord Poole, was conscious that he did not know what ordinary voters wanted; to gain insights, he observed Britons enjoying the then novel experience of shopping at a supermarket. Conservative Central Office turned its back on traditional party institutions and commissioned an advertising agency, Colman, Prentis and Varley (CPV), to produce advertising that was simple in thought, phrasing and emotional overtones. The CPV staff were marketing professionals who were active in the Bow Group and other Conservative organizations. Instead of promoting Macmillan's upper-class visage, CPV advertisements emphasized themes that ordinary people could identify with. The best-known showed a family of indeterminate social class happily washing their new car; the catchword slogan was, 'Life's Better with the Conservatives; Don't Let Labour Ruin It.' In the political equivalent of full frontal nudity, an advertisement in the *News of the World* depicted a cloth-capped East End docker under the caption, 'You've looking at a Conservative.'[7] Labour MPs denounced the Conservatives for trying to sell politics as if it were a soap detergent. They ignored the fact that soap detergent sales were booming as newly affluent voters bought their first washing machine.

Hugh Gaitskell was likewise anxious to boost Labour's chances of victory in the 1959 election. As a rationalist, Gaitskell turned for advice to Mark Abrams, a well-known leader in market research and long-time Labour supporter. A proposal to sample voter opinion was put to the Labour Party's National Executive Committee. It was rejected after the party's deputy leader, Aneurin Bevan, who had risen from the coal face to the governing class, claimed it was unnecessary: 'We don't need a survey to know what the working class thinks; I know what it thinks.' The survey was carried out independently of the Labour Party, financed by well-to-do friends of Hugh Gaitskell at a cost of £500.[8]

Innovators in the Labour Party did capture the committee responsible for party political broadcasts at the 1959 election, and produced lively programmes modelled on news magazines that had high viewership ratings. The presenters were young Labour MPs experienced in television current affairs: Anthony Wedgwood (subsequently, a peer and then plain Tony) Benn; Christopher Mayhew (subsequently a Liberal Democrat peer); and Woodrow Wyatt (subsequently a Thatcher peer). Conservative television programmes were conventional, being prepared by a committee dominated by Cabinet ministers. The climactic programme featured Harold Macmillan as a statesman, outlining foreign policy with a large globe as an awkward prop. After viewing this programme in an Oxford common room, my immediate reaction was to turn to an older don and ask, 'Was this how they campaigned in the 1920s?'

The 1964 election campaign confirmed the commitment of both parties to popular electioneering. Loss of the 1959 election reduced obstacles to innovation in the Labour Party. Mark Abrams's reports on which issues voters thought were important and which they thought unimportant were read attentively by Labour's new leader, Harold Wilson. In a show of pseudo-puritanism, the Labour Party did not hire an advertising agency. Instead, it solicited free help from four senior advertising agency executives; three of them were later rewarded with peerages. Instead of publicizing socialist themes or specific policies, Labour used the ideologically directionless slogan, 'Let's Go with Labour.' The Conservatives had the harder task, as their Prime Minister, Alec Douglas-Home, consistently ran 20 percentage points behind Wilson in the Gallup Poll rating of party leaders. Moreover, changes of personnel at Central Office had given a key role to a Beaverbrook-trained journalist of the old school, who took pleasure in saying that public opinion surveys were a waste of money since he already knew what the voters thought. *The Times*, while not putting news on its front page, did hire me to advise its readers about what voters thought. A memo I circulated to reporting staff accustomed to the world of Westminster contained such necessary, and even provocative guidelines as: 'Remember, one-third of the electorate are working-class women.' Defeat made the Conservatives ready to become more populist.

Party leaders have specially welcomed the new style of campaigning because it puts in their hands the weapons used to target voters. An old-school campaign was very decentralized. In more than 600 constituencies each parliamentary candidate put his or her own spin on what the party stood for, and local activists could say whatever they wanted or do nothing. New-style mass media campaigning not only enables a leader to speak to millions, it also gives him or her control of the party's message, whatever it is. Decisions about spending millions of pounds on advertising space are centralized. Every advertisement, poster and television film that goes out in the party's name is approved in writing by the party leader or by an authorized deputy. Through control of paid advertising and party political broadcasts, the public face of the party can stay on the leader's message.

Party leaders differ in the extent to which their personality or ideas are the chief message for target voters. Harold Wilson was ready to adapt his behaviour to make the most of new methods of targeting voters. While Ted Heath could understand the clinical analysis of an election strategist, he did not have the personality of a salesman. Margaret Thatcher approached campaigning with a missionary zeal for selling her brand of Conservatism, while aides had to remind her that some of her radical principles were more likely to scare off than attract voters.

The Blair revolution in campaigning began with the transformation of Labour into an electable party. The Blair campaign group benefited from observation of the 1992 Clinton presidential campaign, which was pragmatic in its strategy and flexible in 'crossover' appeals to voters who had not previously supported his party. American campaigners also made use of state-of-the-art electronic technology, such as computerized databases, bleepers, pagers, e-mail etc. When Clinton won in 1992 and gained re-election six months before the 1997 British general election, this added to his appeal to Blair's team. The prospect of winning Downing Street, combined with Blair's desire to be seen as pro-business in his appeal, enabled New Labour to raise the millions of pounds needed to finance a high-technology election campaign.

3 A fickle electorate

The frequency with which a Prime Minister must act – or be seen to be acting – results in political capital being constantly reassessed. During the life of a Parliament, public opinion polls and by-elections produce both good and bad results for Downing Street.

At some time in a Parliament, almost every Prime Minister suffers a slump in popularity due to events, necessary but unpopular policy decisions, or the arrogance that comes from taking office for granted. An alert Prime Minister can regard a loss of popularity as a signal to switch policies; for example, moving from a deflationary economic policy to financing a pre-election boom, or reshuffling the Cabinet to get rid of unpopular ministers.

Fluctuations in opinion polls

Polls reporting the current state of public opinion are media events beyond the control of Number Ten. The standard Gallup Poll question – 'Are you satisfied or dissatisfied with . . . as Prime Minister?' – was first asked about Clement Attlee in August 1945, and intermittently in the following decade. Since 1955 satisfaction with the Prime Minister has been monitored almost every month by the Gallup Poll and the number of published polls has increased greatly since then. Almost every week there is a media story about the ups and downs of prime ministerial popularity. As long as the Commons was dominated by old-school MPs, the effect of polls on the Prime Minister's political capital was slight. But by the 1970 general election, election campaigns had changed from jousting between knights in armour to electronic warfare.

Even though a Prime Minister's personality is relatively constant, popular support varies greatly within each individual's term of office (figure 6.1). The most extreme swings were experienced by Harold Macmillan. His lowest approval rating was 30 per cent, reached shortly after he became Prime Minister in 1957, and the highest, 79 per cent, in May, 1960. It then fell again to a low of 35 per cent three years later. Harold Wilson similarly experienced dramatic ups and downs in popularity in his first six years in Downing Street.

On average, the gap between the peak and trough in the popularity rating of the Prime Minister is 28 percentage points. The spread would be greater still if Prime Ministers who had generated widespread dissatisfaction had also been able to reach the heights of a Macmillan or a Wilson. For example, Edward Heath's popularity was relatively steady – the distance between his peak and trough was only 14 percentage points – because at no time in his premiership did Heath ever gain the approval of as much as half the electorate.

122 *Winning Elections*

Figure 6.1 Highs, means and lows in approval of prime ministers

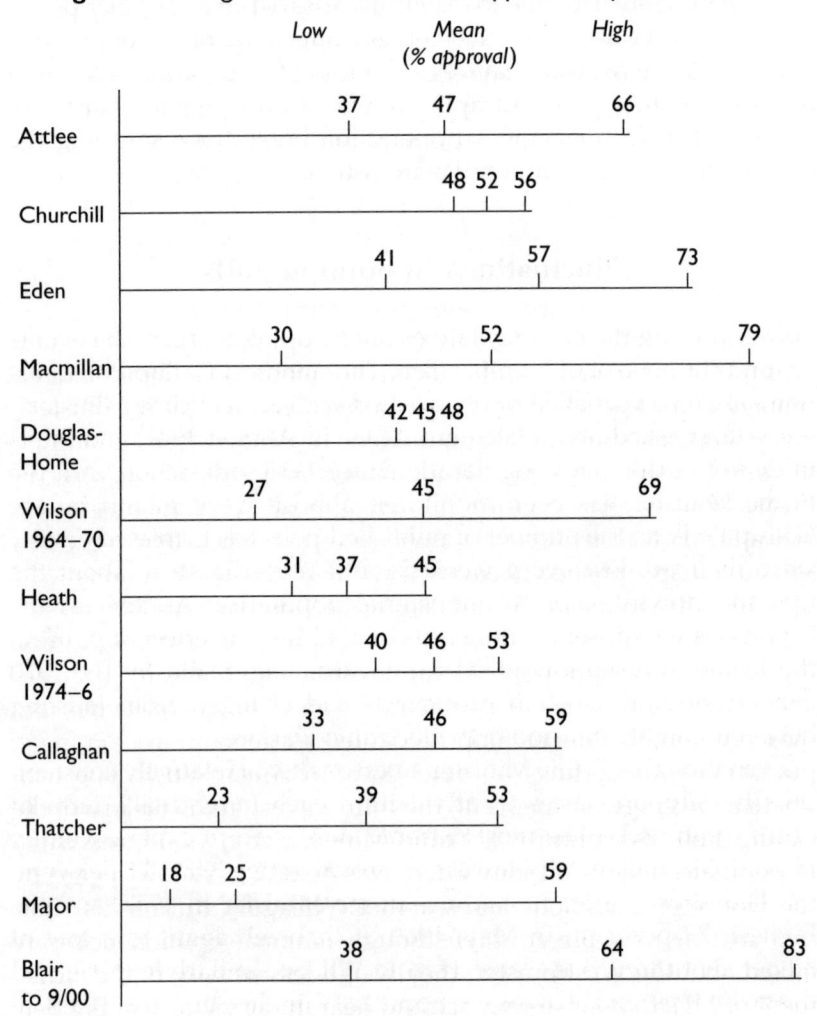

Prime Minister	Low	Mean (% approval)	High
Attlee	37	47	66
Churchill	48	52	56
Eden	41	57	73
Macmillan	30	52	79
Douglas-Home	42	45	48
Wilson 1964–70	27	45	69
Heath	31	37	45
Wilson 1974–6	40	46	53
Callaghan	33	46	59
Thatcher	23	39	53
Major	18	25	59
Blair to 9/00	38	64	83

Source: Calculated by the author from British Gallup Poll monthly survey data.

Since a Prime Minister is likely to be at the peak of popularity on entering Downing Street and to have worn out his or her welcome on leaving, we would expect each incumbent's rating to show a steady downward trend. But this is not the case; most postwar Prime Ministers have seen their satisfaction fluctuate both *up and down* during their stay in Downing Street.[9] The normal pattern is to peak early in the term of office and reach the trough around the mid-point, before showing a significant recovery by the time of the next election. Nor has the shift from a deferential media to the politics of denigration caused satisfaction with successive prime ministers to fall continuously. Instead, satisfaction has fluctuated up and down. John Major had the lowest rating in the history of the Gallup Poll, averaging approval by only 25 per cent, but his successor, Tony Blair, set a record high, being approved by 83 per cent.

Shortly after Tony Blair entered Downing Street, Peter Mandelson boasted that there would be no mid-term slump in Labour's support. Up to a point, Mandelson was correct. Two years after Blair entered Downing Street he enjoyed the approval of 70 per cent of Gallup Poll respondents and the New Labour Party had a 27 percentage point lead over the Conservatives. But the pride of Downing Street was subsequently humbled. In the forty-first month of Blair's premiership, demonstrations against petrol price increases pushed Blair's approval rating down to 38 per cent, the biggest fall in Gallup Poll history, and, for the first time since 1992, the Conservative Party pushed ahead of Labour in the opinion polls.

While any politician would like to be popular with the public, a high rating in public opinion polls is *not* the same as a good reputation in Westminster. Within Westminster Margaret Thatcher was able to impose her personal views on Cabinet colleagues and the Commons to a degree unprecedented for generations. Yet in the public eye her standing was much lower. Popular satisfaction with Thatcher averaged 39 per cent, the third lowest in the history of the Gallup Poll. By contrast, a Prime Minister who stood very high in popular esteem, Anthony Eden, was held in very low regard by the House of Commons and Cabinet colleagues during his short stay in Downing Street. Even though national opinion polls are talked about in Westminster, they weigh less heavily in the judgement of MPs than what they see and hear in the vicinity of Big Ben.

The personal popularity of the Prime Minister is not the same as popular support for the governing party – and it is the latter that is crucial if the Prime Minister is to remain in Downing Street. The critical Gallup Poll question is: 'If there were a general election tomorrow, which party would you support?' The replies show ups and downs during the life of a Parliament, but the distance between the highest and lowest level of support is much less than that for the popularity rating of prime ministers. On average, a Prime Minister's highest personal rating has been 12 percentage points above his or her party's best poll result. For half a century after 1945 no party had ever been endorsed by more than 53 per cent of the voters, but Clement Attlee, Anthony Eden, Harold Macmillan and Harold Wilson were each endorsed by two-thirds or more of Gallup Poll respondents. Since then, both Tony Blair and New Labour have set Gallup Poll records for popularity, and at his peak Blair has been 20 percentage points more popular than his party.

Messages from by-elections

MPs put more weight on by-election results than opinion polls, because they are not answers to hypothetical questions but hard evidence of how real voters are behaving. By-elections are usually *not* held at a time or place chosen by the Prime Minister; the most common reason for a by-election is the death of the sitting MP. When a by-election falls in the middle of a Parliament, the result is vulnerable to 'mid-term blues' – and local circumstances may add further complications to the government holding the seat. The governing party has more seats at risk than the Opposition, because it has more MPs. When the governing party loses a by-election, this reminds its MPs that they are vulnerable to losing their seats.

Old-school Prime Ministers gave little thought to by-elections, since the governing party did not lose a single seat for a decade after 1945, and in 1953 the Conservative government actually gained a seat. In the following decade, seats occasionally changed hands, most notably Liberal gains from the Conservative government. But such shifts were exceptions. Between 1955 and 1966, the incumbent party held the seat in 87 per cent of by-elections.

Since 1966 by-elections have often been bad news for Downing Street. In the 1966–70 Parliament, the Labour government lost all fifteen seats that it defended, twelve to the Conservatives and one each to the Liberals, the Scottish Nationalists and the Welsh Nationalists. Under Margaret Thatcher the Conservatives lost twelve seats, but the official Opposition party, Labour, gained only five and the Liberals and the Social Democrats gained seven. Between 1992 and 1997 the only by-elections held in Conservative seats followed the death of the sitting MP; the governing party lost all eight seats. Even when seats do not change hands, by-elections tend to embarrass the government, because they register a swing in votes against it. In the 1966–70 Parliament, the swing against the Labour government averaged 12 per cent. In the disastrous 1992 Parliament, the governing party's vote fell by an average of 24 per cent in Conservative seats.

The Prime Minister may dismiss losing a by-election to the Liberals as lacking significance, since the Liberal leader is not a competitor. But such arguments are only half-truths, for the government's loss of a seat to a third party reduces its overall majority in the Commons by one. By-election defeats caused Jim Callaghan and John Major to lose their Commons majority. If the turnout is low, the result can be described as unrepresentative, but it leaves unanswered the question: why are the governing party's supporters staying at home? Since there can be dozens of by-elections in each Parliament, all of them cannot be dismissed as freaks.

A by-election swing shows a protest against the governing party, since its vote goes down more than the official Opposition's support rises, and third parties do relatively well. The pattern of protest has followed a cyclical pattern since 1966. The governing party's vote drops in the initial years of a Parliament and recovers substantially in the run up to the next general election. By the end of its second year in office the by-election vote for the Prime Minister's party averages 10 percentage points less than at the preceding general election. The third year is usually the worst, with the fall in support averaging 18 percentage points. The government's vote recovers substantially in the fourth year of a Parliament, reflecting efforts made by Downing Street to recover ground in preparation for a forthcoming general election. Between 1966 and 1992, the governing party won back more than two-thirds of the seats that it had lost at by-elections. The recovery from by-election defeats is a tendency not a certainty, for in 1997 the Major government failed to regain seven of the eight seats lost at by-elections.

The ballot that counts

A mid-term slump will depress the Prime Minister's stock of political capital, but need not be fatal. The Prime Minister can remind supporters that a slump in opinion polls is not the same as an election defeat, and a seat lost at a by-election can be regained at a general election. Current difficulties can be glossed over with a rosy scenario promising that the government's electoral fortunes will improve before the next general election. An optimistic forecast of future events cannot be shown to be false until a few months or weeks before polling day, when it is too late to change leaders.

A Prime Minister does not need to be in the lead for most of a Parliament to win re-election. In more than 500 monthly opinion polls since 1945, the governing party has *trailed* the opposition 70 per cent of the time, and in ten of the fourteen Parliaments the Opposition has been ahead in a majority of monthly polls. Notwithstanding unpopularity during the life of a Parliament, since 1950 the Prime Minister has emerged victorious on election day in eight of fourteen contests. Not only was victory secured in the four Parliaments when the government of the day was normally ahead in the polls (1964, the short Parliament of 1974, 1983 and 1987) but also when the Opposition party was ahead of the government in most monthly polls taken in the Parliaments of 1945, 1951, 1955 and 1979.

To win re-election, the Prime Minister need 'only' call an election for a month in which the government is ahead of the Opposition. In the halcyon days of Keynesian demand management, the Prime Minister could try to stimulate the economy to promote prosperity and a 'feel good' factor before calling an election. The 1966 victory of Harold Wilson is a textbook example of a well-timed election. Six months after winning re-election, devaluation sank the Labour government's economic policy, but Wilson was safe in Downing Street for four years. In 1970 the Prime Minister's power to call an election boomeranged. When the economy showed signs of recovery, Wilson called an election almost a year earlier than required and the Conservatives won an upset victory. Since economic issues are not the only influence on voting behaviour, a short-term upturn in the economy does not guarantee victory, as John Major learned in 1997.

The right to name the date of the election can become the sword of Damocles, terminating a Prime Minister's career. Six general elections since 1945 have been called when the Prime Minister had no choice but to do so. In 1945 the Labour Party was unwilling to agree with Winston Churchill terms for continuing the wartime coalition after VE Day, and in 1964 and 1997 the five-year limit on the life of a Parliament ran out. In autumn, 1951 Clement Attlee led a tired and divided governing party without a working majority in the Commons; and in February 1974, economic confrontation between Ted Heath and the mineworkers required a general election to decide the question 'Who governs?' In 1979 the Callaghan government was defeated on a vote of confidence in the Commons. In each instance, the Prime Minister forced to call an election lost office.

While an election is a life-or-death matter to the Prime Minister, satisfaction with the Prime Minister is *not* a major determinant of how people vote. Studies of voting behaviour consistently show that the most important influences on electoral choice are long-standing political values, economic interests and party identification. The leader's personal appeal affects only a few per cent of voters. The 1992 election provides a specially dramatic illustration. Knowing whether a person voted for the Thatcher-led Conservative Party in 1987 made it possible to identify 88 per cent of the support for the party led by John Major. Adding to this the rating given John Major as against Neil Kinnock accounts for only an additional 1 per cent of Major's vote.[10] Furthermore, the impact of a leader may be negative rather than positive. In 1964 Alec Douglas-Home was a liability to the Conservatives, and the same was true of Ted Heath in 1974. As each election was decided by a small majority of seats, the governing party would have stood a better chance of winning if it had dumped the Prime Minister.[11]

In considering personal appeal, it is important to measure the Prime Minister's popularity against that of competitors. In 1983 Margaret Thatcher enjoyed a 32 percentage point lead in approval, because of the *un*popularity of Michael Foot, who was endorsed by only 18 per cent in the Gallup Poll. In a complementary manner, Tony Blair had a 35 per cent lead in 1997, because the endorsement of John Major was the lowest of any Prime Minister on record at the start of an election campaign. When a general election is called, the Prime Minister is usually more popular than the Opposition leader. But a personal lead does not guarantee victory to the governing party. In 1970 Harold Wilson's Gallup rating was above that of Ted Heath, in 1974 Heath was above Wilson, and in 1979 Jim Callaghan's was well above Margaret Thatcher. Yet in all three elections the less personally appealing leader won Downing Street.

The popularity of the Liberal Party leader shows the limitation of treating personal approval as tantamount to an election outcome. Since October, 1974 the Gallup Poll has asked the electorate: 'Do you think ... is or is not proving a good leader of the Liberals (or, subsequently, Liberal Democrats)?' The Liberal leader normally has a higher approval rating than either the Prime Minister or the Leader of the Opposition, averaging approval by 61 per cent of respondents between 1974 and 1995.[12] In 1997 Paddy Ashdown was as popular as Tony Blair, reaching 79 per cent in the Gallup Poll. But no Liberal party leader has been able to convert high personal approval into a big Liberal vote. A large majority of those approving the Liberal leader vote Conservative or Labour.

Notwithstanding efforts of Tony Blair to transform Labour into a party in his own image, two-thirds of the vote putting him in Downing Street came from old Labour voters who had supported the party before Blair became its leader (figure 6.2). The typical Labour supporter (including, presumably, Blair himself) had voted for Labour when it was led by Neil Kinnock, Michael Foot, Jim Callaghan and Harold Wilson, leaders whom Blairites have Tipp-Exed out of their picture of the New Labour party. The additional third of the vote, which provided the margin between victory and defeat, was drawn from four different sources: a minority of former Conservatives, Liberal Democrats, supporters of other parties, and those who didn't vote or were too young to vote at the previous election.

The Prime Minister's greatest impact is indirect, the effect he or she has on the government's record. When Margaret Thatcher

Figure 6.2 Old Labour core of 1997 New Labour vote
(*How Blair's voters behaved in 1992*)

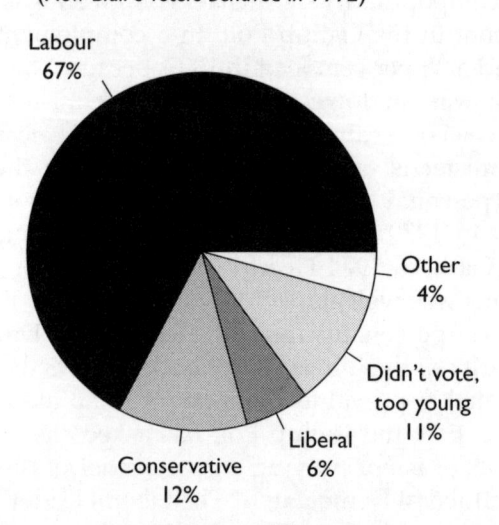

Labour 67%
Other 4%
Didn't vote, too young 11%
Liberal 6%
Conservative 12%

Source: 1997 British Election Study.

launched a British military offensive to regain the Falkland Islands in 1982, Conservative support stood at only 31 per cent in the Gallup Poll, and the alliance of Liberals and Social Democrats was in first place. Military success boosted Conservative support to 45 per cent in eight weeks and deflated the third party challenge. When John Major failed to anticipate the vulnerability of the pound after his upset 1992 election victory, this caused an abrupt collapse of the pound and his chances of winning re-election, as John Smith and then Tony Blair reformed the Labour Party to make it electable. But once in office Blair has faced a very different challenge: facing up to responsibility for British government.

7

Managing Parliament and Party

> It's carrying democracy too far if you don't know the result of the vote before the meeting.
>
> Eric Varley, former Labour Cabinet minister

The Prime Minister enters Downing Street by winning the support of the majority party in Parliament. While MPs and activists like to see their party in government, election victory creates the expectation that policies advocated in opposition will become government policies. Once in Downing Street, the Prime Minister must deal with difficult policy issues, subject to constraints that are hardly imagined by an Opposition leader writing a 'wish list' for government. Commitments inherited from the past, pressures from within British society and commitments to the European Union limit what any British government can do. In a lecture delivered in 1970, shortly after a new government came to Downing Street, the chief Whitehall Mandarin, Sir William Armstrong, described the forces limiting the room for manoeuvre of any British government as 'ongoing reality'.[1]

There is inevitably a tension between what partisans want and what the government of the day is able to do, for partisan aspirations are not limited by the burdens of office. Yet whatever the government does is immediately considered party policy. In the words of Herbert Morrison, a senior Labour minister for eleven years, 'Socialism is what the government does.' If government actions are consistent with party expectations, support is readily forthcoming. However, when 'ongoing reality' is in conflict with what partisans think is the right thing to do, party ideologues may attack their Prime Minister for betraying the party's ideals by surrendering to something stronger than party. This is the dilemma that faced Barbara Castle, a leftwing MP and Cabinet minister: 'It's hell when your party's in power. You don't know whether to follow your conscience or your party.'[2]

Since British political parties are confederations of institutions, MPs disagreeing with the Prime Minister's leadership can try to bring pressure on Downing Street from the party organization outside Parliament: constituency associations, the annual conference of the party, and in the case of the Labour Party affiliated trade unions. Old-school Conservative prime ministers tended to treat their party organization as their servant, as the parliamentary party was organized more than half a century before a nationwide network of constituency associations was created. A pre-1914 party leader, A. J. Balfour, reportedly said he would sooner take orders from his valet than from a Conservative Party conference. The Labour Party was formed outside Parliament to secure the representation of the working class in Parliament. But when Professor Harold Laski, the chairman of the extra-parliamentary party, tried to claim authority over a Labour Prime Minister, Clement Attlee replied, 'You have no right whatever to speak on behalf of the government and a period of silence on your part would be welcome.'[3]

In resolving conflicts between what government does and what the party expects, the Prime Minister is in a strong position. He or she can marshal information from Whitehall in efforts to persuade backbench MPs that the policy being followed is for the best or, even if patently unpalatable, it is the only possible policy that the government can follow. If the government introduces legislation that goes against the grain, party loyalty can be invoked to prevent rebellion, and this is especially so when the Opposition moves a vote of no confidence. If necessary, the whips can offer stronger sanctions and inducements to secure support. A combined assault on the hearts, minds and other parts of the anatomy of backbench MPs almost invariably results in voting for the government.

Managing MPs is central to maintaining the Prime Minister's political capital. Promoting policies that reflect the party's traditional commitments helps, and a high standing in public opinion polls promises that sacrifices of traditional commitments will reap election victory. Participation in party activities in Parliament, in the country and annual conference is symbolically important, showing that the Prime Minister has not forgotten the people who put him or her in Downing Street. A failure to manage MPs and party activities will stimulate criticism in the press and backbench rebellions in the Commons, revealing that Downing Street's victories in formal votes of confidence are a sham.

1 The House is no longer a home

Old-school Prime Ministers regarded the House of Commons as their political home, for before entering Downing Street, they had spent decades there. Winston Churchill, for example, was an MP for thirty-nine years before becoming Prime Minister. Until the Second World War, prime ministers such as Stanley Baldwin kept in touch with MPs on a continuing basis, acting as Leader of the House as well as Prime Minister. Being Leader of the House requires ongoing discussions with the Government Chief Whip that take into account the interests of backbench MPs and the Opposition front bench. Even in wartime, when there were many demands on his time, Churchill was attentive to the House. An aide noted, 'At no time was Parliament's right of criticism restricted and, if anything, he seemed over-sensitive to parliamentary opinion, insisting on debates and votes of confidence even when it was clear that he enjoyed the support of the overwhelming majority.'[4] Clement Attlee was attentive to the Parliamentary Labour Party mood during wartime; when the Labour government had a large majority from 1945 to 1950; and even more when its majority was wafer thin in 1950–1. Harold Wilson took advantage of having an office in the Palace of Westminster to do much of his afternoon and early evening work there. This also provided him with a refuge from quarrels in Downing Street between political staff and civil servants.

An old-school Prime Minister saw the House as the forum for maintaining political capital nationwide. The classic Westminster view was expressed by Marcia Williams, Harold Wilson's longtime aide:

> The Prime Minister, if he is to maintain his authority in his own party, has to demonstrate his authority over the Opposition. If he does it well, it impresses first his Cabinet colleagues and also his back-bench supporters. Then it has its repercussions on television and in the newspapers. There is nothing like a good press on the following morning [after Prime Minister's questions] for heartening a party leader. Afterwards, it is possible to sense the reaction in the

country as the effect of newspaper stories and the reports of MPs to their constituencies have their effect throughout the rest of Britain.[5]

New-style Prime Ministers have spent less time as an MP. Whereas Jim Callaghan had been in the Commons for thirty-one years before becoming Prime Minister, Margaret Thatcher had been there twenty years before entering Downing Street, and John Major only eleven years before succeeding her. In his fourteen years in the Commons, Tony Blair had never been a minister answering questions from the government benches. Less experience of life in the Commons goes along with a Prime Minister being less inclined to treat the House as his or her political home.

An absentee MP

Participation in divisions in the House of Commons is normally not necessary for the governing party to win a vote. However, it does indicate the importance that the Prime Minister attaches to party solidarity. Unlike the situation in countries where legislators can vote by proxy or electronically, a division in the House of Commons is a social occasion. All MPs walk past the tellers in a queue with colleagues. An alert backbench MP can collar the Prime Minister and the Prime Minister can chat informally with backbench supporters, listening and dispensing friendly and sympathetic comments.

The median MP participates in 64 per cent of parliamentary divisions. The Prime Minister has good reason for a lower attendance record, because of urgent problems in Whitehall or attendance at meetings abroad.[6] Therefore, the Prime Minister's voting record should not be compared with that of the average MP but with other prime ministers'. From 1946 until the mid-1980s prime ministers usually voted in more than a third of all divisions. The level of participation fluctuated with the size of the government's majority, the health of the Prime Minister and other factors (figure 7.1). When Churchill returned to Downing Street in 1951, he paid his respects to the Commons by participating in more than half of the divisions in his first session, and after his stroke he none the less participated in one-quarter of the divisions in the Commons. In the last session of the 1992–7 Parliament, when the Conservative government's majority was often uncertain, John Major voted in 42 per cent of

134 *Managing Parliament and Party*

Figure 7.1 Participation in divisions in the Commons
(% in which Prime Minister participated)

Prime Minister	%
Attlee 1946	32
Churchill 1951	55
Eden 1955	48
Macmillan 1959	32
Wilson 1969	35
Heath 1970	32
Wilson 1974	43
Callaghan 1976	39
Thatcher 1979	41
Thatcher 1989	17
Major 1990	20
Major 1996	42
Blair 1997	6

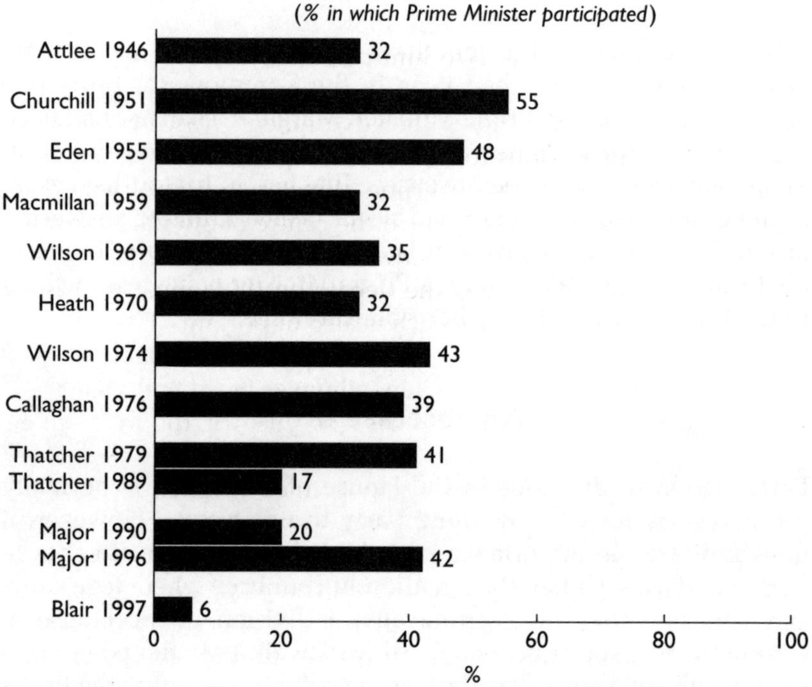

Sources: From 1969: averages of annual figures compiled by the House of Commons Library, and reported in Andrew Tyrie, *Mr. Blair's Poodle*. London: Centre for Policy Studies, 2000, p. 31. For Churchill, Eden and Macmillan, figures compiled by the author from a sample of divisions in the first session of Parliament. For Attlee, figures made available by George W. Jones and June Burnham, from their research on the parliamentary activity of prime ministers.

divisions, and Jim Callaghan voted in 39 per cent of divisions when his government lacked a working majority. Even though having a comfortable majority, in her first session as Prime Minister Margaret Thatcher voted in 41 per cent of divisions. By her last session as Prime Minister, Thatcher's attendance in division lobbies was less than half that – and MPs' criticisms of her remoteness multiplied.

Tony Blair has stood out in avoiding divisions in the House of Commons. In the first session of the 1997 Parliament Blair voted in only 5 per cent of divisions, and in the second session in only 8 per cent. Only a handful of Ulster MPs, including Sinn Fein abstentionists, voted less often than Tony Blair. The Foreign Secretary, Robin Cook, who has even more reason to be frequently abroad, voted almost twice as often as the Prime Minister. By not rubbing shoulders with Labour MPs in the division lobby, Blair increased the distance between himself and more than 150 Labour MPs new to the House and unknown to him personally.

Debates are classic parliamentary occasions, and when the Prime Minister speaks he or she puts the government's case and answers attacks from MPs anxious to make their reputation by showing up the Prime Minister. When the Prime Minister speaks or intervenes in the House, he or she is ex officio the centre of attention. Foreign affairs is the chief subject that draws the Prime Minister to speak at length in the Commons, and the debate on the annual legislative programme in the Queen's Speech is also important.[7] From 1945 to 1979, the Prime Minister averaged six speeches in major debates annually, except for Anthony Eden, who was faced with a demand to make even more major speeches because of the Suez crisis. Although Margaret Thatcher was ready to lecture many audiences about her convictions, she was less inclined to attempt lecturing the Commons. She averaged three major speeches a year, less than half the rate of predecessors. Even though John Major faced major foreign policy crises such as the Gulf War and the Maastricht Treaty, he spoke scarcely more frequently. In his first eighteen months in office, Tony Blair has set a new low, making a major speech only once a year on average (figure 7.2).

Because the Prime Minister is accountable for the government as a whole, he or she could participate in debates on almost any topic, but as a non-departmental minister, it is only necessary for him or her to do so when departmental issues are of central importance to the government's programme as a whole, or a departmental crisis threatens the Prime Minister's political capital too. Consistently, the Chancellor and the Home Secretary each make more Commons speeches annually than the Prime Minister. The Chancellor of the Exchequer answers for the budget; prison riots are the responsibility of the Home Secretary; and so forth around the Cabinet.

The Prime Minister can also make impromptu interventions in debates, scoring points off the Opposition or squelching criticisms as soon as they are voiced. But to intervene, a Prime Minister has to spend hours listening to what other MPs are saying rather than dash in to answer questions or make a statement and then dash out. Old-school Prime Ministers such as Churchill, Attlee and Eden intervened about once every ten days the Commons was in session, and Edward Heath even more often. Although Margaret

136　*Managing Parliament and Party*

Figure 7.2　Major speeches by Prime Minister in the Commons
(Number of speeches per year)

Prime Minister	Speeches
Churchill	7
Attlee	6
Eden	11
Macmillan	6
Douglas-Home	6
Wilson	7
Heath	6
Callaghan	6
Thatcher	3
Major	4
Blair	1

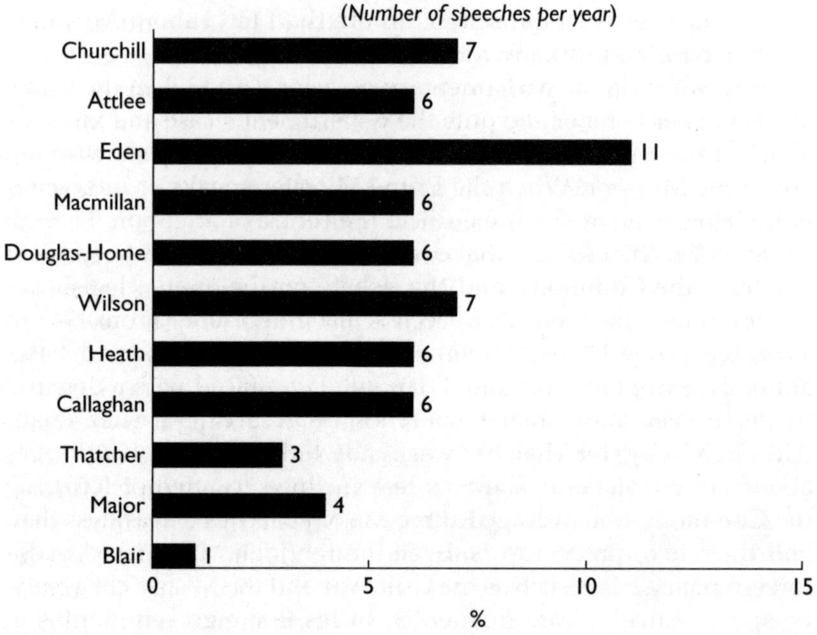

Sources: George W. Jones, 'Presidentialization in a Parliamentary System'. In C. Campbell and M. J. Wyszomirski, eds, *Executive Leadership in Anglo-American Systems*. Pittsburgh: University of Pittsburgh Press, 1991, table 10, supplemented by data supplied by June Burnham and George Jones. Blair data is for the period up to November 1998; the data for Churchill and Wilson combines two periods in office.

Thatcher did not hesitate to interrupt her Cabinet colleagues in public and private, she intervened in parliamentary debates only three times a year on average, and John Major slightly less frequently. Tony Blair has totally avoided participation in the cut and thrust of debates. In his first eighteen months in office, he did not make a single impromptu intervention.[8]

From fielding to dodging questions

Questions in the House are the primary means by which MPs can try to hold the Prime Minister accountable. When procedures for questions were first formalized in the late nineteenth century, MPs could ask questions of the Prime Minister any day when the House was sitting. Neville Chamberlain answered parliamentary questions on three-quarters of the days when the House sat, and Clement Attlee fielded questions on half the days that the Commons was in session.[9] By the 1950s Winston Churchill's ill health reduced questions to twice a week. In 1961 major procedural changes revised the rules for Prime Minister's Question Time. Two periods of fifteen minutes were set aside each week specially for the Prime Minister to answer questions submitted two weeks in advance. By 1990 the volume of questions had reached more than 13,000 a session, far more than could ever be answered orally.

The Prime Minister's appearance at Question Time is considered the high point of the week at Westminster. Awkward issues raised by Opposition questions can make the Prime Minister aware of shortcomings that departmental ministers may try to hide. The political priorities of Question Time have nothing to do with the spending priorities of departments. Questions about the most costly programmes of government – social security, health and education – are very rarely put to the Prime Minister. The Prime Minister seeks to raise the morale of backbench MPs in the governing party and the Leader of the Opposition seeks to show that he or she would make a better Prime Minister than the current incumbent. The Prime Minister carefully rehearses 'impromptu' replies to possible supplementary questions. Harold Macmillan nearly became sick during these preparations.

The nature of Question Time has changed radically over the years.[10] Until well into the 1960s, the primary aim of questions was to get the Prime Minister to address clearly specified issues. But this allowed the Prime Minister to pass questions to the departmental minister immediately responsible. To avoid this, questions have increasingly concerned personal activities of the Prime Minister; for example, whether he or she plans to visit a particular town. The sting is revealed by the supplementary question, giving an Opposition MP a chance of catching the Prime Minister unprepared. Since questions must be put down a fortnight in advance, vague questions can also be adapted to newsworthy topics of the moment. Downing Street staff devote significant effort to identifying booby traps in seemingly innocuous questions from the Opposition.

Harold Wilson led the way in turning Question Time into an opportunity to score points off the Opposition by fair means or foul. Exchanges between the Prime Minister and the Opposition have developed into uninformative slanging matches aimed at creating sound bites for the media. The Prime Minister can welcome abuse that raises the political temperature, for then he or she does not need to address the substance of a question but reply, as John Major did to Neil Kinnock, 'The right honourable gentleman has just revealed to the House why he is unfit to be in government.'[11]

Government whips have shown increasing readiness to prompt backbench MPs to promote the Prime Minister's and their own interests by asking questions that show both in a favourable light. An analysis of twenty-one appearances at Question Times by Tony Blair found that on thirty-five different occasions he replied to an obliging backbench Labour MP with the phrase, 'My honourable friend is absolutely right.'[12] The tactic will backfire, however, if a backbench MP asks a question that is 'too fawning', and draws a laugh from a disrespectful House.

The practice of planted questions led the then Speaker of the House of Commons, Betty Boothroyd, herself a Labour MP, to express disquiet at the readiness of newly elected Labour MPs to be 'toadies'. Clare Short, an old Labour Cabinet minister, has claimed, 'In opposition, I found toadying Tories creepy. I wouldn't have expected Labour MPs to be the same, but they are.' The Prime Minister views such behaviour differently; he told a *Woman's Hour* interviewer that Labour MPs who put questions to him about the positive achievements of the government were being 'constructive' and 'self-disciplined'.[13] The Speaker's complaints were ignored or met with 'half-hearted attempts to destabilise the Speaker'. The attempts were half-hearted, because 'in their view she does not matter enough to put too much effort into getting rid of her'.[14]

Mud-slinging has dulled the critical faculties of MPs. During the Suez crisis Anthony Eden's refusal to answer the Leader of the Opposition's question asking if Britain was at war with Egypt caused such an uproar that the Speaker suspended the sitting for half an hour to allow tempers to cool.[15] However, when Tony Blair responded to a Conservative question about neglecting attendance at Cabinet meetings during the Kosovo conflict by saying, 'Obviously with the war on, I haven't been able to attend two or three Cabinets.' MPs failed to notice that he had described what was officially an 'international armed conflict' as a war, with all the latter term implied in national and international law. Journalists were left to pursue the slip, and civil servants to explain it away.[16]

Tony Blair has shown no taste for Question Time. One of the first steps he took after entering Downing Street was to alter the routine from twice a week appearances of fifteen minutes each to a single weekly appearance of half an hour. While the amount of time for questions remains the same, the number of days that the Prime Minister is obliged to be questioned is halved. Scheduling a day trip to Brussels for a Wednesday gets the Prime Minister out of one-quarter of a month's parliamentary obligations. When William Hague, an experienced Oxford Union debater, showed he could often get the better of the Prime Minister in an exchange of facts, wit and insults, Downing Street blamed departments for shortcomings in the Prime Minister's responses. It asked for 'killer facts' to silence awkward questioners. In the absence of such facts, Blair sometimes resorts to bluster.

When Blair's parliamentary involvement is compared with prime ministers since 1868, he appears heading for a new record in distancing Downing Street from the Palace of Westminster only a few hundred feet away. Ministers have followed suit. Departmental ministers are now releasing statements likely to invite criticism in 'friendly' settings outside Parliament rather than giving them first to MPs. This pattern of behaviour earned public rebukes from the Speaker of the House, Betty Boothroyd.[17] Peter Mandelson has justified ignoring Parliament by saying, 'the era of pure representative democracy is coming slowly to an end'.[18]

2 Whipping MPs

The Prime Minister can tolerate debate in the Commons, since the government rarely risks losing a vote there. Old-school MPs almost invariably voted the party whip from a sense of collective party loyalty. Clement Attlee was fond of quoting a Labour MP who had been a firebrand socialist before 1914 and then a committed loyalist: 'When I was young I always talked a lot about my conscience. When I got older, I learned it was just my blooming conceit.' New-style MPs can be equally ready to follow Downing Street's direction, but the motive is often different: ambition for personal advancement.

The Chief Whip literally and symbolically lives between the Prime Minister and the parliamentary party at 12 Downing Street. The Chief Whip and assistant whips try to operate a two-way system of communication, advising the Prime Minister about the morale of MPs as well as telling MPs what is expected of them by Downing

Street. For the Prime Minister to ignore the whip's early warning of deteriorating morale is a symptom of political hardening of the arteries. The whips are also responsible for delivering votes from recalcitrant backbenchers. An awkward MP who ignores the offer of an attractive committee assignment or overseas trip and embarrasses the government is likely to feel the whip's mailed fist. One whip gloried in the motto, 'Kill the bastards before they kill us.'

Thanks to the loyalty of MPs to the party whip, up to 99 per cent of bills that the government introduces are enacted into law. In addition, 99.9 per cent of government amendments to bills are approved, compared to less than 10 per cent of amendments from backbench MPs in the governing party. The Opposition's activities have virtually no impact on legislation; less than 5 per cent of amendments from Opposition MPs are approved.[19]

To maintain political capital, the Prime Minister also needs the uncoerced confidence of MPs. In mid-Victorian times, Walter Bagehot described the House of Commons as weighing men as well as weighing measures; having a good personal reputation remains important today. A vote count may lull the Prime Minister into a false sense of security, as votes can be produced for policies about which MPs have substantial doubts. John Major was haunted by the apparent agreement that ambitious MPs offered, for he knew that they were toadying to him in hopes of gaining a ministerial post, and their loyalty could not be relied on. In order to stay in touch with what MPs really had on their mind, Jim Callaghan made it a point of principle never to refuse a meeting requested by a backbench Labour MP.

Brute votes yield brute support

Old-school Prime Ministers did not expect agreement but they did expect MPs to vote the party whip whether or not they agreed with the government. From 1945 to 1979, the proportion of divisions with a very high degree of cohesion (that is, at least nine-tenths of all MPs vote the party whip) occurred more than 95 per cent of the time in each Parliament, and in some sessions more than 99 per cent of the votes showed parties very cohesive. A division in which the government's support is 'only' 99 per cent is not a cannon pointed at the Prime Minister; it signifies that the governing party has a few loose popguns in its midst.

An often overlooked reason for cohesive votes is that old-school Prime Ministers tended to avoid putting issues to a vote that were likely to cause divisions, whether within the governing party or between government and opposition. Since 1945 there has been a cross-party consensus favouring a big majority of government measures. The Opposition does not vote against most bills on second reading, for it does not want to oppose measures popular with the public, including its own supporters and negotiated to the satisfaction of interest groups.[20] Under Margaret Thatcher there was an increase in the number of government bills voted against by the Opposition on principle, but they remained a minority. Tony Blair has reverted to normal practice, avoiding policies likely to attract opposition. When issues such as abortion or divorce create intense divisions within and across party lines, the Prime Minister can sidestep a challenge to authority by declaring a free vote.

The bark of individual backbenchers is not a threat to a Prime Minister as long as he or she can dismiss criticism as the views of a handful or group of MPs lacking widespread support in the governing party. For example, the 1945–51 Labour government was faced with repeated attacks from a group of leftwing MPs for aligning its foreign policy with the United States. When I interviewed Clement Attlee about this for my doctoral thesis, and explained that I wanted to discuss the problems his government had had with MPs, Attlee's laconic reply was, 'No problem. Just a few silly people.' Attlee could afford to dismiss criticism as long as his Foreign Secretary, Ernest Bevin, was dominant, and government was delivering welfare state legislation much welcomed by Labour's core voters.

Since there are usually more than a thousand divisions in the life of a Parliament, there are many occasions when one backbench MP can rebel against the party whip. In the 1970 Parliament, the median Conservative MP voted against the party's whip once. In the much more fractious 1974–9 Parliament, the median Labour MP voted against the party's whips half a dozen times. Another way of interpreting these figures is that the median MP votes with the government whip several hundred times for every time that he or she goes against it. When individual MPs vote against the whip, they rarely threaten the government's majority, for usually they express extremist sentiments, and thus are likely to be isolated in the division lobby. Labour MPs frequently voting against the Blair government on leftwing grounds, such as Tony Benn, Dennis

Skinner and Tam Dalyell, are unlikely to attract Conservatives to join them.[21]

Backbench MPs can question the Prime Minister off the floor of the House in parliamentary party meetings and informally. The Prime Minister can use such occasions to cultivate understanding for government decisions at variance with party aspirations. For example, Harold Wilson was ready to meet backbench Labour MPs outside the Commons chamber, and more than twice as likely to address the Parliamentary Labour Party as to make a major speech in the Commons.[22] When push comes to shove, the Prime Minister has much the stronger position, and can bludgeon down critics. Harold Wilson once told the Parliamentary Labour Party:

> All I say is 'watch it'. Every dog is allowed one bite, but a different view is taken of a dog that goes on biting all the time. If there are doubts that the dog is biting not because of the dictates of conscience but because he is considered vicious, then things happen to that dog. He may not get his licence renewed when it falls due.[23]

In the light of the experience of previous Labour prime ministers, on becoming Opposition leader Tony Blair began forging rules to prevent public criticism of his leadership. New vetting procedures were introduced for prospective parliamentary candidates, and activists deemed 'off message' because of their leftwing views were excluded from selection lists. The great increase in Labour MPs in 1997 brought a flood of new Blair loyalists to the Commons. MPs have been encouraged to stay away from the House and spend more time in their constituency talking to voters rather than asking questions of ministers. They are meant to obey strict disciplinary rules about avoiding any conduct that could bring 'the party into disrepute'. Violation of this ill-defined rule could lead to an MP being declared ineligible for readoption as a New Labour parliamentary candidate. A backbench Labour MP who criticized a government measure in a debate noticed that the Labour whip on duty in the chamber ticked a box against his name marked 'unhelpful'.

New-style Prime Ministers have embraced their party organization in order to suffocate critics by preventing extra-parliamentary arenas from being used as platforms for criticism. The advent of television has made a party's annual conference an occasion for addressing a mass television audience – and the chair seeks to prevent critics within the party from producing sound bites that would spoil those of the Prime Minister. In marking the centenary of the Labour Party, Tony Blair spelled out his idea of the relation of party and leader:

> Political parties require unity and leadership. Of course, leaders must listen. And we do. But remember, there's only one thing the public dislikes more than a leader in control of his party, and that is a leader not in control of his party. The whole party has to be engaged in telling the story of the government, not just the ones at the top.[24]

Tony Blair has argued that individual MPs have been elected 'to put through our programme' and not to question how the government implements the party's election manifesto.[25] Three generations of the Benn family illustrate the change in relations between MPs and Prime Minister. William Wedgwood Benn was a radical Liberal MP from 1906 to 1927, and then joined the Labour Party, becoming a Labour peer and government minister under Clement Attlee. The only electrical device he ever relied on was a hearing aid to follow debates in the House of Lords. His son, Anthony Wedgwood Benn, was elected a Labour MP in 1950 and was a Cabinet minister for eleven years. His chief electrical device has been a dictating machine for his political diary. When the grandson, Hilary Wedgwood Benn, was elected a New Labour MP in a by-election in 1999, he was issued an electronic bleeper to keep him on message.

3 From Butskellism to Blatcherism

The Prime Minister's party is more united by interest than by ideology. MPs want to remain the governing party, and they want to remain MPs. Armchair philosophers write about parties as united by a distinctive ideology, but there is no agreement about what the party label represents. The Conservative Party has claimed to represent British traditions rather than a fixed set of principles. When defined as a state of mind, conservatism should be spelled with a small 'c' – and it can be found in the Labour Party as well as in its opponents. When Hugh Gaitskell proposed removing the party's constitutional commitment to socialism in Clause IV after the 1959 election, Harold Wilson opposed it on the grounds, 'We were being asked to take Genesis out of the Bible.'[26] The century-long history of the Labour Party has been a study in disagreements about whether the party is 'socialist' and what the term means.

In so far as MPs and voters have political principles and ideological commitments, these divide the governing party, and the Opposition too. It is misleading to describe the electorate as divided into left and right. When voters are asked to place themselves on a left–right scale, the largest group place themselves in the centre, and for many voters this is not a description of political principles but the reflection of a desire to avoid ideological pigeonholes. While the Prime Minister needs the support of some centrist voters to gain and hold office, this is not easy, for there is no unity of outlook or ideology among voters who so place themselves. In the electorate as a whole, surveys find that political principles consistently divide the electorate into as many as half a dozen different groups that can be characterized by attitudes towards morality, libertarianism, authority and equality, as well as commitment to the welfare state or the market.[27]

A party leader's task is to create a coalition of MPs and voters with more or less diverse views – and to manage that coalition once in office. Coalition politics is consensus politics. But consensus politics is not static: the pressure of events from the world beyond Westminster sees to that, and so too does the intensifying effect of long-term structural changes. The response of each Prime Minister leads to changes in public policy, and to the political values by which government policy is justified. As each Prime Minister accepts much of the legacy of predecessors, the result is a *moving consensus*.[28] Movement has come from prime ministers as different as Clement Attlee and Margaret Thatcher. Consensus has followed when their successors, respectively Winston Churchill and Tony Blair, have accepted their innovations.

Butskellism: a move to the centre

The inter-party consensus that dominated Downing Street for more than a generation after 1945 is an amalgam of names of two leading political figures who never made it to Number Ten.[29] R. A. Butler, a one-nation Tory, presided over the postwar transformation of the domestic policy of the Conservative Party, and Hugh Gaitskell was a social democrat whose premature death in 1963 deprived him of the opportunity of becoming Labour's Prime Minister.

Butskellism reflected agreement about the means of policy as well as consensual goals. Full employment, security in old age, free secondary education and a right to health care are prime examples of consensual goals. A consensus on goals was forged in the wartime coalition led by Winston Churchill, with Clement Attlee as his deputy. The coalition endorsed the Beveridge plan for social security and the Keynesian Full Employment White Paper, both named after Liberals, and the 1944 Education Act was promoted by Butler himself. The Attlee government extended the welfare state by creating the national health service and added a socialist dimension to the mixed economy, nationalizing major industries.

Butskellism was institutionalized as part of the 'ongoing reality' of government by the Conservative government returned in 1951 carrying on the measures it inherited from the Attlee government. The groundwork was laid in Opposition, when Churchill directed R. A. Butler to produce a consensus 'one-nation' domestic programme based on Benjamin Disraeli's definition of 'a sound Conservative government', namely, 'Tory men and Whig measures'. The motive for doing so was simple: a desire to win votes rather than lose them. In a BBC broadcast, Churchill declared that on social services, foreign affairs and defence 'nine-tenths of the people agree on nine-tenths of what has been and will be done'.[30] The lengthy tenure of Harold Macmillan as Prime Minister extended the grip of Butskellism, for Macmillan had advocated a one-nation 'middle way' in the 1930s.

The premierships of Harold Wilson and Ted Heath marked a change of emphasis but not a break with Butskellism. Both Wilson and Heath stressed managerial activism and expertise, which they presented with slogans that were so non-ideological that they were interchangeable. The 1964 election slogan of Harold Wilson, 'Let's go with Labour', left the direction of change unspecified. In 1970 Edward Heath led the Conservatives to an election victory with an equally vague slogan, 'Action not words.' Both were ready to endorse the welfare state and take responsibility for Keynesian economic policies. The results were not as intended, for while Heath and Wilson shared a preference for managerial goals, each experienced frustrations and failure, as the national economy threatened to become unmanageable, and domestic problems were exacerbated by difficulties in the international economy. Inflation and unemployment rose and the economy contracted.

The economic turbulence of the 1970s brought about an end to the Butskellite consensus, revealing limitations of Keynesian

In the 1979 election, Jim Callaghan campaigned unsuccessfully against Margaret Thatcher to conserve the Butskellite consensus.
Reproduced by kind permission of Keith Waite.

economic policies and a growing imbalance between public spending and tax revenue threatening the funding of welfare state programmes. Before his early death, Tony Crosland told a gathering of welfare state proponents, 'the party is over', and Jim Callaghan warned the 1976 Labour Party conference, 'You cannot now, if you ever could, spend your way out of a recession.' The Callaghan government accepted monetarist conditions laid down by the International Monetary Fund as a condition for its support.

Filling the vacuum with Blatcherism

At the 1979 general election Jim Callaghan campaigned as the conservator of the Butskellite consensus. However, Margaret Thatcher campaigned against it, charging that the Heath government, in which she had served as a Cabinet minister for four years, pursued 'the most radical form of socialism ever contemplated by an elected British government'. On entering Downing Street Thatcher felt the exhilaration of an 'inner conviction' voiced by an eighteenth-century predecessor, the Earl of Chatham: 'I know that I can save this country and that no one else can.'[31] The route that she saw leading to salvation was not a consensus path. Ideological conflict was intensified when the Opposition adopted as its leader Michael Foot, whose attachment to socialist rhetoric was supported by his detachment from everyday problems of policy.

Uniquely among twentieth-century prime ministers, Margaret Thatcher gave her name to an 'ism'. She believed that a market economy was better than a mixed economy based on close cooperation between government, industry and trade unions. She also believed that individual citizens, rather than the state, should be responsible for their own welfare. Her outlook owed more to the ideas of nineteenth-century laissez faire Manchester Liberalism than to her immediate Conservative predecessors.

The first converts that Thatcher had to win were within the Conservative Party, for when she entered Downing Street many senior party leaders were still 'wets', that is, one-nation Conservatives. From his seat in the Commons, Ted Heath's facial expression showed what he thought of 'that woman'. From the House of Lords, Harold Macmillan poured scorn on Thatcher's privatization measures by likening them to selling the family silver to raise cash. When prices and unemployment continued to rise, backbench MPs voiced unease. After victory in the Falklands War and a triumphant re-election in 1983, Thatcher dropped wets from her Cabinet. The patronage resources of Downing Street were used to create a Cabinet in which she felt ideologically comfortable; three straight election victories brought to the Commons hundreds of younger MPs with no commitments to a 'socialist' past; and Downing Street was used as a 'bully pulpit' to preach her views to the country, and the world, at large.

The Opposition began to move toward Thatcherism when Butskellite MPs led a split from Michael Foot's Labour Party to form the Social Democratic Party, which, under David Owen's leadership, replaced socialist rhetoric with an explicit commitment to both market economics and the welfare state. Neil Kinnock gradually moved the Labour Party back from the 'loony left' fringe, and John Smith continued to do so. However, he rejected arguments put forward by Peter Mandelson and Philip Gould that the way to fight Thatcherism was to abandon Labour's social democratic principles; the two men were left out in the political cold.[32]

The 'fundamental and irreversible shift in the balance of power' called for in a 1974 Labour Party manifesto was achieved when Tony Blair became leader, and then Prime Minister. It was a shift in the direction of Thatcherism. To use an American parallel, Mandelson and Gould have been the Colonel Parker of British politics. Just as the discoverer of Elvis Presley was looking for a white boy who could sing black, so they were seeking for a Labour leader who was a red MP but could sing blue. In Tony Blair they found their leader, for Blair had arrived at the same conclusion that they had: the way to beat the Conservatives at election time was to abandon Labour (and Butskellite) commitments to taxing and spending and accept the great bulk of Thatcher's legacy, and that of her successor, John Major, including privatization and trade union law reform. Old Labour adherents complained that Blair had jettisoned not only electorally risky commitments to taxing and spending, but also the values of liberty and equality.[33]

The 1997 Labour Party manifesto echoed Thatcher's rejection of Tory socialism by rejecting historic Labour government achievements. 'We have rewritten our constitution, the new Clause Four, to put a commitment to enterprise alongside the commitment to justice. We have changed the way we make policy, and put our relations with the trade unions on a modern footing.' The manifesto accepted that much of Thatcherism worked. A few weeks after

Figure 7.3 Moving consensus in party manifestos

On the scale plus 100 is extreme right; minus 100 extreme left.

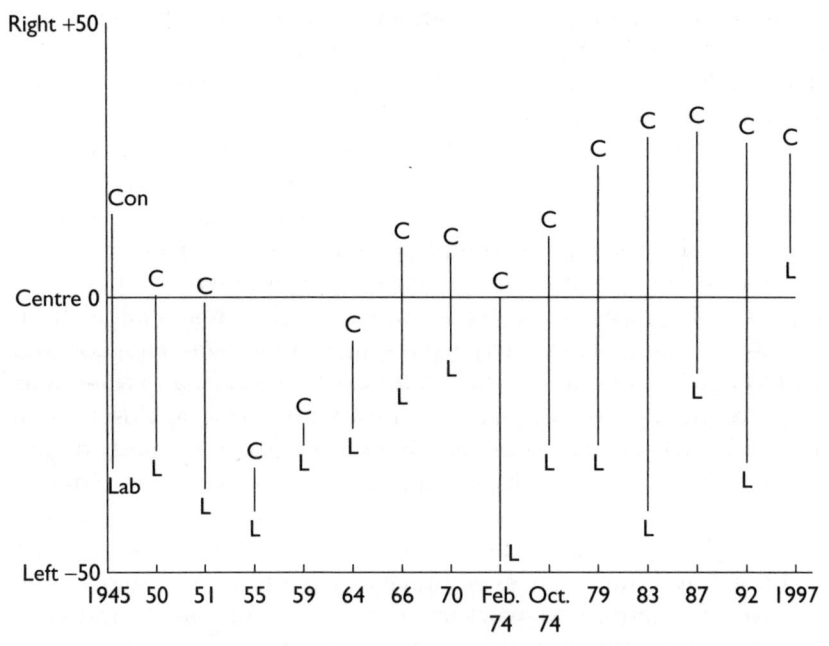

Source: Right–left classification based on a content analysis of party election manifestos by Ian Budge, University of Essex, as reported in his 'Party Policy and Ideology: Reversing the 1950s?', table 1. In G. Evans and P. Norris, eds, *Critical Elections*. London: Sage, 1999, pp. 1–21.

entering Downing Street Blair invited Thatcher to Downing Street for a consultation prior to a meeting with European Union leaders.

The extent to which Blatcherism has replaced Butskellism is shown by a content analysis of party manifestos since 1945 classifying the manifestos of parties on an ideological left–right dimension (figure 7.3). Between 1945 and 1955 Conservative manifestos moved well to the left of centre in order to catch up with Labour. In the following decade, the two parties stayed close together and moved back to the centre together. A big gap opened up after Margaret Thatcher took the Conservative Party to the right in 1979 and Michael Foot took the Labour Party to the left. Under Callaghan, Kinnock and Smith, Labour sought to reduce the gap between the manifestos of the two parties while remaining in left-of-centre positions close to those taken when Attlee and Wilson won landslide victories in 1945 and 1966. However, Thatcher tilted the ideological seesaw in the other direction. The 1997 Labour victory came only after Tony Blair had produced a New Labour manifesto that was to the right of centre. Blair's manifesto was not only further to the right than anything produced by any of his six predecessors, but also further to the right than the one-nation manifestos of Conservative prime ministers from Anthony Eden to Ted Heath.[34]

Blair's 'rebranding' of the Labour Party scored a spectacular electoral success in 1997, but his New Labour platform caused disquiet among those loyal to Butskellite policies and social democratic or socialist principles. To pre-empt post-election charges of reneging on traditional Labour commitments, Blair adopted in opposition a policy of 'getting our betrayal in first'.[35] The great shibboleth of socialism, Clause IV of the party's constitution, was repealed and New Labour's manifesto was endorsed by more than nine-tenths of party members in a November 1996 vote. Working closely with Peter Mandelson and select allies, Blair restructured the party organization so that its capacity for attacking the leader was blunted, and his people filled all the posts that counted. Robert Harris has described Blair's strategy as that of 'Trotskyite entryists, only of the right: a tiny bourgeois revolutionary cell that unexpectedly took control of a moribund workers' party, transformed it, and then used it to take power in the country as a whole'.[36]

Although Blair has seized control of decisionmaking organs of the Labour Party, he has not seized its heart. The traditional heart of the Labour movement, the trade unions, has been bruised by Blair's treatment. Although he has formal meetings with trade union leaders at Downing Street, they create puzzlement; in the words of one trade union leader, 'Why does he hate us so?' Tom Sawyer, a trade unionist whom Blair backed to become general secretary of the reorganized party, has expressed doubts about the makeover of the party.

> When somebody comes up with the 17 most important people in the Labour Party and there's hardly any MPs or Cabinet members among them, Labour people want to be reassured that the most important people in the party are its elected representatives, people who the rank-and-file members put their trust in.[37]

Old Labour dogs sometimes bark, or even bite. When Peter Mandelson sought election by party activists to Labour's national executive committee, he was defeated. Downing Street failed to stop Ken Livingstone from running for Mayor of London in May 2000, and its own candidate was ignominiously beaten into fourth place. A big loss of local council seats around the country was attributed to apathy among core Labour voters (cf. figure 6.2 above). When addressing the annual dinner of the Confederation of British Industries a few weeks later to firm up New Labour support, Blair made a gesture to old Labour supporters, dropping references to New Labour in the prepared text of his speech. But Blair did not revert to using the party's historic name. Instead, he invoked a vague, non-party 'we' and in some cases substituted 'I'.[38] In his speech to the party's pre-election annual conference at Brighton in September 2000, Blair was four times more likely to refer to the Labour Party than to the New Labour Party. His much more frequent use of the perpendicular pronoun 'I' left listeners in no doubt about who called the shots in this Labour government.

Party competition need not be a conflict of ideologies; it can simply be a conflict of ambitions. When a mischievous Conservative MP posed the parliamentary question, 'Can the Prime Minister tell the House what Blairism is?', Tony Blair had no difficulty in giving a clear, unambiguous reply: 'It had its first outing on 1 May 1997 and resulted in an election victory and a majority of 179.'[39]

8

Managing Colleagues and Bastards

> Every French soldier carries in his cartridge pouch the baton of a marshal of France.
>
> Napoleon Bonaparte

> Where do you think most of this poison is coming from? From the dispossessed and the never-possessed. You can think of ex-ministers who are going around causing all sorts of trouble. We don't want another three more of the bastards out there.
>
> John Major, off camera to a television interviewer

In theory, British government is collegial, and the Cabinet is its prime expression. In practice, ministers have both individual ambitions and collective ties. Whereas Napoleon's subordinates could rise in their career by fighting their country's enemies, an ambitious Cabinet minister enters Downing Street by elbowing past colleagues or running over them.

The Prime Minister's relations with Cabinet ministers are primarily political, a means of holding the government of the day together. Because every governing party has several aspiring prime ministers, the Prime Minister seeks to co-opt potential rivals by offering them positions in Cabinet. As President Lyndon Johnson explained his appointment of an awkward critic, 'I'd rather have him inside the tent pissing out than outside the tent pissing in.' Old-school prime ministers used more decorous language, but their thoughts were the same. New-style prime ministers have developed a fresh twist. While bringing rivals within the tent of Cabinet, Number Ten staff can brief against them. In the cruel metaphor of a Nixon aide in the

White House, this leaves the minister hanging there, twisting in the wind.

The doctrine of collective responsibility requires ministers to be loyal to all decisions of Cabinet. While disagreements may be voiced in private, public disagreement is deemed tantamount to resignation. The doctrine binds more than one hundred MPs in government posts to the Prime Minister. Once collective responsibility is invoked, the substance of a decision becomes unimportant. As Lord Melbourne said at the end of chairing a Cabinet meeting in the 1830s, 'Bye the bye, there is one thing that we haven't agreed upon, which is, what are we to say? Now is it to make our corn cheaper or to make the price steady? I don't care *which*, but we had better all tell *the same story*.'[1]

Each minister devotes far more time to his or her department than does the Prime Minister. Because departmental interests differ, Cabinet ministers compete against each other for public money, attention in the Commons and media headlines. As Barbara Castle has related, 'I entered the Cabinet believing in my innocence that it would make major policy decisions in collective deliberation. But I was soon disabused of that ... I was faced by departmental enemies.'[2] A Cabinet minister's frustrations are easily explained by a Washington epigram: 'Where you stand depends upon where you sit.'

The Prime Minister does not need to be an expert in managing institutions; he or she must be an expert in political management, reconciling the opinions and ambitions of Cabinet ministers with Downing Street's interests. This type of management is not taught at Harvard or the London Business School. It is what a Frenchman has called *la politique politicienne*, that is, 'political activity in which only politicians are interested because it has no link with actual life'.[3] If ministers are skilfully managed, Downing Street can claim credit, while if things go wrong failure can be blamed on the departmental minister responsible. However, if ministers are mismanaged, colleagues become bastards. John Major's frustration reflected the fact that when he challenged disloyal colleagues to fight him in a leadership contest, they refused to do so. However, ministers continued boring below the waterline of the ship of state. The result was, in the words of Norman Lamont, whom Major sacked as Chancellor of the Exchequer, the Prime Minister gave the impression of 'being in office but not in power'.[4]

1 Why the Prime Minister needs other ministers

There is not world enough and time for anyone to be informed about all that is done in the name of Her Majesty's Government, let alone influence all its activities. When the Prime Minister spends time on one problem, there is less time to spend on other activities of government. In 'time-sharing' burdens with Cabinet ministers, a Prime Minister is necessarily engaged in power-sharing. As Tony Blair found out, dealing with the Kosovo crisis greatly reduced the time he had available for the 1999 European Parliament election, a Cabinet reshuffle and sleep. A Prime Minister who boasts, as Harold Wilson did, that he digested 500 policy briefs in a weekend can do so only by spending a minute or two with each.[5] Tony Blair's appointment of some three hundred task forces to identify policies that work appears impressive, until one does the arithmetic calculation, 'How much time does he have to give to their reports?', and the political calculation, 'What will happen to their reports if the Prime Minister does not actively promote their recommendations?'

The Prime Minister is a non-departmental minister. After moving from the Foreign Office to Number Ten, Jim Callaghan found:

> I had nothing to do. Ministers were busy with their departmental work; the telephone did not ring for, generally speaking, people do not telephone the Prime Minister – the Prime Minister phones them ... For a brief period I savoured the suspicion that as everyone else was doing the government's work, I could be the idlest member of the Administration if I was so minded.[6]

As Callaghan soon learned, the appearance of calm was illusory, as an economic crisis forced him to go, once again, cap in hand to the International Monetary Fund. None the less, Callaghan was correct in highlighting the fact that the Prime Minister's unique position allows him or her more discretion about deciding what to do and what not to do than is allowed the typical Cabinet minister.

Picking and choosing what to do

British government centralizes in Whitehall responsibility for legislation, public expenditure and administration to a degree unusual among modern democracies. However, the load is so large that the Prime Minister must rely on departmental ministers. Most of the hundreds of policies of British government run by routine; they are part of the Queen's Government that is carried on regardless of the party in office. Every Act of Parliament enacted by predecessors, recent or long dead, remains in effect when control of Downing Street changes hands. Responsibility for dealing with everything from agriculture to transport is gladly offloaded.

The memoirs of politicians are revealing in what they omit as well as what they include. While every Prime Minister's memoir is full of references to foreign affairs and economic difficulties, the great majority give very little attention to the biggest spending programmes of government. In Edward Heath's memoirs, each of the indexed references to health refers to personal health, such as an army vaccination, an appendectomy, or injuring a leg in a sailing race.[7] Pensions, the most costly programme of government, receive little or no attention in memoirs. Nor do the memoirs of spending ministers make many references to developing policies with the Prime Minister. When the Prime Minister offers an MP a Cabinet post, little or no direction is given the minister about what is meant to be done. This was true of a 'bossy' Margaret Thatcher as well as of John Major.

At any one time the constraints of the clock limit the number of issues that the Prime Minister can deal with. Management by exception is the only way to find time to deal with high priority matters. Departmental ministers carry on the great bulk of government programmes without personal direction from the Prime Minister. The routine can be interrupted by Downing Street staff monitoring departmental activities and flagging items for the Prime Minister's attention. Even more likely, a department will become the object of the Prime Minister's personal attention when something goes wrong; for example, petrol prices become a public concern. But giving time to a crisis event means there is less time to devote to other things.

An effective Prime Minister is a *potential* presence in each department. The possibility of intervention by Downing Street makes it prudent for ministers approaching a decision to ask: 'Is Downing Street in or out on this one?' Old-school prime ministers almost invariably gave their ministers great latitude. While Harold Wilson liked to portray Downing Street as a beehive of activities, much of the activity involved buzzing around the Prime Minister rather than Wilson interfering with ministers with the political authority of Roy Jenkins, Denis Healey or Tony Crosland.

New-style prime ministers are much readier to intervene on policy issues, and Margaret Thatcher actively relished doing so. With youthful enthusiasm and inexperience, Tony Blair has sought to change the culture of Whitehall to 'join up' disparate policies, and established an elaborate system of monitoring departmental performance through bureaucratized reporting and reviews of checklist items. But this has not been effective. In Blair's own words:

> You try getting change in the public sector and the public services. I bear the scars on my back after two years in government and heaven knows what it will be like after a bit longer.[8]

The personal initiative of a single individual is insufficient, when bureaucracies employing tens or hundreds of thousands of people are involved. To influence the shaping of policy it is necessary to be involved in lengthy deliberations that go into formulating measures that can be enacted by Parliament and have significant impacts on both public expenditure and British society.

Just as a Cabinet minister cannot carry a policy if the Prime Minister of the day vetoes it, the Prime Minister too is caught up in a system of 'mutual blackball', a term coined by Nigel Lawson to describe practices in place long before he became Chancellor of the Exchequer. A departmental minister can ignore a suggestion from the Prime Minister, if the minister deems it unsatisfactory. If the Prime Minister repeats the suggestion, the department can establish a committee to 'sit' on it. If the Prime Minister asks for detailed plans, a lengthy memorandum can be forwarded listing all the difficulties in making any changes from current policy. All this can lead to the Prime Minister losing interest in the subject or attention being distracted by events elsewhere. Only if the Prime Minister has strong views and persists in voicing them must the minister cooperate or risk losing office.

For generations, the doctrine of collective Cabinet responsibility has been used by prime ministers to secure the public support of ministers who have not been consulted about a policy (for example, moving troops in an emergency) or who have no direct responsibility for an issue (for example, decisions about Northern Ireland). However, old-school prime ministers saw the prudential political value of consulting Cabinet ministers on problems of great political importance and uncertain outcome. The rationale is described by a peacetime private secretary of Winston Churchill:

> It is almost always more important for a decision to be well considered than to be expeditious. He wanted to be sure that everything was exactly right, that everyone who should be consulted had had his say and that all the consequences of the proposal had been thought out. That was the way he liked to work, and a thoroughly statesmanlike way it is; a good deal of the tranquil success of his second Prime Ministership can be ascribed to it.[9]

Whether or not compromises arrived at by collective deliberations produce better policies is debatable, but they certainly produce more political support for whatever is decided and more political insurance if the outcome is unsatisfactory.

2 The glue of patronage

The art of Cabinet-making is to assemble politicians who will stick to the Prime Minister from conviction, calculation, hope of further preferment or cowardice. The Prime Minister uses patronage as the glue to hold together a governing party with diverse views and ambitions. The choice of MPs for ministerial posts is not a management selection task in which first the skills required are determined, and then individuals recruited who match these requirements. It is a closed competition, for the qualification for a major post is already being an MP. Appointing ministers is about matching individuals to posts where they can do the most good (or threaten the least harm) to the Prime Minister.

Dangling bait

A ministerial post is the bait that every Prime Minister uses when trawling for support. Ambitious backbench MPs can call attention to themselves by scoring points off the Opposition in debate, putting the case for the government in the House and its committees, or making themselves so awkward that they are brought within the government tent. As Aneurin Bevan famously advised Richard

Crossman, 'There are two ways to get ahead: grovel or kick people where it hurts.' (He then added, 'The trouble with you, Dick, is that you do both!') Frontbench politicians are normally ready to adjust their political views in order to remain in government. Thus, wets who had followed the lead of Harold Macmillan and Edward Heath were willing to dry out in order to be in a Thatcher Cabinet, and Tony Blair found many MPs from the old left who were glad to become ministers in his New Labour government.

The ministerial patronage at the disposal of the Prime Minister offers a ladder of opportunity. It starts with the lowly unpaid post of Parliamentary Private Secretary (PPS), rising to a junior ministerial post as Under-Secretary of State, promotion to Minister of State with defined responsibilities under a Cabinet minister, to twenty posts in Cabinet, the penultimate stop for a wouldbe Prime Minister. The supply of ministerial posts has expanded greatly in the past century. In the third Marquess of Salisbury's Cabinet in 1900, forty-two MPs held ministerial posts, just over 10 per cent of the governing party's membership in the Commons. In addition, twenty-seven hereditary members of the House of Lords held posts. In Ramsay MacDonald's second minority government, seventy-six Labour MPs held posts, 26 per cent of the governing party, and the number of peers who were ministers was down by two-thirds. Since 1945, the number of MPs holding ministerial posts has risen from ninety-five under Clement Attlee to 129 under Tony Blair (figure 8.1). The proportion of MPs holding ministerial posts fluctuates around one-third with the size of the government's majority.

The number of Cabinet posts has remained virtually constant for a century; there were nineteen Cabinet ministers in 1900 and twenty-two a century later. The increase in ministerial posts has been concentrated on the lower and intermediate rungs of the career ladder, thus changing the 'shape' of a government. The number of entry-level appointments as a PPS, an unpaid dogsbody liaising between a minister and the governing party in the Commons, has increased from twenty-seven in 1950 to forty-seven in 2000. The number of 'real' appointments as a minister with civil service staff and insider involvement in Whitehall has increased from sixty-three in 1950 to eighty-three today.

The demand for ministerial posts has also increased substantially. The Labour benches are no longer filled with ageing trade unionists who left school at the age of twelve or fourteen. A majority

Figure 8.1 Growth in Prime Minister's patronage
(Number of MPs with a position in government)

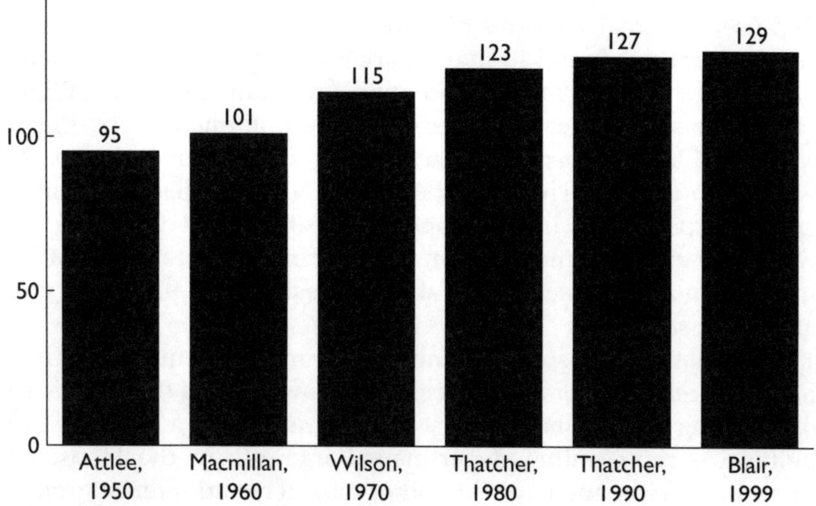

Attlee, 1950	Macmillan, 1960	Wilson, 1970	Thatcher, 1980	Thatcher, 1990	Blair, 1999
95	101	115	123	127	129

Source: Derived from David Butler and Gareth Butler, *Twentieth-Century British Political Facts, 1900–2000.* London: Macmillan, 8th edn, 2000, p. 71.

of Labour MPs are university graduates with professional skills and ambitions that they see as qualifying them for a ministerial post. The Conservative benches no longer have a solid bloc of gentry who see a seat in the House of Commons as a social role along with others, such as being a Master of Foxhounds. Conservative MPs are much more likely today to see politics as a full-time career. A chief whip has complained, 'We suffer from what I call pol-flation. We have too many MPs – and they all want office.'[10]

The great majority of MPs who are aspiring to office, and who have not disqualified themselves by their political or personal behaviour, gain at least a junior government post today. In the first part of the twentieth century, only a sixth to a quarter of MPs ever held a government post. Since then, the proportion receiving Downing Street patronage has risen. Among MPs in the House between 1945 and 1974, 45 per cent at some point had a government appointment. From 1974 to 1992, more than half of MPs had a government job, notwithstanding the long period of Labour in Opposition.[11] Whilst a post as a PPS or a junior minister in a minor department does not carry much weight in Whitehall, it does bind recipients to support the Prime Minister or risk instant dismissal.

Matching horses to courses

Because the great majority of Cabinet ministers must be MPs, a requirement not found in many parliamentary systems, Downing Street does not engage in nationwide recruitment as the White House does when making presidential appointments. The Prime Minister's task is to match leading MPs in the governing party with Cabinet posts. The institutionalization of the Shadow Cabinet creates expectations in the Opposition party about who will get which job in government. When a new Prime Minister gains office midway in a Parliament, the Cabinet is reshuffled rather than created from scratch.

The amateur ethos of Westminster means that ministers rarely have any relevant, let alone specialist, knowledge of their ministry on arriving there. The primary skills required of a minister are political – representing departmental interests in the House of Commons, to the media and to other ministers and interest groups – rather than technical. The Chancellor of the Exchequer is more likely to have studied law or history than economics, and it is exceptional for the Foreign Secretary ever to have lived abroad, let alone worked in an embassy. A minister is expected to learn about a department on the job. Up to a point, coming to a subject with no prior knowledge can be an asset, for a minister can then ask the 'idiot' question about established policies: 'Why are we doing this?' MPs are less concerned with a department's subject matter than with the position it gives them on the ladder of ministerial opportunity.

The appointment of the Chancellor of the Exchequer is particularly important, for the work of the Treasury is of major concern to Downing Street too. The Treasury is a large and complex department covering tasks often split between two or three agencies in other countries. Therefore, it is hard for Downing Street to monitor everything done there. Because many of the activities of the Treasury are technical, it also requires more economic expertise than a Prime Minister or most Downing Street staff will possess. But for the same reason, there is always a danger that the Treasury (and the Chancellor) will go into business for themselves, pursuing a line of policy that may make economic but not political sense. Since macroeconomic policies of the Treasury have an impact on micro-level spending decisions of departments, this can cause friction within government. Since the Chancellorship usually goes to a political heavyweight, he is much less susceptible to direction from Number Ten than is the case with most ministers.

The Foreign Secretaryship is also a high status position, and the responsibilities of the Foreign Office are of major concern to Downing Street. However, it is much easier for the Prime Minister to adopt a hands off attitude towards the great bulk of Foreign Office business, because it is of no domestic political significance. As and when a crisis erupts and gives an issue high political salience, it is easy for the Prime Minister to trump the Foreign Secretary, because crisis talks often involve discussions between heads of government – that is, the White House rather than the US State Department – and because the Foreign Secretary cannot on his own commit Her Majesty's Government to action abroad, whereas the Prime Minister can and does.

The limited overlap in policies between the Treasury and the Foreign Office is politically useful to the Prime Minister. Senior ministers who are scarcely on speaking terms with each other can be given different jobs in order to keep them from fighting running battles that detract from the Prime Minister's political capital. Thus, Clement Attlee separated Ernest Bevin from chancellors Hugh Dalton and Stafford Cripps, and Tony Blair has separated Gordon Brown and Robin Cook, who have been quarrelling since their student days at Edinburgh University. The growth of intermestic politics makes it harder for the Prime Minister to keep quarrelling rivals apart, as Tony Blair has found on issues such as the euro.

A Prime Minister juxtaposes senior ministers so that ambitious personalities check and balance each other in ways that enhance his or her own job security. Jim Callaghan was elected Labour leader in 1976 in a contest against five other Cabinet ministers. On entering Number Ten he named Michael Foot, the front runner on the first ballot, as Lord President of the Council and Leader of the House of Commons, where Foot regularly had to defend the Callaghan government's record to critical Labour MPs. Roy Jenkins was removed from Westminster by being named President of the European Commission in Brussels. Denis Healey remained Chancellor of the Exchequer, where he shortly became responsible for defending the acceptance of economic conditions from the International Monetary Fund. Tony Crosland was made Foreign Secretary, where he had no direct responsibility for economic issues on which he had a specialist knowledge and could differ from Healey. Tony Benn remained nominally in charge at the Department of Energy, in an attempt to make him share responsibility for the collective decisions of the government.

When Margaret Thatcher became Prime Minister in 1979 she prudently filled her Cabinet with senior Conservative 'wets' who begrudged her the job, so as to prevent the formation of a faction against her on the back benches. For example, Jim Prior was made Secretary for Employment, even though Thatcher considered that his outlook 'was, indeed, fundamentally different from mine'. After gaining confidence in office, she appointed Norman Tebbit as Employment minister, 'a true believer in the kind of approach Keith Joseph and I stood for'. Prior was offered a post remote from economic issues, the Northern Ireland Office, and he took it rather than be sacked from Cabinet.[12] After three years in that job, he headed for the quieter life of the corporate board room.

Tony Benn was exceptional in irrepressibly advancing his personal leftwing agenda while a Cabinet minister for eleven years under Harold Wilson and Jim Callaghan. Benn was surrounded by politically reliable junior ministers and civil servants who would alert Downing Street if Benn threatened a leftwing policy inconsistent with that of the Labour Cabinet. Benn continuously politicked within the Labour Party on behalf of leftwing causes, thus stretching to the limit the bounds of collective responsibility. On the Lyndon Johnson principle that it was better to have Benn inside the Labour tent than outside, Downing Street tolerated his behaviour. Immediately after Labour went into Opposition in 1979, Benn became leader of a leftwing faction denouncing the errors of the Wilson and Callaghan governments in which he had served.

When the political situation dictates it, the Prime Minister will appoint a 'bridge-builder' minister with specially good links with those in the governing party most likely to challenge the Prime Minister's leadership. William Whitelaw served as Margaret Thatcher's bridge to the 'wet' wing of the Conservative Party, and was sometimes able to curb her convictions when party considerations made this desirable. Because Whitelaw was unique, there was no replacement when he retired from the Cabinet in 1986, and Thatcher's political judgements increasingly irritated her own MPs. John Prescott, a trade unionist, ran second to Tony Blair in the contest for the Labour leadership in 1994. Blair named Prescott Deputy Prime Minister as well as putting him in charge of a broad Environment remit. Prescott has been described as 'Blair's bridge to the Labour Party. Prescott is like the Jewish rabbi. It is only once he has blessed Tony's goods that the membership accept them as kosher.'[13]

The Prime Minister tries to represent political interests and social groups from which the governing party gains, or hopes to gain, support, such as women, trade unionists, farmers or Scots. Clement Attlee explicitly valued the presence in Cabinet of ministers close to ordinary working-class people, as a balance for Oxbridge colleagues. In a Cabinet discussion he would call on George Tomlinson, who had left school at the age of twelve. If Tomlinson responded, 'It sounds all right but I've been trying to persuade my wife of it for the last three weeks and I can't persuade her', the Prime Minister could refer the issue back for further consideration.[14] Tony Blair named six women to his first Cabinet, and has been ready to name ethnic minority MPs to ministerial posts too. But he has found it difficult to identify trade unionists whom he could or would appoint to Cabinet posts.

To balance political competitors and enemies, every Prime Minister has personally loyal ministers who know that they have no future in government if their leader falls. In response to a politician who said, 'I will support you when you are in the right', Lord Melbourne replied, 'What I want is men who will support me when I am in the wrong.' Until devolution, the posts of Scottish and Welsh secretaries were specially suitable for loyalists, and non-departmental posts are so too. Tony Blair was acting in accord with precedent in initially making his top aide, Peter Mandelson, Minister Without Portfolio.

The House of Lords is also used to bring loyalists and friends into government. When Churchill formed his 1951 Cabinet, he named Lord Cherwell, his trusted and controversial scientific adviser during the war, as Paymaster-General. Harold Macmillan brought his old companion from Minister of Housing days, Lord Mills, into Cabinet as Paymaster-General. Tony Blair has appointed a large number of peers, many of whom are personal friends of his, such as the Lord Chancellor, Lord Irvine (who first employed Blair at the bar), and the Minister of State at the Cabinet Office, Lord Falconer (an old school chum). Some ministers in the Lords are known on the Labour scene, such as the Leader of the House of Lords (Lady Jay, daughter of Jim Callaghan) or the Minister of Transport (Lord Macdonald, a journalist and then a media businessman). Lord Levy, who raised millions of pounds for the Labour Party, was asked to undertake special missions for Blair in Israel, without reference to the departmental minister responsible.

In common with his predecessors, Tony Blair likes to appoint people he likes. However, Blair's preference for peers in government is abnormal. Not only has Blair appointed more peers to the House of Lords than any predecessor but also he has appointed a larger number of lords to ministerial posts than any peacetime Prime Minister since the days of the third Marquess of Salisbury. Blair's use of peerages to install dozens of New Labour ministers who are solely dependent on him for their political career gives him many ministers with whom he can feel comfortable. But because peers are usually given posts subordinate to a Cabinet minister, jealousy and friction can be created when ministers find that their nominal subordinate has stronger links with the Prime Minister than they do.

At some point in the process of appointing more than one hundred people to ministerial posts, the Prime Minister runs out of friends, enemies and MPs whom he identifies as having a claim on a ministerial post. At that point he or she turns to the Whip's Office or other trusted advisers for names to fill junior posts. This can result in a junior minister being surprised to learn that the Prime Minister barely recognizes who he or she is or what his or her post is in government.

Reshuffling people up or out

Reshuffling Cabinet posts occurs much more frequently in Britain than in other established democracies, for two years in a ministerial post is a long time. When European coalition governments change the Prime Minister, most Cabinet ministers are likely to remain in place. The opposite is the case in Westminster, for Cabinet ministers are reshuffled much more often than prime ministers are changed. Since 1970 there have been twenty different politicians in charge of the Department of Trade, an average stay of eighteen months.

The expectation of a reshuffle tends to keep ambitious MPs loyal, in hope of rising up the ministerial ladder and fear of being dropped if they step out of line. From the Prime Minister's point of view, a reshuffle is an opportunity to change the balance of abilities and ambitions in Cabinet to her or his advantage. As Margaret Thatcher has explained:

> Planning a reshuffle is immensely complex. There is never a perfect outcome. It is necessary to get the main decisions about the big

offices of state right and then work outward and downward from these. Nor is it possible always to give the best positions to one's closest supporters. Not only must the Cabinet to some extent reflect the varying views in the Parliamentary Party at a particular time: there are some people that it is better to bring in because they would cause more trouble outside. Peter Walker and, to a lesser extent, Kenneth Clarke, are examples, precisely because they fought their corner hard.[15]

The Cabinet's balance can be maintained by reshuffling senior ministers between posts of comparable status. For example, when Nigel Lawson resigned as Chancellor in 1989, John Major was moved from the Foreign Office to the Treasury and Douglas Hurd from the Home Office to the Foreign Office. An alternative is the promotion of an individual sufficiently junior within the party so that the Prime Minister can take command as and when Downing Street wishes to do so. Foreign Secretaries have often been appointed for their pliability. When Tony Crosland died unexpectedly a year after Jim Callaghan had named him Foreign Secretary, the post was given to a minister of state at the Foreign Office, David Owen. This avoided upsetting the balance of the Cabinet, and allowed Callaghan, as an ex-Foreign Secretary, to step in whenever he wished to take charge.

The threat of resignation by a senior minister is a double-edged sword, for it can end an ambitious minister's career or destabilize the Prime Minister – and it is often not clear in advance what the outcome will be. The resignation of Aneurin Bevan and colleagues in 1951 helped bring down the Attlee government a few months later and embittered but did not prevent Harold Wilson's subsequent advancement. While Margaret Thatcher managed to survive the resignation of Michael Heseltine over the Westland helicopter affair, Geoffrey Howe's subsequent resignation in protest at her handling of European affairs helped bring her down. Most ministers blunt the political impact of their resignation by clinging to office long after their political capital has begun to wane. A shrewd Prime Minister such as Harold Wilson was content to let his rivals destroy their own careers. While George Brown was a formidable Labour figure in Opposition, by the time he became Foreign Secretary his behaviour when drunk had exhausted his following, so that Brown's resignation in protest at the way Wilson was conducting government business was welcomed with relief in the Labour Cabinet.

The Prime Minister must be a butcher, cutting off the ministerial careers of individuals who are inadequate in Parliament, the media and Whitehall. While journalists like to write speculative columns that dispose of ministers, most Prime Ministers find dismissing a colleague distasteful. For example, Tony Blair's well heralded reshuffle of July 1999 turned out to be a night of the rubber knives, as few changes were made. A conspicuous exception was the 'night of the long knives', when Harold Macmillan dismissed seven Cabinet ministers in July 1962. However, this detracted from Macmillan's political capital because it was interpreted as a sign of weakness. Jeremy Thorpe commented, 'Greater love hath no man than this, that he lay down his friends for his life.'

At the start of a Parliament, many new recruits are hopeful of office and show this by being ultra-loyal. By the end of a Parliament, some have become disappointed and frustrated, as cheering their leader has not been rewarded by even a lowly post on the ministerial ladder. The bigger the governing party's majority, the greater the potential for frustration. The back benches also accumulate ex-ministers with grievances against the Prime Minister who terminated their ministerial career. If not discredited by their mistakes in office, ex-ministers can make telling criticisms when the Prime Minister is vulnerable.

3   Diminished collegiality and diminished responsibility

There are many ways in which the Prime Minister can handle Cabinet colleagues – gently, roughly, with kid gloves or with a ten-foot pole – or by a combination of all these means. In handling ministers, the Prime Minister has the advantage of not being committed to a departmental point of view. The Prime Minister's goal is to promote policies that will add to the reputation of the government, or at least, not discredit it by ministerial quarrels or plots threatening his or her political capital. To achieve these goals, the Prime Minister deals with ministers informally as well as through formal Cabinet channels.

In handling colleagues the Prime Minister has the authority of office, a claim to shared party loyalties and powers of patronage. An individual minister can claim greater knowledge of departmental business, due to his or her continuous involvement with experienced departmental civil servants. A minister is also in the position of obstructing the implementation of a measure, for Downing Street has no administrative capability. Economic policies are in the hands of the Treasury, the Board of Trade and other ministries; foreign policies are in the hands of departments engaged in overseas relations; and the delivery of health and education services is dispersed by Whitehall departments to many more or less detached public agencies the length and breadth of the land. The lower the Prime Minister's political capital, the harder it is for him or her to influence ministers.

The decline of Cabinet

Cabinet meetings are the paramount symbol of the collegiality of ministers, and it is politically significant that their frequency and length has been decreasing. Under old-school Prime Ministers, the full Cabinet met once and often twice a week. The Leader of the House of Commons presented a review of the coming week's parliamentary business; the Foreign Secretary reviewed international issues; and the Chancellor often made a statement about economic problems. The Cabinet discussed 'hot issues', such as a colonial crisis or the political implications of a threatened strike, reports came up from Cabinet committees and annual activities such as the defence White Paper. Between 1964 and 1970 Harold Wilson had full Cabinet meetings usually twice a week when the House was sitting, a total of about seventy-five a year.

Since Margaret Thatcher arrived in Downing Street, the significance of full Cabinet meetings has been eroded, as she was more interested in setting out her own views than listening to those of others. Cabinet meetings have also become much shorter. Whereas Wilson's Cabinet often lasted three hours in order to allow all ministers to talk themselves out, Thatcher's were not so long and the weekly Cabinet meetings of John Major could run for as little as an hour. Tony Blair has further downgraded Cabinet: its meetings can take no more than a perfunctory thirty to forty minutes. Moreover, Alastair Campbell can use the meeting to deliver the media line that Cabinet ministers are meant to present afterwards.

Cabinet today is a dignified rather than efficient part of the Constitution, as new-style Prime Ministers have decided that lengthy discussions among twenty MPs with diverse views and departmental responsibilities are a waste of time. In a complementary way, ministers prefer to get on with their own departmental responsibilities rather than listen to discussions about matters that are decided over their heads or behind their backs. Nigel Lawson went so far as to claim, 'I always looked forward to the weekly Cabinet meeting immensely because it was, apart from the summer holidays, the only period of real rest that I got in what was a very busy job.'[16]

The need to co-ordinate policies between departments and share collective responsibility continues to require frequent meetings between departmental ministers and Number Ten. Patrick Gordon Walker, who served in both Attlee and Wilson Cabinets, has described these as *'partial Cabinets'*.[17] Meetings are partial because they leave out ministers who have no responsibility for action, and the selection of those attending will be weighted to suit the purposes of Downing Street. The meetings are Cabinets inasmuch as those involved are departmental ministers with personal stakes in the outcome. Partial Cabinets are specially useful in a crisis, because they enable the Prime Minister to draw on the knowledge and judgements of senior colleagues and permit quick responses.

Cabinet committees are a formal expression of partial Cabinets. Each committee includes a limited number of ministers whose departments are directly involved with an issue, and a non-departmental minister whose task it is to resolve conflicts between departments. Committees permit collective deliberation and impose collective responsibility. When contentious issues arise between departmental ministers, a non-departmental chair can exert pressure to arrive at a compromise so that the decision cannot be overturned by 'amateur' colleagues in a full Cabinet discussion.

The Prime Minister can influence committee deliberations by deciding its terms of reference, who serves and who is excluded, and who chairs. If a committee has problems, the Prime Minister can be kept informed by the committee chair, the Cabinet Office official who serves as its secretary, or a Policy Unit staff person who attends. The Prime Minister normally chairs a few standing and ad hoc committees concerned with foreign affairs, security matters, and issues of immediate and personal concern to Number Ten. In a crisis, the Prime Minister can use a small committee to take control of action. During the Falklands crisis, Margaret Thatcher constituted a War Cabinet that included, in addition to ministers directly involved in operations, the Home Secretary, William Whitelaw, 'my deputy and trusted adviser', and the Paymaster-General and Chair of the Conservative Party, Cecil Parkinson, 'who not only shared my political instincts but was brilliantly effective in dealing with public relations'.[18]

The Prime Minister avoids serving on a majority of Cabinet committees. In 1994 John Major was a member of only nine of twenty-one Cabinet committees dealing with policy issues, while the Chancellor of the Exchequer was on fourteen, and the Foreign Secretary, the President of the Board of Trade and the Home Secretary each belonged to thirteen committees. The need to save time is one motive for staying away from many committees. Another is a desire to economize political capital by avoiding committees that involve conflicts between ambitious departmental ministers or discussions of problems for which Downing Street can identify no solution.

Informal meetings in which individual Cabinet ministers negotiate issues directly with the Prime Minister are evidence of what Nigel Lawson has described as *'creeping bilateralism'*.[19] If an agreement is reached, there is little chance that it will be upset subsequently by Cabinet. If the Prime Minister fears that a department is trying to 'bounce' Downing Street into an agreement that has not been fully thought through, a formal Cabinet committee can be set up whose members will include opponents as well as proponents of a departmental minister's plan of action.

On entering Downing Street, Tony Blair promoted informality as part of his youthful style of government, discussing policy with colleagues while sitting on sofas around a coffee table. The Prime Minister quickly learned the advantages of formal meetings at a table full of briefing papers, with his position central in the seating plan.

Blair has also introduced new committees to deal with the so-called 'wicked issues' that cut across conventional Whitehall departmental jurisdictions, such as social exclusion or single parenting. The intent is to encourage departments to think laterally about problems where responsibilities are spread across many departments. Blair has also appointed more than 300 task forces, mixing experts, public sector officials from outside as well as inside the civil service, private industry, producer interests, media people and a few trade unionists.[20] Blair's belief is that broad-based committees can come up with better proposals for promoting 'joined up' government. However, whatever is decided can only be implemented by departmental ministers and a mixture of institutions that are responsible for delivery of public policies in local communities from one end of Britain to the other.

Taking charge

How the decision is arrived at – through formal committees, informal networks or a combination of the two – is subordinate to the political outcome. The Prime Minister does not need to make decisions, but to ensure that decisions made are to the advantage of Downing Street. If this is not possible, then the Prime Minister has a direct interest in limiting damage by getting ministers to agree a course of action that they will defend collectively as the best possible decision in the circumstances.

Old-school Prime Ministers such as Clement Attlee gave Cabinet ministers much leeway to deal with problems within their department or in committees. As Attlee said of his Foreign Secretary, Ernest Bevin, 'If you have a good dog, you don't bark yourself.' When the government faced a difficult decision, Attlee gave ministers time to state their case to colleagues – and to have it opposed by other colleagues. In that way, every minister was involved in consultations, and each was aware that his or her own views were controverted by colleagues. If a Cabinet discussion reached an impasse, Attlee adjourned for further discussion. But when he sensed a consensus, Attlee was quick to sum up.

> The job of the Prime Minister is to get the general feeling, collect the voices. And then, when everything reasonable has been said, to get on with the job and say, 'Well, I think the decision of the Cabinet is this, that or the other. Any objections?' Usually, there aren't.[21]

Jim Callaghan learned from Attlee 'the advantage of keeping your mouth shut , and of not exposing your point of view if you wanted to get your business through'. When his government faced an economic crisis in 1976 that led to an International Monetary Fund loan, Callaghan was acutely aware that this was a political crisis.

> I knew it was quite possible for the government to break up, and it could have been another 1931, so I was determined to allow the

Cabinet to talk itself out. They could talk and talk and talk as long as they liked; everybody had a fair chance, and I told them to put in memoranda. We discussed their memoranda, we re-discussed their memoranda and so on, and eventually, by allowing them to talk themselves out, they all came to a common conclusion. Some were unhappy about it, but they did come to a common conclusion, and we preserved the unity of the Cabinet and of the party.

In an effort to keep the governing party together, Callaghan held twenty-six Cabinet meetings to discuss how the Labour government could deal with the crisis confronting it. The Prime Minister encouraged Tony Benn, an 'impossibilist' in economic terms, to prepare a Cabinet paper on an alternative economic strategy. It was presented along with a paper from the Cabinet Office that shot down Benn's paper.[22]

By contrast, Margaret Thatcher found it hard not to express her point of view, believing her convictions would lead to the right policies. She told a journalist prior to winning the 1979 election, 'It must be a conviction government. As Prime Minister, I could not waste time having any internal arguments.'[23] A Foreign Office diplomat described her approach to discussions with colleagues thus:

With her, there was often not even the prelude of reasonable discussion. She would begin a ministerial meeting by saying that she wanted to hear the views of X and Y, but wished first to make a few points of her own, at the end of which the invitation to X and Y had usually lapsed.[24]

When Margaret Thatcher sought advice, it was not about what to do but about how to implement decisions to which she was committed, such as the privatization of nationalized industries or the poll tax.

While Margaret Thatcher often compelled ministers to go along with her by force of personality, robustness of arguments, and the unspoken threat to ministerial careers of crossing her, there was not time enough to apply her will to all the activities of government. Thus, many departmental measures were not in harmony with her own views. A former minister, David Mellor, noted, 'There were moments when Mrs. Thatcher would privately rage so ferociously against something the Government had done that you almost forgot she was Prime Minister.'[25] When Thatcher's political capital was low and ministers pushed their case hard, she recognized that it could be politically necessary to set aside her own views, as happened with British entry to the European Exchange Rate Mechanism:

> I had too few allies to continue to resist and win the day. There are limits to the ability of even the most determined democratic leader to stand out against what the Cabinet, the Parliamentary Party, the industrial lobby and the press demand.[26]

Tony Blair has accelerated the decline of Cabinet, reducing the frequency and duration of meetings, but he cannot dispense with Whitehall departments that have the expertise, the formal responsibility and the organizational capacity to carry out public policies. For that reason, he cannot dispense with departmental ministers. In place of the formal and informal networks of committees and bilateral discussions, Blair has sought to create a hierarchical system of command and control, giving greater political authority to his enlarged staff at Number Ten. Peter Mandelson has described the situation thus:

> It requires much tighter co-ordination in government. Management theorists among you will know, or instantly be struck by, the analogy of a rowing eight as a perfect team. When they are well coordinated and have confidence in each other, they pull strongly on the oar, even though they cannot see where they are going.[27]

From this perspective, 'joined up government' is about yoking ministers and ministries together, with the tiller in the hands of someone at Number Ten, and ministers and civil servants applauding what he says.

Downing Street staff sit on committees dealing with departmental business to make sure each oar is being pulled as it should. Soon after the 1997 election, David Miliband and Alastair Campbell briefed a Fleet Street paper on how the Blair system is intended to work:

> Downing Street has agreed objectives with every Whitehall department and each Cabinet minister is held responsible for those targets being met. In the DFEE [Department for Education and Employment] there is a named official responsible for every target. If we don't drive these changes through they will never get done. Tony Blair regularly calls in each Cabinet minister and his permanent secretary and monitors progress. Everybody knows his head is on the block.

Tony Blair marshalled Cabinet ministers and senior civil servants in the rose garden of Number Ten to applaud his presentation of his government's first annual report.
Photo: PA Photos/Keiran Docherty/Reuters.

Without a reshuffle, Downing Street staff can undermine the authority of a minister by casting doubt on their capacity. In the extreme case of Mo Mowlam as Northern Ireland Secretary, her political standing in London was undermined and the Prime Minister used her headquarters at Hillsborough to hold meetings from which Mowlam, nominally the responsible minister, was visibly excluded.[28]

When asked in 1997 about the need to reconcile political differences through Cabinet deliberations, Miliband commented, 'In the past Cabinets were important when governments were factionalized and divided. This government is neither.' Alastair Campbell concurred, 'When they had big cabinets they spent their day doing one of two things: tearing lumps out of each other or writing diaries.'[29] Yet when the interests of competing Cabinet ministers are great and divisions are deep, the command-and-control system is no more than a conflict management system, as Blair has since learned in the debate about Britain's relationship with the European

Monetary Union. Although he has privately written memos calling for a 'firmer, certain, clearer' policy line on monetary union, his primary public concern is staying out of the battle on this issue between the Cabinet's most senior ministers and potential bastards. Euro-enthusiasts such as the Foreign Secretary, Robin Cook, and Peter Mandelson intermittently speak as if British entry is 'inevitable'. However, the Chancellor, Gordon Brown, repeatedly insists that entry will only happen if five economic conditions that he has laid down are met. Brown's supporters have briefed the press that speeches made by Cook and Mandelson are 'garbage'.[30] The fight is not only about what government does, but also who calls the shots.

9

Running – and Running After – the Economy

> In a free-for-all economy, we want to be part of the all.
> Frank Cousins, general secretary, Transport and General Workers' Union

> This is anti-British and derogatory to sterling but, on balance, if one is free to do so, it makes sense to me.
> W. J. Keswick, director of the Bank of England, advice to a City banker during 1957 sterling crisis

The Prime Minister is a politician not an economist; the economic activities that matter most are those that affect his or her political capital. Because British government must raise taxes equal to two-fifths of the gross domestic product to finance public spending, the Prime Minister cannot be indifferent to the state of the economy. A buoyant economy makes it possible to claim credit for greater prosperity, lower taxes and increasing expenditure on popular public services such as health care and pensions. For these reasons, the Prime Minister does not need a visit from a political adviser of Bill Clinton to think, 'It's the economy, stupid.'

However, markets are not organized like Whitehall; decisions are made in many different places. In the board rooms of banks and trade union headquarters the self-interest of organizations come first, as the remarks above by Frank Cousins and William Keswick illustrate. Equally, when retailers set out their stalls or people go shopping, they are not thinking about the interests of Downing Street but about their own particular household needs. The state of the economy also reflects what is done North of Watford and beyond Dover. The ups and downs of the business cycle and cumulative structural changes in the international economy influence economic changes from the beginning to the end of a Parliament. Hardly a business day goes by without something happening in the market place that is of interest in Downing Street.

The Prime Minister makes political judgements about major economic issues, such as the priority to be given to fighting inflation or fighting unemployment. The Prime Minister wants to promote the 'feel good' factor, that is, a sense of prosperity in the electorate. But sometimes circumstances dictate unpopular decisions, and the Prime Minister must seek to minimize the 'feel bad' factor by claiming current pains are necessary in order to realize future gains. The long-term dynamic of the British economy since 1945 enables prime ministers to claim that the national economy has grown while they have been in Downing Street. But inflation and unemployment can follow short-term up-and-down cycles during the life of a Parliament; both Labour and Conservative prime ministers have learned to their cost that managing the economic cycle is not so easy as it looks. Economics is called the dismal science because it imposes costs as well as benefits. The costs are often immediate and political, while the benefits are long-term (that is, after the next election) and conjectural.

The Prime Minister's job is not to manage the economy, nor are incumbents of Number Ten particularly qualified to do so. The only economist ever to become Prime Minister was Harold Wilson, and the economic record of his governments was not positive. Margaret Thatcher approached economics in political and moral rather than technical terms: 'Economics are the method; the object is to change the soul.'[1] Of the eleven post-war Prime Ministers, eight had never served as Chancellor of the Exchequer. The three Prime Ministers who had done so, Winston Churchill, Jim Callaghan and John Major, were each identified with major economic failures at the Treasury, at Number Ten or at both places.

The domestic arrangements of Downing Street give expression to the Prime Minister's balancing role, for the Chief Whip normally lives at Number Twelve and the Chancellor at Number Eleven. Both owe their place to the occupant of Number Ten. The Prime Minister's first economic priority is to appoint a Chancellor of the Exchequer. Alec Douglas-Home, who famously referred to using matchsticks to understand how an economy worked, had no difficulty in making clear that the responsibility for the economy rested with his Chancellor of the Exchequer, Reginald Maudling. By contrast, Harold Wilson could not avoid being publicly identified with economic decisions. Tony Blair is well suited to play a balancing role, for he has no background in economics or financial matters. Moreover, disengagement reduces friction with his Chancellor of the Exchequer, Gordon Brown, whom Blair leapfrogged over in the race for Labour leadership. A quarrel between Prime Minister and Chancellor could lead to one or both leaving Downing Street.

When issues become serious, no Prime Minister can avoid becoming involved in economic decisions threatening the political future of the government as a whole. Jim Callaghan appointed Denis Healey Chancellor in the hope that Healey would save him from immersion in difficult economic issues. But within months, the economy was in a tailspin and the Prime Minister's ease was disrupted: 'I found, as other Prime Ministers had done before me, that the Prime Minister can't keep himself or herself aloof.'[2]

But *which* economy should the Prime Minister pay attention to – the economy that immediately affects voters in their role as employees and shoppers or the national economic concerns on which the Treasury primarily focuses? An old-school Prime Minister could think first in terms of the national economy, as the Attlee government did when it nationalized industries. However, the historic position of Britain as an importing and exporting country faced old-school prime ministers with international economic issues too. Over the decades, the terms of trade have changed greatly in the international economy. The dollar, the yen and the euro now speak louder than sterling; the major 'British' automobile-makers are Ford, General Motors and Japanese-owned firms; and the contents of computers made in Britain are as cosmopolitan as the food on offer in Sainsburys. In a very real sense, it can be questioned whether the economy for which the Prime Minister is responsible is still a British economy.

When it became open to world trade in mid-Victorian times, the British economy was the dominant participant in the international economy. The Prime Minister could therefore put the national economy first. Today, Downing Street must be extroverted, for what happens in the world outside Westminster has great impact on the economic concerns of Downing Street. International events, such as the 1973 oil price shock, interact with domestic events, such as the confrontation between Ted Heath and the National Union of Mineworkers. Heath's failure to adapt to international events, like John Major's inability to see international pressures on the pound two decades later, illustrate the rueful view of a senior Treasury official, 'We were never much good with foreigners.'[3]

To manage the economy, the Prime Minister must catch hold of it first. In narrowly political terms, the Prime Minister appears well placed to do so, for the Treasury has the power to make a wide range of economic decisions, and the Prime Minister has the last word about what the Chancellor proposes. But Downing Street does not have command-and-control powers over the activities of banks, business and trade unions. With a fine show of non-partisanship, British firms have ignored the urgings of successive Prime Ministers to invest and export more, British unions have ignored Downing Street requests to lower their demands for wage increases, and youthful workers have ignored repeated Downing Street exhortations to get more education, training and job skills to compete in the twenty-first century. The decentralized nature of a market economy results in the Prime Minister expending much energy running after the economy.

New-style prime ministers concluded that it was impossible to manage the British economy as their predecessors had done, because rules of thumb deduced from new-style economic theories no longer produced the results that they wanted. As a Labour Treasury minister ruefully explained to me in autumn 1975, 'The old laws of economics that we studied in school haven't been suspended just because we are in office.'

In the twenty-first century the Prime Minister must change direction in order to catch up with events. The economic laws that matter are not those of national economics, which focus on supply and demand in an economy closed to international influences. Instead, the economy of Great Britain is integrated in an increasingly competitive and open international economy.

1 Planning the mixed economy

For three decades after the Second World War, successive Labour and Conservative prime ministers were committed to economic planning within the framework of a mixed economy in which government played an important role. Downing Street accepted responsibility for full employment, prices and economic growth. The political backlash against the 1930s made one-nation Conservative prime ministers ready to agree with their Labour counterparts that maintaining full employment came first. The Treasury assured prime ministers that Keynes's economic theories made it possible to manage the economy to achieve these goals. Keynesian principles appealed to the Prime Minister and Chancellor because they emphasize decisions about taxation, public expenditure and interest rates, decisions that the government of the day must in any event take. From abstract theories, simple rules of thumb could be deduced that a Prime Minister without any economic literacy could understand, and these rules could be used to identify meaningful policy options and prescribe how to alter policies when the economy got in trouble.

Giving direction with confidence

When Clement Attlee became Prime Minister in 1945, confidence in economic planning was high in Whitehall, for Britain had won the war and planners were anxious to show that they could convert a wartime into a peacetime economy. The Labour government nationalized major economic institutions, including the Bank of England, and the coal, electricity, gas, railway, road haulage, steel and civil aviation industries. Controls were maintained on foreign currency exchange and dollar imports such as tobacco and Hollywood movies. Food rationing was maintained and at times even tightened. Public expenditure approached half the national product – and tax rates were equally high. In 1946 the standard rate of income tax was 50 per cent, and the marginal tax on high incomes rose to 95 per cent.

To deal with the ups and downs of the economy, Clement Attlee appointed Chancellors of the Exchequer who were experienced in dealing with economic issues – Hugh Dalton, Stafford Cripps and Hugh Gaitskell. Attlee also showed skill in securing the departure of Dalton and Cripps when each ran into economic difficulties. Attlee's fortunes turned sour in 1951, as he was in hospital when rows broke out between Chancellor Hugh Gaitskell and Aneurin Bevan, and his deputy, Herbert Morrison, failed to keep both in Cabinet. During the Attlee government there was transition from a wartime to a peacetime economy without a recession. The gross domestic product rose by a fifth compared to the last year of peace. There was full, even over-full employment. The unemployment rate averaged only 1 per cent and inflation averaged 3 per cent a year.

The return of the Conservative government under Winston Churchill in 1951 did little to alter government's involvement in the economy. Most of the industries nationalized by the Attlee government remained in public ownership. Rationing finally ended and controls were reduced but not eliminated. Politically, the most significant change was an increase in the role of the Chancellor of the Exchequer, as Churchill and Eden concentrated on the 'high' politics of diplomacy and defence, while leaving R. A. Butler and Harold Macmillan to look after the counting house side of government.

Harold Macmillan brought to Number Ten a strong commitment to government managing the economy, having seen unemployment at first hand while representing a North of England constituency between the wars and coincidentally having published Keynes. Within twelve months of taking office, Macmillan showed his commitment by accepting the resignation of his three Treasury ministers, Peter Thorneycroft, Nigel Birch and Enoch Powell, rather than approve their monetarist policies. Macmillan made political capital of increased mass consumption of refrigerators, cars and television sets, proudly proclaiming, 'Most of our people have never had it so good.' But Macmillan also saw need for government initiatives to prevent good times being followed by bad. In 1961 he established the National Economic Development Council in the hope it would encourage a faster rate of economic growth. In the same year, he put forward an application for Britain to join the newly created European Common Market.

Under four Conservative prime ministers between 1951 and 1964, there was an increase of more than a third in the real gross domestic product per person, unemployment was between 1 and 2 per cent and, after a rise, inflation fell to under 3 per cent. A booming economy meant that job losses in traditional industries such as coal, shipbuilding and cotton textiles were offset by increased employment in automobiles, health, education and office jobs. There was even scope to finance economically irrational investment decisions. Confronted with the choice between subsidizing investment in the steel industry in either South Wales or Scotland, Harold Macmillan made a political judgement of Solomon, dividing the money so that part of the investment went to Scotland and part to Wales. The Conservatives fought the 1964 election with a manifesto promising to increase public spending on popular social programmes at a rate of 4.1 per cent annually, financed by a forecast annual economic growth rate of 4.0 per cent.

Harold Wilson fought the 1964 election by attacking 'thirteen wasted years' of Conservative government and confidently promising that a Labour government would do better, since it would base plans on scientific principles consistent with its socialist philosophy. Instead of old-fashioned nationalization, Wilson promised to take positive government action to promote new technology under a National Economic Plan to increase economic growth. Although Alec Douglas-Home was presiding over a rapidly expanding national economy, disarray among Conservatives over his appointment as Prime Minister gave Wilson a narrow election victory.

Losing confidence

Unusually among politicians, Harold Macmillan was a reflective man given to seeing the dark side of life as well as positive achievements. In the same 1957 speech in which he heralded the arrival of the 'you've never had it so good' economy, he also said:

> What is beginning to worry some of us is, 'Is it too good to be true?' or perhaps I should say, 'Is it too good to last?' Amidst all this prosperity, there is one problem that has troubled us one way or another ever since the war. It's the problem of rising prices.

Macmillan's remarks reflected anxiety over an increase of more than 25 per cent in prices in the first five years of the Conservative government returned in 1951. While inflation fell to an average of 2.6 per cent while Macmillan was in office, his diagnosis correctly forecast troubles that confronted his successors.

The confident Keynesian policies of Downing Street were undermined by pressures from the world North of Watford. Full employment created shop floor union pressures for wage increases in a free for all economy, and a booming economy led employers to pay higher wages to prevent strikes. Increased wages gave people more money to spend, and demand rose faster than the productivity of British firms. Prices began to rise, and rising prices stimulated demands for bigger wage increases, thus increasing the upward inflationary spiral. As an employer of more than a quarter of the labour force, the government was directly involved in wage negotiations; it was also responsible for cost-of-living increases for pensioners. More tax revenue was needed to finance higher public sector wages, increased pensions and higher interest rates on public sector borrowing. When consumer demand was met by importing cars, television sets and other consumer goods from abroad, this created a balance of payments problem too.

Because Conservative governments had been associated with inter-war unemployment, prime ministers from Churchill to Macmillan sought the goodwill of unions – their critics called it appeasement – and looked to faster rates of economic growth as the means of breaking the wage–price spiral. As the leader of a party that was integrally allied with trade unions, Harold Wilson saw himself well placed to get trade union leaders to compromise wage demands over beer and sandwiches at Number Ten. But trade union general secretaries had trouble delivering compliance by their members; shop stewards organized unofficial strikes for higher wages. When exhortation failed and inflation increased, Downing Street hit the 'stop' button of the 'stop–go' economy, raising interest rates, pushing up unemployment and reducing the rate of economic growth. When these constraints showed evidence of success, the 'go' button was punched, relaxing fiscal policy, stimulating the economy to faster growth and fuller employment, and pushing up prices.

In efforts to bring order to 'free for all' economic pressures, prime ministers from Macmillan to Callaghan invited representatives of unions and employers from the world North of Watford to join government-sponsored corporatist institutions. A Council on Pay, Productivity and Incomes was set up in 1957, and succeeded by a National Incomes Commission in 1961, and the Prices and Incomes Board in 1965. This was followed in 1973 by a Prices Commission and a Pay Board, and in 1979 by a Commission on Pay Comparability. Between 1965 and 1977, a total of fourteen different incomes policies were adopted and abandoned.[4]

In his first six years in Downing Street, Harold Wilson tried five incomes policies. In 1964 Wilson proclaimed a planned growth of incomes. After being re-elected with a big majority in 1966, he called for a twelve-month freeze on wages and price restraints. This failed, and devaluation and an International Monetary Fund (IMF) loan followed. Concurrently, the Wilson government set up a Royal Commission on the Reform of the Trade Unions and Employers' Associations. A White Paper, *In Place of Strife*, recommended giving trade unions statutory rights and obligations, measures regarded as desirable by unions in other European countries. However, British unions opposed legislation as an infringement on their rights outside the law; they were supported by a Cabinet faction led by the then Home Secretary, Jim Callaghan. Wilson abandoned the idea. By the time of the 1970 election, prices had risen by almost a third, and unemployment was starting to rise too.

The Heath government offered both stick and carrot to employers and workers. It brought in an Industrial Relations Act that gave unions both rights and obligations, and it promoted tripartite corporatist institutions to discuss prices, wages and employment policies. It sought to moderate wage and price increases through five different policies. As annual wage settlements rose steeply, reaching 16 per cent, the Heath government adopted a series of measures intended to control inflation by stages. But price rises accelerated and unemployment rose towards the dreaded figure of one million. When the National Union of Mineworkers put in a wage demand well above the government maximum, the government, as the owner of the coal mining industry, could not duck involvement, nor did it want to abandon its wage policy. Strikes by miners in early 1974 produced energy shortages, leading to the proclamation of a three-day working week in major industries. Edward Heath sought to break the impasse by calling a general election on the issue 'Who governs?' The electorate's answer was: 'Not you.'

The 1974–9 Labour government inherited its own mistakes, compounded by those of Edward Heath. In the year from June 1974, wages increased by an average of 33 per cent. Wilson promoted incomes policies under the generic heading of the Social Contract, which offered increased public expenditure on social policies to which Labour was anyway committed, in return for unions accepting lower wage increases as inflation under Wilson increased to an annual average of 21 per cent. This led to a cut in real wages and an IMF loan accompanied by stringent anti-inflationary measures. Under Callaghan the inflation rate fell, but none the less averaged 12 per cent per year. Unions were running out of patience with policies of wage restraint, and the 'Winter of Discontent' that began in autumn 1978 was a prelude to Labour's election defeat.

Table 9.1 The economic misery index: inflation plus unemployment

Prime Minister	Inflation	Unemployment (annual average in %)	Total misery
Attlee	3.0	1.1	4.1
Churchill	5.0	1.2	6.2
Eden	4.9	0.9	5.8
Macmillan	2.6	1.4	4.0
Douglas-Home	2.7	1.4	4.1
Wilson 1964–70	4.4	1.6	6.0
Heath	8.6	2.6	11.2
Wilson 1974–6	21.0	3.0	24.0
Callaghan	12.3	5.1	17.4
Thatcher	8.0	8.7	16.7
Major	3.3	8.7	12.0
Blair to June 2000	2.7	4.8	7.5

Sources: *Annual Abstract of Statistics*. Figures for 1999 and 2000 from Office for National statistics: www.statistics.gov.uk/statbase/mainmenu.asp. Inflation rates calculated from the month the Prime Minister entered office to the month of departure; unemployment rates calculated from quarterly averages.

If economic growth were the sole criterion for success, then the Wilson–Heath–Callaghan years could be judged positively, for the gross domestic product grew by a third in real terms between 1964 and 1979. But a very different story is told by the 'misery index', which adds together the annual rate of inflation and the percentage unemployed. The index is particularly apt for assessing the 'feel good' or 'feel bad' consequence of Keynesian policies. The same aggregate level of misery could be achieved by a Labour Prime Minister exchanging a higher inflation rate for lower unemployment, or a Conservative Prime Minister accepting higher unemployment and lower inflation.

For almost a quarter century after 1945, the misery index was stable and low, fluctuating between 4 and 6 per cent annually, depending on national and international pressures rather than the party or Prime Minister in Downing Street (table 9.1). At the beginning of the 1970s, both unemployment and inflation began to rise together. Inflation rose much more, as Ted Heath tried to keep unemployment below one million. Stagflation became the major problem of Downing Street as inflation rose and the economy stagnated or even shrank. By the end of Harold Wilson's first year back in Downing Street, unemployment had passed the dreaded one million figure, and the inflation rate more than doubled. Prices rose the same amount the following year, and by an additional 17 per cent the year after. Since annual rates of inflation are cumulative, the result was that during the term of office of Harold Wilson and Jim Callaghan prices doubled. This produced an intense political demand to reduce the rate of inflation.

2 Trying to take hands off the economy

Margaret Thatcher met the demand for reducing inflation by introducing monetarist policies that lowered inflation at the cost of increasing unemployment. She justified the measures adopted by arguing that Numbers Ten and Eleven Downing Street ought to take their hands off the economy and leave economic decisions to the market place. This turned out to be easier said than done. None the less, after eleven years in office Margaret Thatcher did succeed in changing expectations about what Downing Street should do about the economy, and left behind doctrines accepted by both John Major and Tony Blair.

Although Margaret Thatcher had no formal economic education, she had an intuitive affinity with economic theories based on the classic laissez faire assumption that government should leave the economy to the market. However, accepting the legacy of her Labour and Conservative predecessors would have meant taking responsibility for a mixed economy. The paradox of Thatcherism was that the Prime Minister had to intervene actively in the economy to advance her goal of freeing the British economy from the influence of Downing Street.

Thatcher was determined to distance Downing Street from prices and incomes policy. The Commission on Pay Comparability was abolished. Trade unions and employers were expected to agree wages without the involvement of Whitehall. Removing government from major industrial disputes conserved the Prime Minister's political capital. Privatization removed hundreds of thousands of people from the public sector payroll, making their wages a matter for private sector employers. A new legal framework for trade unions and industrial relations required unions to elect their chief officials and hold a ballot before a strike could be made legal. If a union called an illegal strike, its funds were subject to court action. The effectiveness of Thatcher's hands-off strategy was demonstrated when Arthur Scargill led coal miners in a disastrous year-long strike. It started in spring 1984, when coal stocks were high and coal was least in demand, and ended with the National Union of Mineworkers split. The Conservative government was subsequently able to privatize coal mining.

Margaret Thatcher rejected the even-handed Keynesian prescription of balancing anti-inflation policies with economic stimuli promoting employment. While accepting that government has an obligation to control the money supply, she believed that jobs should be created by the market. On entering office, inflation was her first priority, since the collapse of the Callaghan government's wages policy left behind a wage explosion, exacerbated by a sharp rise in retail prices caused by a big Conservative-sponsored increase in Value Added Tax. In Thatcher's first twelve months in office, prices rose 22 per cent, and the rise did not fall below 10 per cent until her third year in office. Unemployment more than doubled by 1983, passing the three million mark. Over more than a decade in office, Thatcher's misery index averaged 16.7 per cent, far higher than that for prime ministers up to 1970, but lower than that for Harold Wilson and Jim Callaghan.

Thatcher's living legacy

Thanks to Thatcher's efforts to reduce the government's role in the economy, John Major and Tony Blair have been less involved with the specifics of the economy, for there is less for Downing Street to manage. A new-style Prime Minister is no longer expected to take responsibility for everything that goes wrong with the economy. More responsibility and blame can be passed to those outside the world of Westminster.

For better and for worse, John Major carried the legacy of Thatcherism into Downing Street. Ideologically, Major accepted the basic goals of Thatcherite economics. He continued privatization and reduced the government's role as an employer by contracting out the delivery of more public services to private agencies. While Major was not a 'gut' anti-European like his predecessor, a substantial number of ministers and MPs were suspicious of everything emanating from Brussels. Major's disastrous association with an unsustainable high foreign exchange rate for the pound and the Maastricht Treaty, which promised a big expansion in the powers of the European Union, produced bitter divisions between himself and the 'bastards' of his Cabinet. Prices were rising when Major entered Number Ten and so was unemployment, in the prelude to a recession that lasted two years. In 1992, an election year, the rate of inflation was falling but because unemployment was rising the misery index was still 13 per cent. By Major's last year in office, the economy was booming. The misery index during Major's term of office was lower than under Thatcher, but still above that for the Heath years.

In seeking electoral support in opposition, Tony Blair expressed pro-market views, telling business leaders, 'The control of inflation through a tough macroeconomic policy framework is even more important than the Tories have said.'[5] In his foreword to the New Labour government's first annual report to its 'shareholders' (that is, the public), the Prime Minister declared 'In all walks of life people act as consumers not just citizens.' In subsequently describing plans for the national health service, which old Labour MPs see as the birthright of citizens, Blair made the Freudian slip of describing his goal as 'putting the customer (er) the patient, first'.[6] As earnest of New Labour's acceptance of the market, Blair pledged that public expenditure would initially be kept at levels set by the Conservative government's budget, and income tax would not be increased in the forthcoming Parliament.

Once in office, the Blair government gave responsibility for interest rates to the Bank of England, thus directing complaints about it away from Downing Street. The standard rate of income tax has been cut to the lowest level since 1930, while less visible 'stealth' taxes have been increased. Continuing international and national economic growth has increased tax revenue, enabling the government to increase expenditure on popular programmes. In Blair's first three years in office, the misery index was at its lowest since Harold Wilson was in Downing Street in the 1960s.

Just as acceptance by Conservative prime ministers such as Churchill was necessary to establish the mixed economy welfare state, so the long-term dominance of Thatcherite economics has been secured by Tony Blair accepting the market as the prime influence on economic policy. Moreover, Blair has sought to spread the message of the market to other members of the Socialist

International. A joint statement about *Europe: The Third Way* with German leader Gerhard Schröder was introduced with a statement more Thatcherite than Christian or Social Democratic:

> The ability of national government to fine-tune the economy in order to secure growth and jobs has been exaggerated. The importance of individual and business enterprise to the creation of wealth has been undervalued. The weaknesses of markets have been overstated and their strengths underestimated.[7]

Demonstrations and picketing in September 2000 in protest against fuel price increases brought home to Blair the vulnerability of Downing Street to opposing pressures from world markets and angry voters, as the actions of the former pushed British oil prices up while the actions of the latter pushed the Prime Minister's popular support down.

3 The pound at sea in the international economy

In the *longue durée* of the past half century, the British economy has trebled in absolute and real terms. Internationally, however, the relative economic weight of Britain has declined. At the end of the Second World War, the British economy was one of the world's two major economies and sterling one of its two major reserve currencies. Living standards in Britain were half again greater than Germany's and more than three times above Japan's, and also above those of major European economies. Whichever Prime Minister or party has been in office, the British economy has grown slowly compared to that of the United States or the average of member-states of the European Union. This is true of the golden years of the 1960s, when all economies were booming, and of the dire years that followed after the 1973 oil crisis. It is true of periods when prime ministers sought to steer a mixed economy, and when Downing Street pursued market-oriented policies. For example, from 1989 to 1999, when Margaret Thatcher, John Major and Tony Blair were in Downing Street, the British economy grew on average by 1.9 per cent a year. By comparison, countries of the European Union grew by an average of 2.2 per cent and the American economy by almost 3.0 per cent.

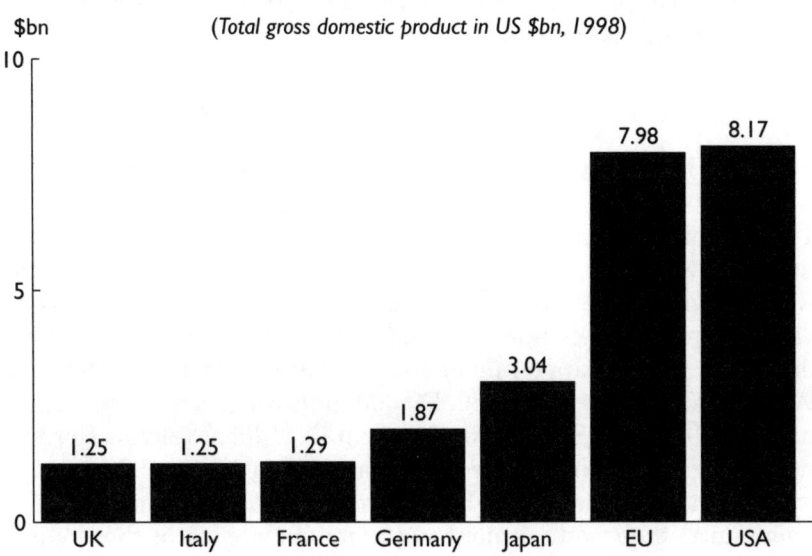

Figure 9.1 Britain's economy in international perspective
(Total gross domestic product in US $bn, 1998)

Country	$bn
UK	1.25
Italy	1.25
France	1.29
Germany	1.87
Japan	3.04
EU	7.98
USA	8.17

Source: OECD, *OECD in Figures*. Paris: supplement to *OECD Observer*. No. 217/218, July 1999, pp. 12–13. All figures in purchasing power parity.

While Britain has never been one of the most populous countries in the world, this was long offset by a wealth greater than that of France, Italy or Japan. In the past half-century, differences in long-term rates of economic growth have enabled many countries to catch up with or surpass Britain. By the end of the twentieth century, the living standards of the French, Germans, Irish, Italians and Japanese had caught up with or surpassed those of Britons. Among the fifteen member-states of the European Union, only Greece, Portugal and Spain have a lower gross domestic product per capita.[8]

On the world economic stage, a British Prime Minister no longer looms large (figure 9.1). An American President does not need to put on cowboy boots to stand tall, for the American economy is more than six times the size of the British. Japan's economy is two and one-half times that of Britain, while its population is double. In the European Union, the Prime Minister can claim to represent one of the big four economies of the EU. When the G-7 group of major world economies meet to discuss problems at their annual global summit, the Prime Minister represents only 7 per cent of the output of the world's seven economic superpowers. Within this group, only Canada has a smaller gross domestic product. The growing pre-eminence of other economies has left prime ministers at sea, uncertain about where as well as how to steer the country's economy.

The pound in a world of kilo currencies

The first of a half-century of international financial crises broke in July 1947 when, pursuant to the terms of the Anglo-American loan, sterling was made convertible into dollars. Six weeks later convertibility was suspended. In September, 1949 the pound was devalued; the exchange rate of $4.03, set at the start of the Second World War, dropped to $2.80. Devaluation was a shock, but it did not alter Downing Street's commitment to a global role for sterling or its reliance on an alliance with Washington (figure 9.2).

Since the devaluation of 1949, successive Prime Ministers have maintained their commitment to the independence of the pound. However, a policy of strict national independence is meaningful only in a closed economy such as North Korea has been. In an open international economy, the international purchasing power of the pound is determined by what happens in markets outside the United Kingdom as well as by what Downing Street does. Whereas in 1945 there was only the dollar to worry about, the decades since have seen a proliferation of major currencies, such as the Deutsche Mark and the yen. The launch of the euro as the common currency of most member-states of the European Union has led pro-Europeans to argue that British independence threatens to turn into isolation.

When Harold Wilson became Prime Minister in 1964, the pound was still valued at the same rate as when the Attlee government left office. However, changes in the international economy were making it increasingly costly domestically to maintain this rate. The Prime Minister announced his 'unalterable determination to maintain the value of the pound';[9] use of the word 'devaluation' was avoided in private as well as in public discussions. Wilson's big victory at the 1966 general election showed his domestic support – but by summer the foreign exchange markets were increasing pressure on the pound. The pressures of intermestic politics on Downing Street led Wilson's trusted adviser, Marcia Williams, to reflect, 'I hated that summer. It all seemed so disillusioning after such a terrific election victory. We had won, yet we didn't seem to have won.'[10]

Figure 9.2 Decline of the pound

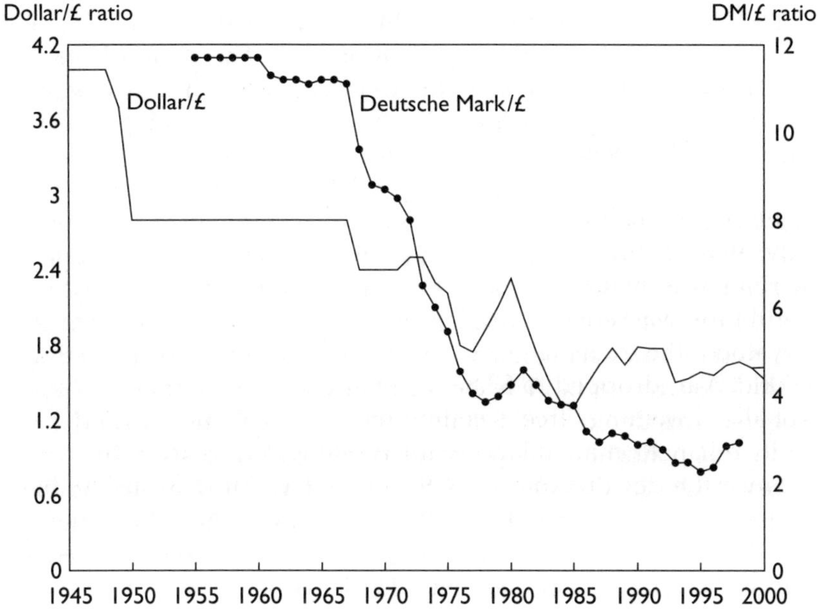

Source: Derived from annual British government statistics.

International markets proved stronger than the Prime Minister's unalterable determination. In November 1967, the pound was devalued to $2.40. A loan was negotiated with the IMF in Washington, and a tough set of economic measures was introduced, including cuts in public expenditure on major social programmes and raising charges on national health service prescriptions. Devaluation accelerated the terminal decline of the sterling area, as other countries that had held large currency reserves in London suffered a devaluation in their pounds too.

The next major change in sterling policy came as a consequence of a decision in the White House. When Washington faced financial problems arising from the Vietnam war, it floated the dollar in the world's currency markets by cutting the link between the dollar and gold in August 1971. The following week Ted Heath's government likewise shifted from a fixed to a floating exchange rate. In a world of kilo currencies, the pound could float both up *and* down, and move in different directions against different currencies. It briefly rose in value against the dollar, while falling against the Deutsche Mark and the yen. The pound's value against the dollar was only a few cents below the level it was at before floating when the miners' strike began in autumn 1973.

The domestic economic crisis that Ted Heath left as a legacy became part of the world recession of 1975. The pound began to float downwards first against the Deutsche Mark and then against the dollar. By the time Jim Callaghan entered Downing Street in March 1976, the pound had fallen by almost a fifth against the dollar since the start of floating and by almost half against the Deutsche Mark (figure 9.2). In an effort to stabilize the pound, Callaghan entered into prolonged discussions in Cabinet and in Washington. In Washington, Britain's weakness was an asset of sorts. Brent Scowcroft, President Ford's National Security Adviser, believed Britain's economic weakness was 'the greatest single threat to the Western world'. The United States Secretary of State, William Rogers, considered that Britain's economic collapse 'would have had great political consequences, so we tended to see it in cosmic terms'.[11] On 28 October 1976 the pound reached a new foreign exchange low of $1.56. The IMF refused Callaghan the generous conditions he sought for a loan, fearing that doing so would reduce the IMF's own political credibility. The letter of intent accompanying Downing Street's request for an IMF loan in December 1976 was not so much a choice made by the Prime Minister as a surrender to international pressures.

The dead cat bounces

A floating exchange rate can go up as well as down. This is captured in the Wall Street maxim, 'Even a dead cat can bounce.' Between 1976 and 1980 foreign revenues from North Sea oil began to roll into the Treasury and OPEC's second big increase in oil prices made Britain's currency a 'petro-pound'. The pound's value rose above $2.30 and it rose against the Deutsche Mark and yen too.

While the logic of a floating currency is that it has no 'right' or 'fixed' price, this has not stopped Margaret Thatcher, John Major and Tony Blair being faced with complaints that the pound is valued too low or too high in relation to foreign currencies. Often, both complaints are heard simultaneously, since a strong pound can be good news for British importers and bad news for exporters, while a weak pound has the opposite effect.

Margaret Thatcher had a laissez faire approach to the domestic economy, but in international economics believed that Britain was (or should be) a major independent economic power. But in a world of intermestic problems, this policy often had awkward consequences. To stop an inflationary spiral inherited from the Labour government, Thatcher pushed interest rates as high as 17 per cent in 1980. High interest rates encouraged an inflow of foreign money, pushing up the value of the pound, leading to cuts in interest rates to stimulate the domestic economy, and a fall in the pound. During Thatcher's premiership, the annual average dollar value of the pound fluctuated between $1.30 and $2.33 and similarly in relation to the Deutsche Mark.

The longer the pound floated up and down in the open international economy, the greater the appeal of a fixed exchange rate. In 1985 Nigel Lawson, Geoffrey Howe and the Governor of the Bank of England began to press Margaret Thatcher to join the European Exchange Rate Mechanism (ERM) formed under the leadership of Germany, perceived as having a very stable currency. At that time, the exchange rate was about DM3.80 to the pound. Thatcher resisted. She saw monetary policy as 'the very heart of economic policy, which itself lies at the heart of democratic politics'. She described proposals for a common monetary policy as a threat to Britain's sovereignty, 'abdicating control over our own monetary policy in order to have it determined by the German *Bundesbank*'. Thatcher told her senior Cabinet colleagues that if they wanted to join the ERM, they would have to find a new Prime Minister.[12]

The pressure on Thatcher to accept membership in the ERM continued for five years, costing her the resignation of the Chancellor of the Exchequer, Nigel Lawson, and of her personal economic adviser, Alan Walters. When her new Chancellor, John Major, continued to press the argument, she gave in 'because I had too few allies to continue to resist and win the day'. In October 1990 Britain joined the ERM with the value of the pound set at DM2.95. At that time, interest rates were above 14 per cent.

The victory that John Major won in the April 1992 was soon made hollow by the fall of the pound. In early September international currency dealers began speculating that the pound would be devalued against the Deutsche Mark. In an effort to create confidence in the pound, John Major told a Scottish audience that it would be a 'betrayal' of Britain to leave the ERM, and £10bn of British reserves was spent in an effort to prevent devaluation. On Black Wednesday, 16 September, the Chancellor raised the bank

Black Wednesday, 16 September 1992. Downing Street pushed interest rates through the roof but world financial markets pushed the pound through the floor.
Courtesy of John Frost Historical Newspapers.

rate to 10 per cent and then 15 per cent; he ended the day withdrawing from the ERM. The pound's exchange rate fell to below DM2.50, public confidence in the Prime Minister halved, divisions within government intensified – and worse was to come.

Most member-states of the European Union saw the Exchange Rate Mechanism as the prelude to European Monetary Union (EMU), which Margaret Thatcher was uncompromisingly against. When member-states met to plan the creation of a European Central Bank with a single European currency, John Major stayed away. In an article published in the *Economist* under the title, 'Raise Your Eyes, There Is a Land Beyond', Major argued that no decision about British participation in a single currency was necessary.

> I hope my fellow heads of government will resist the temptation to recite the mantra of full economic and monetary union as if nothing had changed. If they do recite it, it will have all the quaintness of a rain dance and about the same potency.[13]

When the 'land beyond' was reached and the EMU launched in 1999, Britain was absent.

In dealing with EMU, Tony Blair seeks to protect his political capital. His minimum aim is to avoid John Major's fate of splitting his Cabinet and MPs. The 1997 New Labour manifesto outlined various arguments for and against adopting the euro. It indicated there would be no immediate decision to do so, but said doing so could not be ruled out forever. The only commitment was to hold a referendum on the issue before a final decision went into effect. When the EMU was launched in January 1999 with Britain outside it, Blair greeted this with the unexceptionable statement, 'We can no longer afford to pretend that the euro does not exist.'[14] Subsequently the Chancellor, Gordon Brown, has spelled out five conditions for Britain adopting the euro. Entry should be consistent with: promoting investment in Britain; helping the City's financial services; keeping interest rates down; allowing flexibility to cope with economic difficulties; and promoting growth, stability and employment.

The pound still has the Queen's head on it, but Harold Wilson's claim that the pound in your pocket has not been devalued is patently false. Between Wilson's entry to Downing Street in 1964 and his final departure in 1976, the domestic purchasing power of the pound fell by more than 60 per cent. Notwithstanding the priority Margaret Thatcher gave to fighting inflation, during her time in Downing Street the pound lost more than half its purchasing power. Extending the comparison further shows an even greater erosion in the purchasing power of the pound. The pound notes rustling in the pockets and handbags of Britons celebrating VE Day in 1945 were worth more than twenty times the pound coins in the pockets of Tony Blair's guests at the Millennium Dome at the start of the year 2000. In a less lengthy time period, the value of the pound against the Deutsche Mark has fallen by four-fifths, before bouncing up again to a level that is still three-quarters less than when Harold Wilson entered Downing Street.

Whereas Labour has presided over more big bang devaluations than the Conservatives, Margaret Thatcher has had the dubious distinction of seeing the dead cat (that is, the British pound) bounce up and down much more. In October 1980, the pound was trading at $2.41 to the pound but by 7 March 1985 its value had more than halved to $1.05. The pound then bounced back up to $1.88 by November 1987.

A free market economist can endorse Tony Blair's comment about changes in Britain's place in the international economy being 'the way of the world',[15] in which impersonal market forces decide what happens. An economic historian can see relative economic decline as an unintended consequence of Britain having been the world leader in Victorian times, and now finding latecomers are catching up or surpassing Britain. The most important political conclusion is not one that any Prime Minister would boast about. It is that Downing Street is not so much making Britain's economic policy as reacting to decisions made in the worlds North of Watford and beyond the white cliffs of Dover.

10

Managing Decline in a Shrinking World

> We persist in regarding ourselves as a Great Power capable of everything and only temporarily handicapped by economic difficulties. We are not a Great Power and never will be again. We are a great nation, but if we continue to behave like a Great Power, we shall soon cease to be a great nation.
> Sir Henry Tizard, chief scientific adviser, Ministry of Defence, 1949[1]

> Britain has lost an empire and not yet found a role.
> Dean Acheson, former US Secretary of State

In politics, geography is variable not fixed and as the world changes shape, so too does the position of the Prime Minister. In Shakespeare's time, the English Channel was a 'moat defensive' against continental aggressors, protecting a small, isolated country from more powerful neighbours. When a late Victorian Cabinet minister claimed that Britain stood in splendid isolation, this statement was a half-truth. Britain was not isolated; there were imperial outposts on every continent, it was the world's largest trading nation and sterling was the standard international currency. A century ago Sir Eyre Crowe rejected the idea of isolation but believed that Britain could determine the balance of power in world politics. Prime ministers acted on this assumption, albeit guarantees to defend continental countries did not stop two world wars coming.

In 1945 Winston Churchill characterized Britain's interests as involving three overlapping circles – the Empire, Europe, and the special relationship with the United States. It was the Prime Minister's duty to maintain harmony between the three circles. This view of Britain's global co-ordinating position was shared by Clement

Attlee, who considered himself 'very happy and fortunate in having lived so long in the greatest country in the world'.[2] At each step in the process of adjusting the balance between Britain's three circles of involvement, old-school prime ministers preferred to walk backwards, seeking to maintain past British commitments and maintain an independent British nuclear bomb. The Suez War of 1956 was an extreme and unsuccessful example of this outlook. Those who questioned whether Britain could remain a Great Power, such as Sir Henry Tizard, were lonely voices. In Downing Street, Harold Macmillan was exceptional in recognizing that postwar international developments involved irreversible structural changes to which Britain had to adapt.

Successive prime ministers have retreated from global commitments. Domestic pressures to do so came from the limited economic resources of Britain. Ernest Bevin used to claim that if only he had more coal to export to countries ravaged by war, he could have pursued a much different foreign policy, but this was not the case. The rise of superpowers such as the United States and the Soviet Union reduced Britain to a middle-rank military power. The growth of national independence movements on many continents led to the end of Empire.

Adaptation is an activity, not a strategy. Four decades ago, Dean Acheson, an adviser of Presidents Roosevelt and Truman, recognized this when he noted that Britain had not yet found a role in a shrinking world. Instead of realistically appraising what was practicable with limited resources, Downing Street continued to adapt on an ad hoc basis. William Armstrong, a senior Whitehall civil servant saw this adaptation as 'the orderly management of decline'. However, when Armstrong used this phrase in a conversation with politically oriented Downing Street staff in 1973, they were appalled by the suggestion that the Prime Minister's influence was declining in the world beyond Dover.[3]

New-style prime ministers continue to define their role in global terms. Margaret Thatcher felt more at home in Washington than anywhere in Europe, and when Whitehall officials look for ideas about public policy they are more likely to turn to the United States or New Zealand than to the two countries that are geographically closest, France and Ireland. Tony Blair has echoed Churchill's three circles doctrine, claiming 'We are uniquely placed, with strong partnerships with the EU, the US and in Asia, to create a distinctive global role.'[4] Blair, like Prince Charles or Margaret

Thatcher, feels closer to Australia than to the German-speaking lands of *Mitteleuropa*.

The Prime Minister's diary shows that Downing Street sees its role in world affairs as being there. He or she makes frequent day trips to Europe, a turn of phrase that emphasizes the insular integrity of Britain. It also leaves vague where the Prime Minister is coming from. The supersonic Concord made it easy to spend part of the day in London and part in another continent. During his first eight weeks in office, Tony Blair travelled 26,800 miles to meetings in Amsterdam, Bonn, Denver, Hong Kong, Madrid, Malmö, New York, Noordwijk and Paris twice. Considerable time is also devoted to preparing for meeting foreign leaders who visit London, and to daily contacts with world leaders by telephone. Of the photographs in Jim Callaghan's memoir about Number Ten, two-thirds concern meetings with foreign leaders. In Margaret Thatcher's memoir of government, the number of photographs with foreign leaders is more than double those concerned with domestic politics.

The claim is advanced that the Prime Minister's dealings with foreign leaders 'enhances his or her power', because Downing Street is less restrained by Cabinet or by Parliament when representing the country as a whole.[5] But when dealing with foreign governments the Prime Minister is much more constrained by what happens in the world beyond Dover. While a British Prime Minister may appear important in a gathering of small Commonwealth countries, in the White House a Prime Minister is much reduced in size. When guns are the measure, undemocratic leaders of China and Russia have more explosive power. When money is the measure, the yen and the Deutsche Mark outweigh the pound – and the merging of the Deutsche Mark into the euro increases this disparity. Journalists writing about football do not make the mistake of believing that an English football team that wins the League Cup is thereby assured of victory when competing in the European Cup or the World Cup, and international political competition takes the measure of national governments too.

1   Scaling down commitments

At the end of the Second World War Westminster claimed to rule a fifth of the land area of the world, the territories of the British

Empire. The role of a British Prime Minister was to decide imperial policy; the role of other countries was to follow, as Australia and New Zealand did in going to war in Europe because Britain went to war. In 1942 Winston Churchill told a London audience, 'I have not become the King's First Minister in order to preside over the liquidation of the British Empire.'

From singular eminence to a special relationship

After the fall of France in 1940, Britain had a singular eminence – but it was also a perilous eminence, standing alone against Hitler. President Roosevelt decided that German conquest of Britain was not in the American national interest and launched a lend–lease programme to give material support to Britain. When Hitler declared war on the United States after the Japanese attack on Pearl Harbor, Britain and the United States became military allies, and a special relationship was born, replacing the often supercilious British view of America, and Washington's sometimes anti-imperialist view of Britain.[6]

'Special relationship' is an elastic phrase that can be stretched to fit many purposes. In Washington the vagueness of the term enables it to be used without commitment, while in Britain the Prime Minister can use the term to suggest he or she shares power with the President. The old-school British view was set out privately by Harold Macmillan, the War Cabinet's liaison with General Dwight D. Eisenhower in North Africa. Macmillan described Britons as 'Greeks in this American empire', running allied diplomacy on behalf of both countries, 'as Greek slaves ran the operations of the Emperor Claudius'.[7]

The Attlee government had eight ministries with major responsibilities for the world beyond Dover: the Foreign Office, the Dominions Office, the Secretary of State for India and Burma, the Colonial Office, the Admiralty, the War Office, the Air Ministry, and the Board of Trade. By contrast, there were only three ministries to deal with the classic concerns of the welfare state, education, social security, and health, housing and local government. The Attlee government needed lots of ministries because it faced lots of problems in all three of Britain's worlds.

Imperial commitments were resolved by pulling out. The Attlee government promptly withdrew from the Indian subcontinent, where irreconcilable differences between the Indian National Congress and the Muslim League led to its partition into India and Pakistan. In Palestine, British forces were caught in a cross fire between Zionist and Palestinian groups. While the Foreign Office was sensitive to Arab concerns because of Britain's wide-ranging interests in the Middle East, the United States supported Zionist demands. British troops pulled out in May 1948, and the Arab–Israeli war determined how the British mandate of Palestine was partitioned.

When Winston Churchill coined the term 'Iron Curtain' in a speech in America in 1946, he was not speaking officially, but his sentiments were shared in Westminster and Washington. Lacking the economic and military resources to contain Soviet expansion, the Attlee government encouraged Washington to throw its weight into the European balance of power. In early 1947, Downing Street informed Washington that it could no longer maintain troops in Turkey and in Greece, where a civil war was raging. The President announced the Truman Doctrine, pledging the United States to defend independent countries in Europe. In June 1947 economic aid to Western Europe was offered by American Secretary of State George Marshall. The British government led the organization of European cooperation to allocate aid. When the Soviet Union blockaded Berlin in 1948, Britain joined the United States in airlifting supplies there. The creation of the North Atlantic Treaty Organization (NATO) the following year strengthened cooperation, albeit on terms that recognized that Downing Street was no longer able to guarantee self-defence in Europe. Cooperation was not inevitable. The Attlee government developed a British nuclear bomb independent of the United States just in case it was needed in future. The United States also took unilateral actions; for example, creating the ANZUS mutual defence alliance with Australia and New Zealand in 1951 without Britain.

When push came to shove in Korea in 1950, the Attlee government sent troops to fight alongside the United States in support of a UN resolution to repel North Korean aggression. When reports from Washington suggested that the United States had not ruled out the use of atomic weapons in Korea, Attlee flew to Washington and on his return announced to the Commons that the use of nuclear weapons was not contemplated. Agreement was reached easily because the report was garbled; Truman was not planning to use the atomic bomb. In Westminster Attlee's 'success' entered Labour mythology as an example of Britain's great-power influence.

A special relationship involves sacrifices as well as benefits. At the height of the cold war in 1951, the Attlee government risked (and lost) its political life for the sake of the NATO alliance. It gave a higher priority to rearmament than to maintaining the national health service free of charge. Aneurin Bevan resigned from the Cabinet in protest, and was joined by Harold Wilson. Attlee's political capital was diminished and, after Labour lost the October 1951 election, Labour suffered years of factional fighting in Opposition.

Decline, managed and otherwise

When Dwight D. Eisenhower became President not long after Winston Churchill returned to office, this encouraged hopes in Number Ten that the wartime special relationship could continue. After the death of Stalin, Churchill proposed a Big Three conference of America, Britain and Russia to discuss prospects for ending the cold war. There was no positive response and a month later Churchill suffered a stroke that heralded the end of his active premiership. When President Eisenhower commenced discussions with Nikita Khrushchev in 1960, the wartime Big Three had become the Big Two, for Harold Macmillan was not invited to participate.

Anthony Eden unintentionally demonstrated the limits of Britain's capacity to go it alone. Eden saw Egyptian nationalization of the Suez Canal as threatening Britain's vital interest in the sea route to oil resources in the Persian Gulf, to India and Australia. In secret collaboration with the French and Israeli governments, he launched a military invasion of the Canal Zone in late October, 1956. The Egyptian military was no match for the Anglo-French invasion force, but the Suez invasion failed for political reasons. The United States did not see Egypt as threatening its interests. When financial markets started a run on the pound, the International Monetary Fund refused to support it. Within a week, Eden announced a ceasefire, and troops were evacuated in December. The Suez War destroyed Eden's political capital and health, and he resigned in January. Financial retrenchment led the Wilson government to abandon trying to defend Britain's national interests with an East of Suez military force.

Technological developments effectively ended Britain's claim to have an independent nuclear deterrent, for lack of an independent British delivery system. In 1958 Harold Macmillan negotiated the supply of American Thor missiles for atomic weapons under a 'dual key' arrangement that required both partners to agree to their use. Two years later Washington agreed to supply the Skybolt missile system that Britain could use at its sole discretion. However, Skybolt failed operational tests, and Macmillan had to ask President Kennedy to supply Polaris submarines with missile-launching capabilities. When they became obsolete the replacement was a US-designed Trident fleet.

In the 1950s Downing Street sought to control colonial change by legislating new but limited opportunities for political participation in colonies and new federations in East Africa, Central Africa and the West Indies. It also committed military force to put down guerilla movements in Kenya and Malaysia. In 1960 Harold Macmillan travelled to South Africa to warn that a 'wind of change' was blowing across Africa, and 'whether we like it or not, this growth of national consciousness is a political fact'. The limits of Downing Street's power were revealed in Southern Rhodesia in 1965, when the leader of a small group of white settlers issued a Unilateral Declaration of Independence. Harold Wilson's government refused to recognize the action but did not try to suppress it; the illegal regime sustained itself long enough to be a thorn in the side of four successive British prime ministers.

The 1982 Falklands War was the exception that proves the rule about Britain's decline. Margaret Thatcher acted without military allies and in the face of great uncertainties. There was a shooting war, and the result was military victory. However, it was hardly proof of Britain's Great Power status, for Britain's military opponent was Argentina, a country with a less developed economy, an unpopular military dictatorship and about one-quarter the military personnel of Britain. The Falkland Islands is an ironic prize of war, for it has no strategic significance to contemporary Britain and its 1,800 people are subsidized at a per capita cost far greater than the wage of the average British worker.

Victory in the Falklands War did not increase Britain's influence in Washington. Eighteen months later a military junta seized power in the Caribbean island of Grenada, killing the Prime Minister, an event that Washington viewed with alarm. Since Grenada was a member of the Commonwealth, President Reagan consulted with Margaret Thatcher about sending troops in response to a request from the deposed civilian ministers. She 'strongly advised' against doing so. Troops were none the less sent in, and a civilian government restored. Thatcher felt 'dismayed and let down' that her advice had been ignored.[8] Nor did Britain's military victory in the Falklands impress the government of the People's Republic of China. The Thatcher government began negotiations with Beijing about what would happen when Britain's ninety-nine-year lease on Hong Kong expired in 1997. The negotiation was a classic example of the forced management of decline. The pomp and ceremony of the 1997 handover symbolized Britain's past as a world power, and China's future.

Much fell with the Wall

The fall of the Berlin Wall in 1989 and the collapse of the Soviet Union shook the cold war foundations on which prime ministers had based foreign policy since 1945. Margaret Thatcher responded by facing backwards, reflecting beliefs formed before and during the Second World War. Although the Federal Republic's constitution declared a desire for German reunification, Thatcher sought help from Mikhail Gorbachev and George Bush to 'slow up the already heady pace of developments' towards it. In private conversations in London and Washington she made no secret of her anti-German views.[9] When Germany was none the less reunified, President Bush was in the front rank of those congratulating Germany, and President Mitterrand was promoting plans to strengthen French and German links in the European Union. Margaret Thatcher was in the *hundeshütte* (dog house).

The collapse of the Soviet threat to peace in Europe was paralleled by a new generation of policymakers coming forward in Washington, recalculating America's alliances across continents. In the White House, the British Prime Minister must now compete for attention with representatives of emerging new powers in Asia, Africa, Latin America and the Middle East, as well as competing with the German Chancellor in speaking for Europe. When major international issues arise, the pattern is that the Prime Minister supports rather than determines the policy of the President. The 1991 war against Iraq is an example. In response to Iraq's unexpected seizure of Kuwait, President George Bush constructed a diplomatic coalition of many countries around the globe, including Britain. When John Major became Prime Minister, President Bush invited him to Washington to be briefed on American plans.

When Bush told him that military action was likely within a few weeks and asked for his support, 'Major swallowed hard, but he offered his assent.' Bush said he was 'very impressed by his [that is, Major's] total commitment, his "we're with you" attitude'. When military action came, British troops were in action, along with troops from other nations, all under the command of American General Norman Schwarzkopf.[10]

The Kosovo crisis is a more ambiguous example of the special relationship. President Clinton's goal was to act against Serbia with a minimum of risk to American lives and without committing American ground troops in Serbia. While many European countries hesitated to become involved in what was, in international law, a domestic problem of the Former Republic of Yugoslavia, Tony Blair was a hawk in advocating military action. When the bombing campaign did not immediately break the Serb resolve, Blair made a 'gung ho' speech in Chicago endorsing the use of ground troops. However, his policy was shot down in Washington and by European allies. The White House achieved its goal when Belgrade acknowledged the de facto loss of Kosovo without loss of American lives or commitment of American ground troops. The open-ended task of keeping Kosovars and Serbs apart has been left to Britain and European countries.

While Anglo-American relations continue to produce photo-opportunities, the story behind the pictures is very different from that behind meetings of Roosevelt and Churchill. Since the Second World War, American presidents have diversified their repertoire of special relationships. The White House endorses a special relationship with national leaders as diverse as the President of Russia, the German Chancellor, the Mexican President and the Prime Minister of Japan, and each leader has photographs to show this. A British Prime Minister may have more frequent conversations with the President, but decisions are made in Washington not Westminster, for the special relationship is a relationship of unequals. According to one former British diplomat, it verged on 'poodledom' during the Kosovo war.[11]

The view of the Prime Minister from embassies in Mayfair and Knightsbridge is more positive, since most of the ambassadors at the Court of St James represent unpopulous and often poor countries. When senior embassy officials were asked to rate the importance of Britain to their country, those who described it as most important were ex-British colonies. The median ambassador in London sees Britain as one of the five most important countries with which his or her country deals. Britain's membership in the Security Council of the United Nations and its voting strength in the European Union justify a claim to attention – but not to the status of a superpower.[12]

2 Insular politics goes European

Every Prime Minister since Neville Chamberlain has necessarily been involved in European matters, whether seeking to prevent invasion across the English Channel or promoting closer ties between Downing Street and continental countries. But compared to the commitment of neighbouring countries to European integration the involvement has been strictly limited. It has been considered something that is all right for 'them' but not for 'us', because of our special relationship with the United States and the Commonwealth. Churchill's view – 'We are *with* Europe but not *of* it'[13] – has been endorsed by his successors. Contacts between Downing Street and Brussels, Paris and Berlin, are Anglo-European relations.

Joining Europe: goal, defeat or ambiguous destiny?

Britain emerged victorious in the Second World War, whereas France, the Soviet Union and Italy had each been allied with Nazi Germany for part of the war. Postwar British leaders viewed closer ties with continental countries as potentially threatening. Foreign Secretary Ernest Bevin's views were clear in sentiment though mangled in metaphors: 'If you open that Pandora's box, you never know what Trojan 'orses will jump out.' When the French Foreign Minister Robert Schuman set out a plan for the integration of the iron and steel industries of Western Europe in May 1950, the Attlee government refused to join in discussions that would have led to multinational control of newly nationalized British industries. As Herbert Morrison explained, 'The Durham miners will never wear it.'[14] When Schuman Plan partners began discussions that led to the creation of the European Community in 1957, Anthony Eden was equally aloof. In his last speech to a Labour Party conference, Hugh Gaitskell echoed Churchill by invoking Britain's role in three interlocking circles. With an English disregard for the history of the

United Kingdom, Gaitskell warned that joining Europe meant 'the end of Britain as an independent European state. It means the end of a thousand years of history.' Although Gaitskell died in 1963, his arguments remain alive.[15]

For Harold Macmillan, Europe represented an ambiguous destiny. He had seen Europe at its most desperate in the trenches of France during the First World War and in Second World War negotiations in the Mediterranean. Descriptions of Macmillan's job as 'Viceroy of the Mediterranean' were, however, a half-truth, ignoring the dependence of Her Majesty's Government on troops led by General Eisenhower. When the idea of the European Community was broached in 1955, Macmillan sought to avoid rejecting the idea out of hand. However, he showed imperial disdain towards participation in planning meetings, instructing his staff, 'If they ask me, tell them I'm busy with Cyprus.'[16] But by 1961 Macmillan decided that with the Empire dissolving and the American relationship becoming less special, closer links with Europe were preferable to the consequences of remaining outside: 'Of course we shall go on, but we shall be relatively weak, and we shan't find the true strength that we have and ought to have. We shan't be able to exercise it in a world of giants.'[17] President de Gaulle had no wish to have Britain belatedly push its way into the European Community. In January 1963 de Gaulle vetoed Britain's application to join with an impeccably English argument, saying Britain 'is insular, and linked by her trade, her markets and her suppliers to a great variety of countries, many of which are distant'.

Ted Heath is the only Prime Minister of the past half-century who has unambiguously desired Britain to be part of Europe. The stamina and intensity of Heath's commitment shine through his autobiography, *The Course of My Life*.[18] It includes accounts of student visits in the late 1930s to Republican Spain and Nazi Germany and siding with Churchill against Chamberlain's appeasement policy. Heath's photographs show Hitler at a Nuremburg rally; a gutted synagogue in Bavaria; Heath meeting officials of the Republican government in Spain; participating in an Oxford Union debate with the deposed president of Czechoslovakia, Eduard Benes; and gutted German cities in 1945. Heath saw the European Union as an attempt to create something new in place of the disasters that led to the Second World War. Signing the Treaty of Accession in Brussels was for Heath the climax of a lifetime of political commitment.

208 *Managing Decline in a Shrinking World*

Ted Heath in what he called 'the proudest moment of my life', signing Britain's Treaty of Accession to the European Community, 24 January 1972.
Photo: Popperfoto.

To secure Britain's entry to the European Community required negotiations at Westminster as well as abroad. Divisions in the Conservative Party created substantial obstacles on the domestic front. In the key vote on approving membership, Heath had a majority of 112, but thirty-nine Conservative MPs voted against the measure. The votes of sixty-nine Labour MPs and of Liberal MPs were needed to carry the Treaty. Britain joined the European Community on 1 January 1973.

When Heath's successors have been under pressure on European issues, they put domestic politics first. British opinion has been consistently divided on Europe, but not on strict party lines. When the Wilson government presented its cosmetically renegotiated terms for British membership to the House of Commons in April 1975, a big majority of backbench Labour MPs voted against Europe. The median group of Labour ministers, nine, abstained; forty-five voted for continued membership and thirty-eight against. The measure was only approved thanks to Conservative support. The referendum that followed involved cross-party alliances campaigning for and against membership. The lukewarm character of the Labour government's support for Europe is illustrated by Jim Callaghan, then Foreign Secretary, in a BBC radio interview with Robin Day:

Callaghan:	I am not pro, nor am I anti.
Day:	What are you doing on this programme?
Callaghan:	I'm here because you asked me.
Day:	You're here to advise people to vote Yes, aren't you?
Callaghan:	I am here, and the Prime Minister has taken the same line; it is our job to advise the British people on what we think is the right result. Now there are a lot of other people who've always been emotionally committed to the Market. A lot of other people have been, always been, totally opposed to the Market. I don't think the Prime Minister or myself have ever been in either category and that is not our position today. I'm trying to present the facts as I see them and why we have decided in favour of – now Britain is in, we should stay in.[19]

Battling for Britain

For more than a quarter-century since the 1975 referendum, successive prime ministers have had no choice but to be involved in the politics of the European Union on terms laid down by other countries as well as by their Downing Street predecessors. For domestic political consumption, each Prime Minister has claimed to see his or her role as battling for British interests. But this begs the question: 'What are British interests?' It also ignores the strategic question – What is Britain's role in Europe?' – a question that has gained importance as Britain's role has diminished in other circles close to the heart of Downing Street.

Margaret Thatcher approached European Union politics in the same spirit that she approached her Cabinet, as an outspoken British nationalist, proclaiming 'I am a she de Gaulle.' She was sceptical of the good intentions of French and German leaders, especially when they were cooperating. The greatest European achievement of her period in office was the Single Europe Market for more than 370 million customers, removing trade barriers between member-states. Thatcher saw it as 'getting the Community back on course, concentrating on its role as a huge market, with all the opportunities that would bring to our industries'.[20] She believed that the promotion of free trade through the Single Europe Market would leave the sovereignty of Parliament intact.

Unlike Britain, governments of continental countries see the state as having an active and positive role in economic affairs, promulgating regulations to create a social market, a goal shared by social democratic governments and Catholic parties across Europe. The Single Europe Market has given advocates of the social market scope for promoting their views with the argument that a single market requires a level playing field for economic competition, with common EU rules about employment and social security issues that may directly or indirectly influence the stream of European commerce.

When the Prime Minister battles for Britain, he or she risks political capital on two fronts, for the terms of any agreement must be acceptable to other European governments as well as at Westminster. At the EU Maastricht meeting of December 1991, John Major was confronted with European countries seeking to turn the European Community into a European Union in both name and fact. Such moves were anathema to many Conservative ministers and MPs, but a veto of moves towards European integration risked isolating Britain in Europe while other countries cooperated. While Major was unsuccessful in opposing a social chapter of continental-style employment protection policies in the Maastricht Treaty, he secured an opt out clause, so that the social chapter would not apply to Britain, and subsequently secured endorsement of the Maastricht Treaty in the Commons. Major's definition of Britain's national interest was not shared by the Blair government; it has accepted the social chapter of the Maastricht Treaty and put it into force in Britain.

Having seen what European issues did to the Major government, Tony Blair has avoided a clear-cut position on the major European issue facing him, whether or not Britain should join the European Monetary Union. The Prime Minister has declared that this would happen – as and when it is in Britain's national interests, as defined by economic conditions laid down by the Chancellor of the Exchequer, Gordon Brown. Blair repeatedly affirms scepticism about commitments. In what was billed as a 'pro-Europe' speech in Ghent, a site chosen as a symbolic contrast with Margaret Thatcher's anti-European speech at Bruges, Blair asserted it would be inappropriate to offer a vision for Europe as 'the British are too pragmatic to believe in visions'. A *Financial Times* correspondent translated the message as indicating that Blair 'does not care for the EU we have; he does not know what kind of Europe he wants; or if he knows, he does not dare to tell us'.[21]

Blair's hesitancy is consistent with the 'three stage' approach to Europe of his predecessors. The first stage is to take note that European countries are talking about doing something, but to remain aloof and express doubt that anything will ever come of far-fetched ideas of cooperation. Secondly, if a new institution or major policy is adopted, dismiss it as irrelevant or inconsistent with British interests. The third stage is to accept that what was once impossible or irrelevant is now part of the reality of Europe, and that it is in Britain's interest to take the lead in (that is, catch up with) Europe.

3 Turbulence in intermestic politics

The European Union has turned many issues of major concern to Downing Street into intermestic issues, as what is decided in Brussels affects what is decided in Westminster. Interdependence is a two-way street, for the European Union offers the Prime Minister the opportunity to influence the policies of other member-states – but it also offers fourteen other states, plus the European Commission, the opportunity to influence what is decided at Westminster. When there is disagreement between policies decided in Brussels and policy preferences in Westminster, this creates political turbulence, challenging the belief that Westminster is the only arena where decisions can be taken about what happens in Britain.

While the powers of the European Union are limited, they are real within these limits. The European Union is not a state in the conventional sense of the term, for it lacks a military force. Although the expenditure of the European Union is substantial in aggregate, this is because it covers a population almost eight times that of Britain. The total revenue and expenditure of Brussels are a small fraction of the taxing and spending of British government. The power to make regulations and directives that are binding law on member-states is the chief resource of the European Union, and its rules are enforceable by the European Court of Justice. However, the staff of the European Commission in Brussels is not large enough to implement EU regulations; implementation depends on activities of national governments.

The EU's right to make decisions superior in law to acts of Parliament threatens the Prime Minister's political capital, because Parliament and the anti-European media can blame Downing Street for unpopular decisions taken in Brussels. The Prime Minister can point out positive advantages of many features of EU membership, but some policies, such as generous agricultural subsidies, produce more benefits for other countries than for Britain, and regulations about metric measures that are 'non-issues' on the continent force Britons to come to grips with 'new' systems of weights and measures devised at the end of the eighteenth century in France.

Power-sharing as a British problem

The logic of the European Union is that it should do those things that require collective action to achieve goals that national governments cannot achieve on their own. For example, this is the only way to remove pollution in a river system running through several countries. Collective action can also be justified as promoting efficiency; for example, common standards for commercial products avoid fragmenting European markets by creating fifteen different standards for the product of a single manufacturer. As long as the subjects discussed are narrow technical matters of slight public interest, Whitehall officials usually have little difficulty in arriving at a consensus with their opposite numbers in other countries that accommodates British concerns. Difficulties arise when a problem raises the issue: 'How far should the European Union go in promoting joint action to common ends?' Even when a common goal is agreed – for example, promoting the free movement of labour or combating transnational crime – there are disagreements about the best means to agreed ends.

EU meetings are different in kind from the Prime Minister's normal diplomatic discussions, for the EU can make real policy decisions. In a Commonwealth conference, there is no obligation on the Prime Minister or heads of other Commonwealth governments to act on whatever may be recommended. White House meetings between the President and the Prime Minister normally conclude with agreeable words and photographs, but a British Prime Minister cannot commit the American government, nor, for that matter, can the President commit the United States Congress, to anything they jointly endorse. By contrast, EU discussions can arrive at decisions binding in law and enforceable in the courts.

The process by which the European Union arrives at decisions is very un-British. Discussion is often about legalistic or abstract principles that make more sense in French and German than in English or the Mandarin code of Whitehall. No member-state is large enough to dominate the councils of the EU, either formally or informally.

Even after reunification, Germany has less than one-sixth of the membership in the European Parliament, a fifth of the total EU population and the same number of European Commission members as Britain, France, Italy and Spain.

Power-sharing is built into all the institutions of the European Union. Important decisions require a consensus of member-states. Whereas whips at Westminster create majorities by stampeding brute voters, coalition politics is the norm in German federal politics, in smaller European democracies, and in Washington. The introduction of qualified majority voting has reduced the requirement for unanimity, but the 'super-majority' required remains substantially greater than in the House of Commons. The strongest advocates of the European Union are usually frustrated by the delays and infirmities arising in creating consensus through compromise. The use of proportional representation in electing the European Parliament and the plurality of parties across Europe makes it necessary to have a coalition of parties and nationalities to secure a majority there too. There is nothing inherently undemocratic in governing by a consensus that accommodates a diversity of interests.[22]

In the abstract, British prime ministers are just as much in favour of clean rivers and against the internationalization of crime as are their counterparts across Europe. But there is a difference in their understanding of politics. The problem in Anglo-European relations is not the 'dictatorial' threat of Brussels, but the opposite: the threat of power-sharing, a doctrine antithetical to the sovereignty of Parliament. The Prime Minister's authority at Westminster is based on centralizing rather than sharing power. Differences in outlook are illustrated by contrasting uses of the 'f' word, federalism, and the 's' word, subsidiarity. In Europe, and especially Germany, federalism is seen as strengthening democracy by allowing more opportunities to exercise influence at a multiplicity of levels of government. But for a British Prime Minister who has been reducing the scope for debate within Westminster, power-sharing abroad goes against the grain of what happens in Westminster. Similarly, in Europe subsidiarity is understood as keeping responsibility for public policy at the lowest possible tier of government. However, at Westminster, the creation of devolved assemblies in Scotland and Wales has been undertaken without any surrender of the overriding authority of Parliament, and Number Ten insists on having the first and last words on any policy of political consequence for the United Kingdom.

Paying for photo-opportunities abroad

The Prime Minister's meetings with foreign leaders create opportunities for photographs in novel settings around the world. But in a world of intermestic politics, there is no such thing as a free photo-opportunity. Involvement in the European Union has political costs as well as benefits. When benefits fail to materialize or when costs come before benefits, critics of the EU have a field day in taunting ministers to justify accepting unattractive measures. Where national leaders of all parties are committed to the ideal of Europe, costs imposed by Brussels can be justified as the price worth paying to advance the priceless benefits of Europe at peace rather than at war. Among British prime ministers, Ted Heath has been unique in his commitment to Europe as an ideal. Heath's problem is not his idealism but his nationality; Heath's values are more suited to being the Prime Minister of a continental European country.

Exploiting events for short-term political advantage is normal in domestic politics, but not necessarily good politics when this happens at the expense of European governments whose cooperation will be needed another day. Yet prime ministers have a recurring tendency to do so. When Britain took its periodic six-month turn in the presidency of the European Union in 1992, there was a big disequilibrium in the exchange rate between the pound and the Deutsche Mark. At an early September 1992 meeting of finance ministers, Norman Lamont unsuccessfully sought to bully the German *Bundesbank* into altering its interest rates, and compounded the gaffe by telling the British press that he had secured an outstanding victory for British diplomacy. After the markets forced a devaluation of the pound less than two weeks later, Downing Street used leaks and public statements to blame the Germans for the collapse of its policy. The German Chancellor, Helmut Kohl, publicly dismissed these criticisms as 'childishly simplistic'. A former British ambassador to Bonn wrote to *The Times* denouncing 'the sheer professional incompetence' of Downing Street in dealing with a major issue of intermestic policy and politics.[23]

The stage management of Tony Blair's six-months' presidency of the European Union appeared far more professional. But goodwill was lost by Number Ten's blatant attempts to use meetings to project Blair as a victor in battles for British interests. Difficulties erupted just before Britain assumed the presidency at a summit meeting in Luxembourg in December 1997. At issue was Blair's attempt to secure Britain's inclusion as of right in discussions of the 'euro-club' countries belonging to the European Monetary Union (EMU), even though Britain was not a member of it. A television crew caught an ill-prepared and disbelieving Blair being told by the Luxembourg Foreign Minister that members of EMU would not grant his request. The French Prime Minister explained, 'The British should know about clubs; they invented them.' Alastair Campbell pursued a policy that a Viennese newspaper described as, *'Sieg für Blair oder Shut Up'* (Victory for Blair or Shut Up). Another journalist more charitably commented, 'You could say Campbell's rudeness doesn't matter if the guy gave good information, but he actually doesn't know anything.' A diplomat succinctly summed up the Prime Minister's impact on European colleagues in the Council of Ministers, 'Mr. Blair is sometimes seen as an empty nutshell.'[24]

Policymaking is different from setting up photo-opportunities or setting up foreign governments as fall guys in stories in which Downing Street appears victorious. It also requires the Prime Minister to respond to Dean Acheson's challenge: 'What *is* Britain's role in the world today?' From British waters it is possible to sail anywhere in the world – to Australia, to America or to Calais. Old-school prime ministers gave a clear and consistent answer: to be at the centre of the three circles of Empire, Washington and Europe. But two of these circles have been redrawn. Washington now has special relationships with many countries, and Commonwealth countries no longer look to London as the centre of their world. New-style prime ministers have yet to formulate a credible strategy. Margaret Thatcher's view was clear – she wanted other countries to accept policies based on her convictions – but foreigners often did not share her values. Tony Blair's repetition of the mantra 'Globalization, globalization, globalization' reflects his awareness of a need to appear on the world stage. But it tells us nothing about which stage is most important, and whether the Prime Minister will play a leading role, have a walk-on part or be left giving a monologue without an audience.

11

Tony Blair: A Populist Prime Minister

> New Labour is the political arm of none other than the British people as a whole. Our values are the same: the equal worth of all, with no one cast aside; fairness and justice within strong communities.
>
> 1997 Labour Party manifesto

> We can move in and out of the economic cycle with ease.
>
> Tony Blair[1]

Democratic politics is about letting the people decide. An electorate of 43 million people cannot meet in a single place to discuss issues, and the 'people' do not speak spontaneously, nor do they speak clearly with one voice. That is why democratic politics requires representative institutions of government. Elections decide who governs but not what the government of the day does; that is the responsibility of the Prime Minister, Cabinet ministers and Parliament. At elections, parties differ in the policies to which they give priority, the interests they represent, and their past record of achievement, as well as in the personalities of their leaders. Election results show that the British people disagree too. The Parliament elected in 1997 has MPs representing five different British parties plus five Northern Ireland parties.

By contrast with European Union countries, British politics is majoritarian, not consensual. The government of the day does not require a two-thirds vote of the Commons to approve legislation with major constitutional implications; a one-vote margin is enough. The Prime Minister does not have to bargain with coalition partners to secure a majority in the Commons, as is the case in most

European countries. A party does not have to win half the popular vote or even the most votes cast to secure a Commons majority; it simply needs to come first in half the constituencies. The New Labour Party won a big parliamentary majority at the 1997 election, but only three in seven voters endorsed it. Although New Labour won more than 13 million votes, only 0.2 per cent of these votes were cast for the Prime Minister in his constituency. Constitutional practice gives Tony Blair the right to use Labour's parliamentary majority to enact whatever policies he wants. But the division of the popular vote makes it misleading to claim his party is the political arm of the British people as a whole.

Whereas prime ministers from Attlee to Major took it for granted that politics involves differences of opinion about governing the country, Tony Blair explicitly rejects this belief: he seeks to be a populist Prime Minister of all the people. Blair's message to the electorate is inclusive: 'We are on your side. Your concerns are our concerns. Your aspirations are our aspirations.' His polling guru, Philip Gould, has gone further, arguing, 'We must move from third way to one way.'[2] When a veteran Labour supporter challenged Blair with the statement, 'I'm suspicious, I mean, I know *Tories* who are voting for you', Blair proudly replied, 'Well, long may it continue.'[3]

Unlike his predecessors, Tony Blair explicitly questions the traditional idea that Parliament, and especially MPs in the governing party, represent the people.

> The democratic impulse needs to be strengthened by finding new ways to enable citizens to share in decision-making that affects them. For too long a false antithesis has been claimed between 'representative' and 'direct democracy'. The truth is that in a mature society representatives will make better decisions if they take full account of popular opinion.[4]

There is no doubt in the speaker's mind about who is best placed to take account of public opinion. The claim that he is more representative, because Prime Minister of all the people, is a trump card that Blair repeatedly plays.

> An MP's job is to serve his or her constituents. My job is to serve the whole country – those who voted for me, those who didn't, and those who didn't vote at all.[5]

New initiatives such as focus groups or annual reports do not get rid of representation; they simply manage it in a different way. Blair's elaborate communications strategy is a novel means of *managed populism*. The word 'management' is derived from the Latin word for 'hand'. In Tony Blair's Downing Street, there is no doubt whose hands are meant to be on the reins of public opinion. However, just as a horse can take the bit between its teeth and bolt, so public opinion can offer the Prime Minister a rough ride. Blair learned this to his surprise when his speech to the annual general meeting of the Women's Institute in summer 2000 prompted a slow handclap, and protests by motorists and lorry drivers in September of the same year forced the Prime Minister to defend a minority view of petrol taxes.

Inclusive appeals are necessarily vague, for they focus on the limited number of values to which the great majority of British people give assent. The existence of conflicting interests in the economy, the basis of left v. right politics for the past century, is rejected. Nor is there any recognition of the need for tradeoffs between competing goals, such as increasing public expenditure on education and health service or reducing taxation. Nor is there any place for disagreement about the means of policy; the policy to be adopted is the policy that works. Blair's assumption that Numbers Ten and Eleven Downing Street can now manage the economy 'with ease' shows a naive faith in consensual technocratic solutions for enduring problems of public policy.

Vagueness is disabling when hard choices about policy arise. Messages designed to tell the electorate that the Prime Minister is 'on your side' or 'in tune with gut British instincts'[6] fail to tell Whitehall departments what specific policies should be adopted. In default of clear instructions, populist slogans cannot be turned into acts of Parliament. To say that policies should be judged by what works is indiscriminate, for politicians can disagree about whose interests should be served by policies that affect different people differently.

Tony Blair's proclaimed pragmatism actually blunts the cutting edge of policy, because it does not point out the direction in which government ought to go. Nor does it show how government can get there. While Blair's repetition of such mantras as 'Education, education, education' indicates his concern with the subject, it leaves choices unclear, becoming politics without policy.

1 Managing populism

Tony Blair's predecessors, both old-school and new-style, shared a belief in Westminster's institutions of representative government, in which parties competed for votes and party leaders decided public policy. Elections offered citizens a choice between competing interests; there was no pretence that the Labour Party and the Conservative Party represented the same interests. Each party's manifesto told voters what the party intended to do if it gained office. Although most voters never read the manifesto of their party, the government could claim that what was in the manifesto was what the voters wanted. When fresh issues arose, the Prime Minister did not need opinion polls, focus groups or referendums to determine what the people wanted. He or she discussed the problem with Cabinet colleagues and MPs before arriving at a government decision. MPs assumed that the government of the day could 'do any damned thing that it likes' but that the electorate 'must be allowed to feel that they can exercise some control, even if it's only the control of chucking somebody out that they don't like'.[7]

The nearest equivalent to Tony Blair's claim to speak for all the people was Ted Heath's ill-fated proposal for a Government of National Unity after losing his majority in the February 1974 general election. Far from assuming that all voters or parties were agreed on policies, Heath initially saw it as an anti-socialist coalition of Conservatives and of Liberal MPs whose votes were needed to give him a Commons majority. The Liberals rejected the proposal. Heath then broadened the concept to include non-party persons and, if they would cooperate, 'right-thinking' Labour MPs; the government would compromise differences to deal with a national crisis. The Labour Party unreservedly rejected the idea of a 'national' government, and voters did likewise.[8]

Communicating down a one-way street

Old-school Prime Ministers have usually given limited attention to communicating directly with the electorate, let alone attentively tracking public opinion. Tony Blair's strategy is very different. In the words of Peter Mandelson:

A bit of advice offered to us from President Clinton's early period in office has paid off. You need to explain what you are doing, keep describing the big picture, let the public in on the reasons for the tough decisions you are making. The old saying is still apposite. To govern is to choose. But to govern is also to communicate.[9]

Philip Gould has invoked the view of Dick Morris, a chief Clinton adviser, that 'politicians have to win a daily mandate in which strength comes from popularity'.[10] While this argument is meaningful for a President faced with a hostile Republican-controlled Congress, it is not necessary for a British Prime Minister with the biggest parliamentary majority in more than half a century. The largest cluster of staff in Downing Street today concentrate on fighting the battle of the headlines and sound bites, in which you win some but also lose some, rather than preparing legislation that is certain to be endorsed by a vote in the House of Commons.

Communication is about power and influence. An old-fashioned election meeting with hecklers and questions involved two-way communication, in which a speaker had to listen as well as be heard. Managed populism uses modern technology to make communication a one-way street in which Number Ten seeks to control the traffic. It is communication in the primary dictionary definition of the word, transmitting or imparting information. Alastair Campbell pushes this definition to the limits in his hard hitting 'I'm telling you' rhetoric, with its implicit sequel: 'And you had better believe.' The term 'communication' can also refer to sharing information; this is Tony Blair's preferred sense of the term. But given differences in knowledge, resources and status, a 'sharing' of information between the Prime Minister and the electorate is not an exchange. It is a 'soft' form of 'I am telling you', for when Blair shares his thoughts with you, he wants this to make an impression on what you think.

Listening to the people is difficult for the Prime Minister. An old-school Prime Minister could walk about his constituency or dine in a London club. Barriers to communication were social rather than physical. However, new-style prime ministers have political barriers created by a flotilla of staff assistants and, if they 'go public' on a walkabout, there is sure to be a swarm of media people too. The IRA has added security barriers, for in the past two decades there have been more assassination attempts on the Prime Minister than on the President of the United States. At the Labour

Party conference in Brighton in 2000, a special security bridge was built so that the Prime Minister's feet did not touch the ground when he walked from the conference hotel to the conference hall.

If the people ought to decide what the government does, the referendum is a logical means to let voters do so. However, prime ministers have rejected the referendum as inconsistent with the British idea of representative democracy, in which the vote that counts is taken after a full debate in Parliament. The only referendum put to the whole British electorate – the 1975 vote on whether the United Kingdom should remain in the European Community – was called by Harold Wilson because the governing party was divided on the issue. It was not an indication of faith in populist decisionmaking.[11]

Tony Blair has committed himself to holding referendums about the euro and electoral reform before either would become the law of the land. Commitments to 'letting the people decide' enable Blair to avoid taking sides on issues dividing the Labour Party and the public. Since the Prime Minister can hardly avoid taking sides if a referendum is called, Blair has avoided holding any referendum so far. Talk about electoral reform keeps the door ajar for a possible alliance with the Liberal Democrats. A referendum on adopting the euro, in which the Prime Minister could find himself on the losing side, as did his Danish counterpart in September 2000, may never be called.

From a populist perspective, the great disadvantage of any form of referendum is that decisions about whether a vote is called and what the question is are taken by Downing Street to suit the Prime Minister's interests. From Blair's perspective, almost any referendum has the disadvantage that its outcome will show the impossibility of speaking for all the people, since a referendum usually produces substantial votes on opposing sides.

Blair's concern with saying what people want to hear gives focus groups priority over public opinion polls. Opinion polls are still referred to for evidence of the popularity of the Prime Minister and which party leads in the competition for votes. But the chief advantage of polls – the reduction of rambling and discursive popular feelings into precise and reliable statistical measures – does not meet the needs of Blair's communication team. It is looking for symbols and phrases that can project an 'on your side' feeling through a television sound bite or a tabloid newspaper headline. Focus groups, as developed by Philip Gould with the support of

Peter Mandelson and Alastair Campbell, give insights into the feelings and phrases used when ordinary people unfamiliar with the 'in house' vocabulary of Westminster discuss current affairs. Groups can also be used to test market phrases and slogans that Downing Street is considering using, to make sure that they communicate the message that Downing Street wants to convey.

Focus group participants are not a representative sample of the public, nor are they intended to be; they consist of eight people having an informal discussion of topics introduced by a moderator. Focus groups do not let voters decide anything, for people are asked to react to topics rather than to give a simple Yes or No answer to a referendum proposition. Popular reactions are likely to be multiple, disparate, inconsistent and sometimes confused. Moreover, the participants are so few and their composition so non-random that even if a concrete question was put to a group, the result would represent no more than the opinions of fewer than a dozen people spending an evening together.

Philip Gould claims that focus groups 'enable politicians to hear directly the voters' voices', but this is not quite the case.[12] During the 1997 election campaign, the voice that Tony Blair heard nightly was that of Philip Gould telephoning his reactions to a focus group session. Gould continues to report to Blair in Downing Street. His reports contain reactions to themes test-marketed by the moderator, showing, for example, that Blair's invocation of traditional values is seen as 'risible'. Reports contain Gould's judgements about what is happening nationwide: 'I have a sense of government which started with great strength, but has seen that strength ebb away.'[13] There is no statistical basis for generalizations, but quantitative analysis is valued less than suggestions about themes, slogans and symbols that Downing Street can project. Gould brings to his reports specialist skills in public relations, a fervent belief that the New Labour Party needs the support of traditionally non-Labour voters, and the backing of Tony Blair.

The Internet offers opportunities for two-way communication and Downing Street has its own website – http://pm.gov.uk. However, the traffic is heavily in one direction. The site tells visitors a great deal about government, and especially Number Ten, including features about its history; news of activities of the Prime Minister and government business; and summaries of the cut-and-thrust daily media briefings by the Prime Minister's Spokesperson. The interactive potential of the Internet is very carefully managed. When

Blair makes an occasional appearance, questions are selected in advance, and staff are at hand to key in answers, since Blair himself does not type or use the Internet. The website's chat line, where individuals can post comments and questions, is monitored hourly by Downing Street media staff, who immediately remove messages regarded as politically unhelpful.[14]

Television is the best way to reach the largest audience, but it presents problems because Downing Street does not control the networks or interviewers. Downing Street can influence news events and decide which programmes the Prime Minister chooses to appear on and those that are avoided. Television comes in both 'hard' and 'soft' forms. The hardest type is the American presidential debate, with the incumbent and challenger facing each other before a knowledgeable panel of questioners. However, the confrontation and cross-examination central to debate undermine a political leader's claim to speak for all the people. When John Major offered to debate Tony Blair in the 1997 election, Labour negotiators did not accept the offer, so that Blair's views would not be challenged before a mass audience.[15] Contemporary interviewers such as Jeremy Paxman and John Humphrys are confrontational, aggressively barraging their subjects with questions and interruptions. Alastair Campbell and colleagues have denounced programmes such as *The World at One* and *Newsnight* as 'trivia obsessed' and strictly for policy wonks and 'wankers'.

To boost his 'non-political' appeal to all the people, Tony Blair prefers soft television. Whereas Margaret Thatcher welcomed the opportunity of talking about policy even on chat shows, Blair is happy to chat about personal matters, which suits a philosophy of managed populism. As Philip Gould explains, 'Our contract with the British people is as much emotional as it is rational.' When Blair appeared on *This Morning with Richard and Judy*, described by television executives as 'Flopsy Bunny sofa TV', he mingled a discussion of the national health service and Northern Ireland with chat about his wife's swimsuit and the behaviour of his children.[16]

The major print innovation of the Blair government has been its *Annual Report*, setting out *'what it has done; why it is doing it, what it has learned,* and *what it intends to do next.'*[17] In style, the reports are unabashedly populist. There are colour pictures of ordinary people going about everyday routines and of public sector workers issued with disposable cameras to record their activities. Each report includes a coupon inviting readers to write comments on a form that can be posted or e-mailed to the Annual Report Desk in Downing Street. Distribution has been organized through Tesco supermarkets and the W. H. Smith chain, and the cover price of £2.99 is heavily subsidized from public funds. Sales have been disappointing. Of the 100,000 copies printed of the second report, 10,000 were bought by the public, 41,000 by government departments, and nearly half were pulped. The print run for the third report was halved.[18]

The first annual report covered topics such as prosperity, education, health and crime; it discussed the situation the Blair government had inherited from the Conservatives; what had been done in the first year; and what was to be done next. It ended with a list of action on 177 manifesto commitments, claiming that the Blair government had kept fifty commitments; progress had been made on 119 commitments; and only eight had yet to be timetabled for action. Some commitments were not difficult to achieve, such as introducing a budget within two months of the election or appointing a new minister for public health. Other commitments were about abstaining from action; for example, not repealing key trade union reforms brought in by Margaret Thatcher. The second annual report claimed that ninety manifesto commitments had been met; another eighty-five were on course; and only two had yet to be timetabled. The third report dropped the checklist tabulation of progress on manifesto commitments in favour of two-page colour spreads on highlights of the year. In reply to a taunt from William Hague about under-reporting, Tony Blair told the Commons that 104 of the commitments had now been met, seventy-one were on course, and only two had not been timetabled, with further details available on the Internet.[19]

In form each annual report mimics a company report, but it does not do so in content. A company report goes to shareholders who can use it to decide whether to buy or sell shares in the company. The government's report need not meet any accounting standards when describing its achievements. Some 'achievements' are non-events, such as the claim in the 1999 report that the government was supporting Britain's bid to host the 2006 Football World Cup, a bid that failed the following year. The normally restrained journalist Peter Riddell called the third report 'vacuous drivel, a blatant exercise in propaganda' that 'no self-respecting civil servant should have been associated with' and which 'no private-sector company could ever have issued as an annual report'.[20]

Who are we?

Margaret Thatcher divided the electorate and her own government into 'us' and 'them'. The question 'Are you one of us?' was about policy not personality: did the person believe in market principles and policies? If the answer was yes, then you were readily admitted to the company of Thatcherites, whatever your political or social background. But Thatcher recognized that many people did not share her beliefs. She did not attempt to be Prime Minister of all the people, nor did she seek to repress political debate. Like a true non-conformist, Thatcher believed that she could use common-sense arguments to convert people to her beliefs. Those she could not convert, such as 'wet' Cabinet ministers, she disposed of as soon as she had enough political capital to do so.

Tony Blair is very ecumenical; 'we' is the most frequently used word in his speeches.[21] Blair's use of the word is inclusive rather than exclusive. The word 'we' can refer to the British people as a whole, an all-embracing usage that smothers differences of opinion. The parallel with the 'one nation' rhetoric by centrist Conservatives from Rab Butler to Heath is incomplete, for Conservatives spoke of 'one nation' with a sense of the organic unity of a highly differentiated body politic or used it in opposition to divisions between two nations of rich and poor. Another use of 'we' is to refer to the great majority of British people, whom Blair characterizes as sensible, pragmatic, responsible and hardworking. This communitarian 'we' is invoked to justify legislation imposing obligations or penalties on those who shirk their community responsibilities, such as the workshy, football hooligans and lager louts.

'We' also has much narrower uses, as in memorandums to key staff about communication problems (box 11.1). When Blair writes 'We need a strategy', he refers to a handful of Downing Street confidants to whom the memo is addressed. Voters are 'them', people who suffer from 'bizarre' misperceptions about what 'we' are doing in Downing Street. To eradicate misperceptions, Blair recommends that 'we' should 'appear to empathise with public concern and then channel it into the correct course'.

At times the words 'I' and 'we' are used interchangeably. This is communication in the I-am-telling-you sense. For example, in his foreword to the 1997 New Labour manifesto, Blair declared: 'I want a Britain which *we* all feel part of, in whose future *we* all have a

Box 11.1 Tony Blair's approach to touchstone issues

> *(A private memo by the Prime Minister to select Downing Street staff)*
> TOUCHSTONE ISSUES
>
> There are a clutch of issues – seemingly disparate – that are in fact linked. We need a strategy that is almost discrete, focused on them. They are roughly combining 'on your side' issues with toughness and standing up for Britain. They range from the family – where, partly due to MCA (Married Couples Allowance) and gay issues, we are perceived as weak; asylum and crime, where we are perceived as soft; and asserting the nation's interests where, because of the unpopularity of Europe, a constant barrage of small stories beginning to add up on defence and even issues like Zimbabwe, we are seen as insufficiently assertive.
>
> All this, of course, is perception. It is bizarre that any government I lead should be seen as anti-family. We are, in fact, taking very tough measures on asylum and crime. Kosovo should have laid to rest any doubts about our strength in defence. But all these things add up to a sense that the Government – and this even applies to me – are somehow out of touch with gut British instincts. The Martin case – and the lack of any responses from us that appeared to empathise with public concern and then channel it into the correct course – has only heightened this problem.
>
> We need a thoroughly worked-out strategy stretching over several months to regain the initiative in this area.
>
> Each of these issues should be analysed and the correct policy response drawn up. Then each should be dealt with, but with a message which ties it all together. This is precisely the sort of thing AC (Alastair Campbell) and CF (Lord Falconer) should do.
>
> [There follows a canvass of possible measures to improve public perception of the government's handling of issues concerning crime, asylum, arrests and sentencing policy, defence and the family.]
>
> I should be personally associated with as much of this as possible.
>
> TB

Source: A memo dated 29 April 2000 and published in *The Times*, 17 July 2000, under the heading 'We Need Eye-catching Initiatives'.

stake, in which what *I* want for *my* own children *I* want for yours' (italics added). Robert Harris characterizes this outburst of managed populism as 'either breath-taking or sinisterly Orwellian, or both'.[22]

Tony Blair's claim to be Prime Minister of all the people does not produce the end of politics; it is a continuation of politics by other means. Instead of accepting that elections, parliamentary debate and Cabinet discussions involve differences of opinion, Blair seeks to marginalize those whose views disagree with him, since they cannot be speaking for 'all' the people. His response threatens to turn managed populism into repressive populism.

2   Blunting the cutting edge of policy

Politics without policy can take an MP to Number Ten, but it leaves wide open what happens thereafter. Almost a century ago, Graham Wallas cautioned, 'Men feel vaguely that the expedients by which their party is most likely to win may turn out not to be those by which a state is best governed.'[23] When the head of Blair's Policy Unit at Number Ten, David Miliband, speaks of policies in terms of 'stories' that 'keep the core narrative clear',[24] this provides cues to tabloid headlines, but little or no guidance to Whitehall officials actually concerned with what government does. Tony Blair's litmus test for policy, stated in the 1997 New Labour Election Manifesto, is totally non-directive.

> We will be a radical government. But the definition of radicalism will not be that of doctrine, whether of Left or Right, but of achievement. New Labour is a party of ideas and ideals but not of outdated ideology. What counts is what works.

The desire to adopt policies that 'work' is common to every British Prime Minister of the past century.

Policymaking is about discovering and debating what works, and whose interests are served by a choice between workable policies. Larry Summers, head of the United States Treasury, has an apt criterion for evaluating policies – 'If it doesn't have a cutting edge it doesn't have a point' – for every political choice involves differences of opinion. For example, income tax or corporation tax can be raised or lowered, sentences for a given crime may be made longer or shorter, or road charges can be introduced or petrol taxes cut. While all these policies are workable, they are not equally agreeable to everyone. The cutting edge of Thatcherism pointed clearly to policy choices that divided MPs and the electorate. The danger of Tony Blair's managed populism is that he controls not too much policy, but too little, because the cutting edge of policy is blunted by vague rhetoric. A Prime Minister who emphasizes what everyone wants leaves to others the task of figuring out what, if anything, can be done to match words and deeds.

The Third Way: politics without policy

Tony Blair's Third Way can be used to dismiss old-school policies while avoiding commitment to a particular new policy. In the words of the 1997 New Labour manifesto, 'The old Left would have sought state control of industry. The Conservative right is content to leave all to the market. We reject both approaches.' The Third Way differs fundamentally from traditional conflicts between left and right, for it is a confrontation between past and present rather than between Us and Them. From this perspective, the First and the Second Ways are not wrong but simply irrelevant to the twenty-first century. First Way socialist policies promoted by Clement Attlee and Harold Wilson are characterized as just as out of date as travelling to Blackpool by charabanc for a fortnight's holiday. The Second Way, Thatcherite reliance on the market, is rejected as having served its historical purpose of disposing of socialist errors, but no longer being adequate to meet contemporary problems such as social exclusion. If Blair's developmental logic is accepted, the Third Way is the path dictated by historical necessity, the only way to govern today.

Third Way policies are consensual rather than conflictual. In place of battles between the state and market, the 1997 manifesto proposes, 'Government and industry must work together to achieve key objectives aimed at enhancing the dynamism of the market, not undermining it.' 'Agreement' between values is produced by the rhetorical device of endorsing values conventionally seen as opposed. As Blair told the Fabian Society:

> My vision for the 21st century is of a popular politics reconciling themes which in the past have wrongly been regarded as antagonistic – patriotism *and* internationalism; rights *and* responsibilities; the promotion of enterprise *and* the attack on poverty and discrimination.
>
> The Third Way is not an attempt to split the difference between Right and Left. It is about traditional values in a changed world.[25]

'Modernisation'[26] is a criterion, not a policy. It shows a preference for what is new rather than what is old, and for change as against the status quo. But it does not identify what direction change should take. It is possible to modernize by moving in many different directions, and the means of change are likewise varied. However, advocating a specific alternative invites controversy, for each stimulates differences of opinion. Unselfconsciously, Tony Blair invokes the term 'mantra' to describe his goal of 'modernising' government.[27] He does not appear to realize that a mantra is a mystical incantation rather than a plan of action.

Old Left intellectuals dismiss the Third Way because 'what it has to say about contemporary society is often so cloudy it is not much use to practical politicians'.[28] However, the criticism misses the point. In purely political terms, cloudy Third Way rhetoric is useful in so far as it can convincingly demonstrate that First and Second Way principles of social democracy and the market are now irrelevant. But in public policy terms, Third Way rhetoric is empty, offering little guidance about what does work. Civil servants who have been trying for years to find ways to deal with such seemingly intractable problems as the low skills of the British labour force already know what policies do not work. To leave them without instructions invites civil servants and task forces to serve up policies that have been rejected on good grounds before, or that show no evidence of 'working' – unless that term is defined as producing an instant headline.

When focus groups and media interest suggest a popular demand for action, the simplest way to manage populist pressures is to offer a 'micro-wave' policy, that is, a measure that can be served up promptly and attractively, with little attention to what is inside. In the worst case, the policy may be concocted in Downing Street without consulting responsible departments to see whether what works in the headlines will also work in practice. An example is Tony Blair's headline-grabbing suggestion in summer 2000 of 'instant fines for lager louts', a proposal that the police march disorderly and hard-drinking youths to the nearest cash point and make them draw out money to pay on-the-spot fines. The follow-up stories were not what Downing Street expected; they headlined the police and the Home Office dismissing Blair's suggestion as a gimmick that could not work.

When Blair contemplates touchstone issues, he regards 'several months' as ample time to produce a 'thoroughly worked-out strategy' that will regain the initiative on crime (see box 11.1 above). As Blair's leaked memo on Touchstone Issues illustrates, he wants strategies developed by his communications team to change popular perceptions through measures that are 'tough, with immediate bite, and send a message'. Part of the message should be that Blair is 'personally associated with as much of this as possible'. Several months is enough time to prepare and launch a public relations offensive. But it is not enough time to prepare a coherent piece of legislation for the Commons, let alone have it adopted as an act of Parliament. It takes even more time for the effects of an act to have an impact on the perceptions of the public, whether bizarre or otherwise.

Personality fills the gap left by the devaluation of policy. Blair is well aware of this, and so too are his Downing Street staff, for they owe their positions there to personality rather than to appointments by the civil service or the Labour Party. However, when the Prime Minister says 'Trust me', he invites sceptical journalists to examine how trustworthy he is. The professionalization of communications in Blair's Downing Street encourages journalists to write stories about the spin as well as, or instead of, the policies that are being spun. The publicity given to media management contributes to what Philip Gould has told the Prime Minister is a growing perception that Blair is 'pandering, lacking conviction, unable to hold a position for more than a few weeks'.[29]

Policy returns – with a vengeance

In September 2000 Tony Blair's attempt to substitute politics for policy and manage public opinion was challenged in the streets and in the Labour Party annual conference. When the Organization of Petroleum Exporting Countries (OPEC) suddenly pushed up world oil prices, Blair found it was not possible to avoid a conflict between what the British people wanted and what the Treasury would allow. Aggrieved road hauliers, farmers and motorists protested against oil prices being much higher than in the rest of Europe because British petrol taxes claimed so big a slice of the money they spent at the pump – and Blair's government had been pushing up petrol taxes. Protesters called for a cut in petrol tax, and demands were backed up by picketing that stopped most petrol deliveries, producing great queues of the motoring public and anxieties in industry, commerce and public services. Opinion polls showed almost all the people wanted the government to bring down the price of petrol by cutting petrol taxes – but the government was adamantly against this on policy grounds.

Six years of dismissing concerns of old Labour activists with helping the poor produced frustrations that blew up over pensions at the party's annual conference. The 75p inflation-linked increase in Gordon Brown's budget was widely blamed by Labour activists for the loss of core support and seats in the May 2000 local elections. A conference motion to restore the link between pension increases and growth in the national economy, a policy that Labour had supported in Opposition, was carried with the support of major trade unions. Not only were union leaders voting for a policy that they believed in, but by publicly opposing the Prime Minister they were expressing their frustration with the way Blair had snubbed them since he had arrived in Downing Street.

Concurrently, opinion polls shattered Blair's claim to speak for the British people as a whole. They showed the Conservative Party ahead of Labour for the first time since 1992, and more people dissatisfied than satisfied with Tony Blair as Prime Minister. Although not endorsing the demands of the fuel protesters, *The Times* columnist Anatole Kaletsky welcomed the shift in public mood:

> Mr Blair can no longer pretend that the controversial choices he has so long avoided really do not exist – that opposites can always be imperceptibly blended into a Third Way blancmange . . .
> The protesters have forced Mr Blair to become head of government instead of a ceremonial monarch who subcontracts all real decision-making to public relations agents and focus groups.[30]

Fuel tax and pensions are classic issues of policy *and* politics. Since Blair had proclaimed himself an advocate of the interests of voters as 'consumers' of health services, he was even more open to criticisms from voters as consumers of petrol. Critics and defenders of government policy could advance reasoned arguments in favour of their positions. Having been pipped by Blair in the race for Number Ten, the Chancellor of the Exchequer, Gordon Brown, was happy to let the Prime Minister take the heat for policies that he had previously accepted in private.

Tony Blair's response to the challenges of 'Black September' was to switch the argument from policy to personality. Since focus groups have shown that 'toughness' is an admired quality in leaders, Blair appeared tough, and the fact that he was defending policies unpopular with most or all the people countered the impression of Blair being perceived as 'pandering'. Although without respect for doctrines of parliamentary accountability, Blair claimed that making policy by following opinion polls and street protests would be a denial of parliamentary democracy.

232 Tony Blair: A Populist Prime Minister

> The job of a Prime Minister is sometimes to say to people, 'I will do what I can but I can't do everything for you.' At the risk of making people angry or having short-term unpopularity, I have to try and explain to people why it is right that a government cannot come along as a response to a fuel blockage and start dropping fuel duty.[31]

Confronted with criticism from within the Labour Party, Tony Blair sought to heal old hurts in an impassioned annual conference speech that left him sweating profusely, the audience applauding vigorously, and the media full of praise for his 'passionate protests and his confessional style'.[32] In place of the 'tough' touchstone issues that he had stressed in April (see box 11.1), Blair defined his 'irreducible core' in 'caring' terms that could be shared by old Labour activists, juxtaposing his defence of core values with criticisms from the hard right, rather than the old left, so that he could show toughness in response to each Tory demand, saying, 'I can't do it.'

To demonstrate leadership and give substance to core values, Blair identified five 'choices' that he was determined to make. However, three choices were what Americans call 'no brainers', for no politician in his or her right mind would oppose government favouring economic stability, helping employees learn new skills, and making improvements in the health service. A commitment to increasing spending on education as a proportion of the national product does not require any positive government action, for this will happen anyway if the number and percentage of older pupils staying on at school after age 16 increases. 'The fifth choice', Blair declared, was between 'a government that leads in the world or a government that retreats into isolation', a coded reference to the debate on the euro. On this issue, he said, his choice (*sic*) was to keep his options open. In his reactions, Blair was following the public relations maxim of keeping his core narrative clear, with its underlying (Groucho) Marxist personal goal of victory at the next general election.

12

What Comes After Blair?

Are they [the English] not above all nations divided from the rest of the world, insular both in situation and in mind, both for good and for evil?
Walter Bagehot, *The English Constitution*

We might liken England to a ship which, though anchored in European waters, is always ready to sail away.
André Siegfried, *England's Crisis*[1]

The long-term impact of Tony Blair on Downing Street will depend on the circumstances of his departure. A Prime Minister who leaves because of electoral defeat will be immediately discredited and create a reaction against him, and this is also true of a Prime Minister who leaves when colleagues reckon he or she has passed a 'sell by' date. As the youngest Prime Minister since 1801, Tony Blair is unlikely to be forced from office by ill health. The people whose jobs at Number Ten depend on Blair expect him to stay in office well after his fiftieth birthday in 2003. If Blair were to emulate Harold Wilson and retire at the age of 60, he would be leading his party until 2013, almost as long as Clement Attlee did. However, in the past century massive majorities have usually eroded before the governing party could win a third straight election victory, and most prime ministers have left office involuntarily.

Many influences on post-Blair prime ministers will reflect the legacy of Tony Blair's predecessors, and structural developments in the *longue durée*; therefore, much of the legacy left Blair's successors is already evident. The constitutional strengths and limitations of Downing Street will remain in place. The Prime Minister will remain pre-eminent in the world of Westminster, while structural changes in a shrinking world will diminish his or her influence on intermestic policies. Tony Blair has also made significant and irreversible alterations in the new-style Prime Ministership. First, Number Ten now has a far larger political staff than ever before, and the political staff has more authority over civil servants. Such a gain in power is unlikely to be surrendered by Blair's successor. Second, the authority of the Westminster Parliament over all parts of the United Kingdom has been qualified by elected assemblies for Scotland and Wales, an elected mayor for London, and a Northern Ireland government supported by the Republic of Ireland and the White House as well as Westminster. Third, the authority of Westminster is also subject to constraints of the European Convention on Human Rights. Finally, the old ideological battles about the boundaries between state and market have been ended by the adoption of Blatcherite policies.

Institutions are durable; however far one looks ahead, Downing Street will remain the home of a Prime Minister rather than a President. Exuberance on an intercontinental scale has encouraged claims that Downing Street has become the home of the British President. Politicians of the old school rejected out of hand what R. A. Butler once dismissed as 'government à l'Américaine'. Television has made the Prime Minister the centre of British media attention as the President is in Washington. But one similarity does not make an identity.

The political significance of insularity is changing more rapidly than British institutions. England can remain anchored where it was when André Siegfried wrote in 1931, but Europe is on the move. The deepening of the European Union and enlargement down the Danube and along Baltic shores increases the distance between Westminster and political Europe. Yet whatever Tony Blair does (or does not) decide about European Monetary Union, post-Blair prime ministers will be unable to claim that they simultaneously have a big influence in the Commonwealth, Washington and Europe.

Since the impact of Margaret Thatcher has remained more than two decades after she entered Downing Street, the post-Blair legacy should be felt there up to the year 2020. By that time the Maastricht Treaty will be more than a quarter-century old, and the European Central Bank will have passed the twentieth anniversary of its founding.

1 No going back

The uncertainties facing the Prime Minister do not include the possibility of returning to a dimly remembered and artistically retouched 'golden' era. After Blair, the Prime Minister will, as before, continue to juggle politics and policy. However much the Prime Minister dislikes a once-a-week appearance in the House of Commons, he or she cannot ignore this task as long as the Prime Minister is drawn from the House of Commons rather than being directly elected in the American fashion. To ignore Parliament risks loss of confidence and then loss of office. However much the Prime Minister may want to take credit in the media for being tough on crime or generous in health spending, to have any substantial effect political claims must be backed up by policies that are approved by Parliament, financed by the Treasury, administered by Whitehall departments and delivered North of Watford as well as in central London.

Whether Tony Blair's successor is Gordon Brown, William Hague, both of them, or neither, changes in personnel will not reverse the momentum of trends affecting Downing Street. Even though the work of the Prime Minister remains much the same in principle, *how* the Prime Minister goes about these tasks has changed greatly from the days of old-school incumbents. When changes have irreversible causes, there is no going back. Television is not about to stop covering British politics, nor will journalists revert to being deferential, self-effacing figures respecting the privacy of public officials. Even if the electorate gives a 'once in a generation' endorsement of change, this will not be a vote for going back to the austere days of Clement Attlee or the crisis-induced radicalism of Margaret Thatcher. As long as the Prime Minister is successful, the leader of the Opposition has an incentive to mimic him. The character of MPs may alter, but there is no going back to a House of Commons full of backbenchers who regard it as a resting place after years in the trade union movement or as a duty to perform, like being the lord lieutenant of a shire county.

Whatever decisions Tony Blair does or does not take about Europe, the world beyond Dover will have an increasing impact on the intermestic policies that concern the Prime Minister. The British economy will grow slowly but steadily and living standards will rise, with or without generating a sense of material wellbeing in the electorate. However, the British economy cannot evolve into a niche economy such as Norway's or Ireland's, nor can it regain the superpower status it enjoyed when the Bank of England issued gold sovereigns and the Queen's Navy ruled the waves. Within Westminster, the big uncertainty is membership in the European Monetary Union. From a pan-European perspective, this is of limited significance; the big question is the development of the European Union as a whole. If trends to deepen and broaden continue, then Europe will be sailing away from England, and Downing Street will have to find another convoy of countries to join, or pay the costs of remaining anchored while the world moves on.

2 Number Ten is not the White House

Within the world of Westminster, the shift from the old to the new style of Prime Minister is often referred to as 'presidentialization'.[2] The claim is supported by the great media attention given to both the White House and Downing Street. But to rely on television as a guide to government turns political leaders into celebrities. It confuses visibility on chat shows with the authority conferred by constitutional office. Differences between Number Ten and 1600 Pennsylvania Avenue are expressed in constitutional architecture as well as in buildings. There remains an ocean of difference in political institutions between Britain and America. To see whether Number Ten has been or can be 'presidentialized', we need to make careful comparisons. In a shrinking world, the Prime Minister should be compared with the French President too, for the *Palais de l'Elysée* is a constitutional 'halfway' house between Number Ten and the White House, since France has a Parliament and a Prime Minister as well as a President.

One similarity

Television has transformed the media of political communication worldwide, making a country's chief executive the best-known face in politics. Roosevelt, Truman and Johnson were old-school politicians who dealt face-to-face and by telephone with Members of Congress. New-style presidents have used television to go public, projecting their personality and views to a nationwide audience outside the Washington Beltway. In France the first president of the Fifth Republic, General Charles de Gaulle, was of the old school, with a sense of *la gloire* that made him appear grand yet aloof. The break with the past occurred in 1995, when François Mitterrand, who had served in the Vichy regime of France as well as the Third and Fourth Republics, was replaced by Jacques Chirac. Chirac is a president for the television age – and the historic ties between the French state and the broadcasting media give the *Elysée* as many or more opportunities to exploit the medium than Anglo-American counterparts have. The high visibility that all national leaders have gained co-exists with fundamental differences in the institutions by which they govern.

Many differences

The *route to the top* differs radically between Britain, France and the United States. A French president is recruited from the ranks of government insiders, usually high-flying civil servants who are political to the tips of their Gauloises. The launching pad is attendance at the *Ecole Nationale d'Administration* (ENA), a meritocratic postgraduate training school for public administration, which provides its graduates with a network of political contacts more useful for a political career than those of Oxford or Cambridge. A career in a high-prestige ministry such as Finance or Foreign Affairs typically leads to a job as a presidential assistant, then a senior ministerial appointment and sometimes the Prime Ministership, an office incompatible with membership in the French Parliament. An American president, unlike his French and British counterparts, is often a complete outsider to Washington, lacking any prior experience as a Member of Congress or in the executive branch. Since the election of Jimmy Carter in 1976, three out of four presidents have started their Washington careers in the White House, having previously been governors of their state. The paths that led Bill Clinton and Jacques Chirac to the top would have debarred them from reaching Downing Street, where a prerequisite is long-time service in Parliament.

The top job in France and the United States is decided by *direct popular election*. One reason why high-technology campaign

At 1600 Pennsylvania Avenue the White House fills an American-size block.
Photo: Photodisc.

The Prime Minister's official residence in many senses occupies far less ground than the White House.
Photo: PA Photos.

techniques are usually first developed in America and then imported into Britain is that American politicians must devote far more time to electioneering. An ambitious American politician must campaign first in primary elections against other members of his or her party. Learning to 'press the flesh' with hog farmers in Iowa or lumberjacks in New Hampshire is very different from the experience of an aspiring British leader in the House of Commons. By the time an American reaches the White House, he or she has a tight bond with campaign staff – and is distant from the problems that confront a President.

In France primary and presidential choices are combined in a two-stage contest. In the first round half a dozen or more hopefuls compete against each other. If no candidate wins an absolute majority in the first ballot, the two top candidates face each other in a second-round run off election a few weeks later. The victory of a French president is very much a personal one, for winning the second-round ballot requires endorsement of a broad coalition of voters from several parties and none. By contrast, the first election a British politician must win is the endorsement of the party selectorate; at times that is enough to give entry to Downing Street.

Opposition leaders look to *like-minded* winners for tips about how to win themselves. By winning three successive elections, Margaret Thatcher inspired emulation from right-of-centre candidates around the world, and by winning two successive elections Bill Clinton has served as a model for ambitious left-of-centre candidates, including Tony Blair. The relationship between Tony Blair and the White House would be different with a Republican than with a Clinton, just as Clinton was less cordial to John Major than he has been to Tony Blair. The cool relationship between the socialist Prime Minister of France, Lionel Jospin, and Tony Blair is a reminder that in France socialist politicians still lean to the left rather than to the right.

Both the French and the American presidents have the security of a fixed *term of office*; in France the term has been seven years, and in the United States four years. A French president can run for re-election and, if successful as was François Mitterrand, enjoy fourteen consecutive years in office, a record no British Prime Minister has matched since the Earl of Liverpool in the 1820s. An American president who wins re-election can have eight years in office; Margaret Thatcher is unique among post-1945 prime ministers in having served eleven consecutive years in Downing Street. A British

Prime Minister can be turned out of Downing Street unexpectedly during the life of a Parliament – and many have been.

Constitutions are not the stuff of television programmes, but they are critical in determining how much (or how little) power is concentrated in the chief office of government. The American President is constitutionally weakest. The American system of government is federal; fifty state governments and fifty state governors have powers of their own. For example, education is primarily controlled and financed by state and local governments; a president claiming to be an education president has no direct influence on schools or universities. Police powers too are primarily state powers; John F. Kennedy's assassination was handled (or mishandled) by the Dallas police because his murder was an offence under the laws of Texas rather than a federal crime. Both France and the United Kingdom are unitary states. Although each has devolved some powers to regional governments in recent years, the devolution acts of the United Kingdom make explicit that overriding power remains in Westminster.

The separation of powers in the United States introduces *checks* on the President that are absent in Westminster, where leadership of the governing party places control of the executive and legislature in the same hands. The two houses of Congress are directly elected independently of the President; their constituencies and lengths of terms differ from each other and from that of the President. Congress has powers over legislation, the budget, presidential appointees and departments in the President's Cabinet. Members of Congress do not vote their party whip with the regularity of British MPs. When the majority party in Congress is different from that of the President, responsibility for governing is divided between the parties, and this has been the case four-fifths of the time since 1968. The Supreme Court can and sometimes does rule that the President has acted unconstitutionally. While the glamour of the White House impresses foreign visitors, it has less effect on those who work there. President Harry Truman famously defined the job thus: 'I spend all my time trying to convince people to do things that they ought to do anyway.'[3]

The Constitution of the Fifth French Republic is presidential, but not exclusively so. The French President has substantial authority in foreign affairs and national security; decree powers that may be used in an emergency; and a large staff of politically astute civil servants. But there is also a Prime Minister who depends on the confidence of the National Assembly. Because the Assembly is elected for a four-year term, the coalition electing the President can be a minority in the Assembly. If this happens, the President and Prime Minister of different parties must live together in what the French call *cohabitation*. Both Mitterrand and Chirac have experienced such a check on their authority, a check that cannot arise in the British system.

In *domestic policy*, the British Prime Minister is much stronger than an American President. Law is the unique resource of government, and the Prime Minister can expect Parliament to endorse all the government's legislative proposals, an achievement the French President can strive to equal but cannot surpass. An American President has no hope of getting Congress to approve all the bills put to it, and can end up with nothing, as in President Clinton's failure on health care. In so far as the President of France is involved in domestic policy the resources of government are great. French public expenditure, calculated as a percentage of GDP, is a quarter higher than in Britain, and half again higher than in the United States. The French system of taxation is even more centralized than that in Britain, and more than twice as centralized as that in the American federal system. Public employment is a third major resource of government. France has a higher percentage of its labour force in public employment than either Britain or the United States.

Internationally, the President of the United States is without an equal since the collapse of the Soviet Union, and he has much scope for initiatives independent of Congress. America's pre-eminence does not prevent small and large foreign states from defying the White House. While not unlimited, the military power of the United States is far greater than that of any other member of the North Atlantic Treaty Organization (NATO). French Presidents have more constitutional authority in international affairs than the White House, but much less impact internationally. Legally, Britain and France are equal in the EU, but France has more influence in Brussels, as it was a founder state and the French political and administrative ethos permeates the Commission. Moreover, having accepted interdependence as a fact of political life, through collaboration with Germany French leaders have leveraged their influence on EU policies binding on Britain too.

Systematic comparison confirms what picture postcards show: a Georgian house in a side street in Westminster is different from the plantation-style White House and a Paris *Palais* that housed

Box 12.1 The Prime Minister and presidents compared

	Britain	USA	France
Media visibility	High	High	High
Route to top	Parliament	Governor	Civil service
Election	Party	Popular	Popular
Term	Insecure	Fixed: 4 years	Fixed: 7 years
Constitution	Unitary	Federal	Unitary
Checks	Slight, informal	Congress, Supreme Court	Cohabitation
Domestic policy	High	So-so	High
International policy	EU member	Super	EU member

Madame de Pompadour and Napoleon before becoming the home of the French President (box 12.1). On some points of comparison, the British Prime Minister appears stronger than both the American and the French presidents; for example, control of legislation and freedom from divided government. On points such as security of tenure, the Prime Minister is weaker than both. In international affairs, the President of the United States towers above both British and French counterparts. Any attempt to describe the Prime Minister as 'presidential' is misleading, because it allows just one aspect of the office, media visibility, to represent the whole, while ignoring constitutional features that institutionalize fundamental differences between Number Ten and the White House.

What it would take to create a British President

The maxim 'Never say never in politics' is a reminder that what is true of Downing Street at the start of the twenty-first century need not be true by its end. Considering what it would take to turn Number Ten into the home of a British President highlights the current gap between the offices.

The first step would be to reject the monarchy and make Britain a republic, as the authors of the American Constitution did. This would make the Prime Minister head of state as well as head of the government of the day. The fusion of the two offices is technically possible, but that does not make it practical politics. Criticism of the monarchy waxes and wanes, and reform of the monarchy is discussed in the Royal Household as well as in the media, but reforming the monarchy does not imply abolition. Abolishing the monarchy would require assigning the Queen's current duties to another office. If a British Prime Minister campaigned to abolish the monarchy and take on the role of the Queen, this would be likely to increase opposition to the change. Yet to propose that the monarchy be replaced by a head of state chosen by MPs, as the Speaker of the House of Commons is chosen, would be attacked on the grounds that the people should elect whoever holds the highest office of the state. The campaign to turn Australia into a republic stumbled because of these objections.

Democracies that have rejected the monarchy or lack any tradition of royalty normally have a President as their ceremonial head of state. There is a President in eight of the fifteen member-states of the European Union; each also has a Prime Minister accountable to Parliament. In three countries – Germany, Greece and Italy – the President is not popularly elected but chosen by an electoral college in which Members of Parliament have the preponderant say. In Austria, Ireland, Portugal, Finland and France, the President is popularly elected. In Austria and Ireland, the Presidency is usually a resting place for a retired politician or an individual who would never become the effective head of government. The idea of a weak, popularly elected President is inconsistent with the Anglo-American idea of Presidential government. The hybrid French system makes provision for both a strong, popularly elected President and a Prime Minister accountable to a separately elected Parliament. The French system could be grafted on to the existing Westminster system of government, but this would require not only Britain becoming a Republic but also British politicians to accept the risks of *cohabitation*, with all this implies in terms of checks and friction between co-heads of government.

Israel now has a popularly elected Prime Minister. Each Israeli voter receives two ballots, one for the office of Prime Minister and the other for members of the *Knesset* (that is, the Israeli Parliament). The Israeli system requires the Prime Minister-elect to win the endorsement of the *Knesset* for his or her proposed Cabinet. If its endorsement is refused, a new election is held. Since the *Knesset* is elected by an extreme form of proportional representation, coalition government is necessary. This makes life hectic and unstable for the popularly elected Prime Minister, a situation no British leader would welcome.

Any review of the work of presidents and prime ministers in democracies around the world highlights three points.[4] First, there are big differences in the powers of prime ministers. Whoever is in Downing Street is much stronger than a Prime Minister constrained by partners in a coalition government. Secondly, the label 'president' describes offices with very different powers. Thirdly, by the standards of democracies around the world, the British Prime Minister holds a 'strong' office – and much of that strength comes from the fact that he or she is *not* a President, but combines in one pair of hands leadership of Cabinet, Parliament and the party winning a general election. A separately elected Prime Minister and a separately elected House of Commons would create the risk of 'gridlock' in government when the legislature and executive disagree, as often happens in Washington.

3   Adapting to a shrinking world

The sovereignty of the Crown in Parliament is the central doctrine of the British Constitution. Writing at the height of Britain's global power, A. V. Dicey summarized the doctrine in the spirit of Glendower: 'No person or body is recognised by the law of England as having a right to override or set aside the legislation of Parliament.'[5] Such a claim rings hollow in a post-imperial age, yet Dicey's doctrine continues to dominate discussion of the Constitution.[6] While veterans of Westminster know that a Prime Minister's economic policy can be repudiated by turbulence in the international economy, awareness is not the same as acceptance. An outlook that a Treasury official has described as 'a failure to recognize Britain's changed place in the world'[7] has led to the mismanagement of decline.

Living in denial

The world of Westminster still has politicians who echo Glendower's belief that it is possible to call from the deeps a British foreign policy that ignores foreigners. Margaret Thatcher provided a clinical example of denial when confronted by proposals from Jacques Delors, president of the European Commission, for expanding its scope, proposals accepted by every other member-state in the EU. She passionately told the House of Commons, 'No! No! No!'[8]

The illusions of Glendower are fostered by confusion about geography and history. Former Defence Secretary Michael Portillo, who aspires to be a Prime Minister some day, confuses Britain with Iceland when he says, 'Britain stands half way between the Continent and the United States geographically.'[9] When the statement 'Britain's objective situation today is that of a small island off the north-west coast of Europe, with limited resources, a glorious but imprisoning past, and an uncertain future' is offered as a starting point for identifying a role for Britain in the world, it is rejected by prime ministers.[10]

The Glendower approach is fatally flawed because it is a foreign policy without foreigners. Attempts of British prime ministers to cultivate a common Anglo-American view of the world ignore the fact that immigration to the United States is rapidly reducing the proportion of Americans with a European, let alone English-speaking, heritage. American links with Latin America have been greatly increased by immigration, making Spanish a major language in California, Texas, Florida and New York, and immigrants who understand cricket are more likely to come from India or Pakistan than England. Official population projections indicate that in the foreseeable future less than half the population of the United States will have a European heritage, and only a small minority of Americans will have an English heritage.[11]

The collapse of the Soviet threat has encouraged the White House to scan the globe, alert to opportunities and threats from Africa to Siberia. American policymakers no longer see a special relationship with Britain as a high priority. Instead, Washington seeks a one-stop relationship with the member-states of the European Union. The question about Britain's role posed by Dean Acheson has been answered by a former US Ambassador to Britain, Raymond Seitz: 'If Britain's voice is less influential in Paris or Bonn, it is likely to be less influential in Washington.'[12]

In the introverted world of Westminster, British prime ministers can claim powers not acknowledged by foreigners. When the pound was devalued in 1967, Harold Wilson denied the economic logic of devaluation by proclaiming to television viewers that it 'does not mean that the pound here in Britain in your pocket or purse or in your bank has been devalued'. The Major government's devaluation of the pound against the Deutsche Mark in 1992 was a textbook

At a European Union summit the British Prime Minister is only one among a pride of prime ministers.
Photo: PA Photos/EPA.

example of the power of the international over the domestic economy. Yet the Chancellor of the Exchequer, Norman Lamont, claimed that devaluation would produce 'a British economic policy and a British monetary policy'.

Walter Mitty illusions about Britain's international influence are shown by Foreign Secretary Douglas Hurd's claim that Britain's special relations with America, Europe and the Commonwealth allow it 'to punch above its weight in the world'. Whatever its rhetorical appeal, the claim is dangerous if it is challenged by a real heavyweight. The reality of the twenty-first century is that Britain constitutes only 15 per cent of the population of the European Union. If other EU countries maintain faster rates of economic growth in future as in decades past (cf. figure 9.1), Britain's economic significance will lessen. In economic and military terms, Britain is now a middleweight power.

Accepting facts does not tie the hands of the Prime Minister; instead it opens up a multitude of possibilities in a world of interdependence. In military matters, the main choice for Downing Street is whether to rely exclusively on American-led initiatives, as in past decades, or to supplement or complement the American alliance with a European Defence Force focused on trouble spots of particular European concern. In economic affairs, the international acceptance of Anglo-American ideas of a market economy puts pressure for change on the social market economies of the European Union, while the launch of the euro pressures Downing Street to develop a twenty-first century monetary policy, whether or not Britain joins the European Monetary Union. The fall of the Berlin Wall confronts all European Union member-states with major challenges about their relations with each other and with post-Communist states seeking EU membership. There is no agreement among EU member-states about medium-term political objectives; the only consensus is that there ought to be new structures for an enlarging Europe. A post-Blair Prime Minister will have to live with whatever a majority of EU member-states accepts.

A domestic foreign policy

A Downing Street memorandum about touchstone issues of foreign policy is likely to put politics before policy. In a shrinking world, a new-style Prime Minister remains a Marxist in Groucho's sense of thinking first of personal political capital. The result is a domestic foreign policy, giving priority to cheers at Westminster rather than agreements with foreign governments.[13] A domestic foreign policy covers the Prime Minister politically, since it is crafted to secure widespread support in Westminster. But formulating a domestically acceptable policy is only possible if there is popular agreement about Britain's future in a shrinking world.

Public opinion and political parties are divided about Britain's place in the world. When Britons are asked about their identification with other countries, psychological geography triumphs over physical geography and identifications spread over three continents. A total of 29 per cent say they feel closest to Australia or Canada and 23 per cent say they feel closest to the United States. By contrast, 31 per cent say they feel closest to another country in the European Union.[14] These views give greater weight to Britain's past imperial links to English-speaking countries than to current political ties with Europe.

The majority of Britons have abandoned the illusion of Britain being a global superpower. When the Gallup Poll asks about Britain's role, the response is not jingoistic or expansive. Three-fifths consistently say that they would prefer Britain to be a small, rich country like Switzerland or Sweden, outside the mainstream of international affairs.[15] However, the Scandinavian option is not a realistic choice for a United Kingdom that is one of the four biggest countries in Europe. The Scottish National Party can offer this option to five million Scots, but the effective choice for England today is between being a relatively rich or poor big country.

When Britons are asked about the European Union, the median respondent is uninterested, inconsistent or ambivalent. In five elections of Members of the European Parliament, the turnout of British voters has averaged less than 33 per cent, and in 1999 it fell to 24 per cent. The 1975 referendum on continued membership in Europe showed 64.5 per cent in favour, but public opinion has not been stable since. Surveys find the public divided between those in favour of the European Union, those against, some undecided, and some wishing that Britain had never joined but accepting that Britain will not withdraw from the European Union.

The Prime Minister can make a domestically acceptable response to a divided public by issuing a vague call for a European policy that puts British interests 'first, second and last', as Tony Blair has done.[16] However, this call may be ignored by representatives of fourteen other countries in the 'vasty deep' of the European Union. Six prime ministers have attended more than one hundred EU summit meetings, yet even when agreements are reached on points of detail, the British Prime Minister is often not there in spirit. It is a case of being in the same bed with different dreams.

Making policies with foreigners

There is always a case for the status quo: the fact that it is there. Tony Blair fought the 1997 election with a carefully balanced manifesto endorsing Europe as 'an alliance of independent nations choosing to cooperate to achieve the goals they cannot achieve alone. We oppose a European federal superstate.' Blair's view of Europe *à la carte* has been shared by all prime ministers since Harold Wilson replaced Ted Heath. It is a 'pick and mix' strategy of adopting EU measures that are viewed positively in British politics, and avoiding those that are unpopular at Westminster. The cumulative effect divides the European Union into two groups: countries that consistently accept policies endorsed by a large majority of EU member-states, and countries that sometimes opt in and sometimes opt out. By choice, Britain is in the latter group, which constitutes the outer circle of the European Union, with less than a fifth of its population. In a world of interdependence, avoiding participation in EU policies is not the same as avoiding their impact.

The trouble with relying on the status quo is that Europe is not static. Structural change sometimes proceeds incrementally and sometimes by fits and starts; both have the effect of increasing integration. In selected areas, Downing Street accepts the logic of change; Tony Blair's government, for example, is promoting the strengthening of European defence forces and the admission of up to a dozen member-states from Eastern and Southern Europe.

To achieve Tony Blair's proclaimed goal of seeing Britain 'at the heart of Europe' requires a foreign policy that appeals to foreigners as well as Britons. Because the future of the EU is an intensely political issue, there are competing ideas about what should and should not be done. Differences between and within continental countries offer Downing Street a choice of allies. But a choice requires the Prime Minister to enter a coalition with foreign leaders to advance both their interests and British interests, however defined. Coalition politics come naturally to prime ministers realistic enough to see they need allies in order to form a majority in a union of many countries. But coalition politics is not Westminster winner-take-all politics; it offers something, but not everything, for everyone. In Europe compromise is regarded not as evidence of weakness but as showing that leaders of national governments combine policy and politics.

As long as Britain chooses to remain outside the European Monetary Union (EMU), responsible for a common currency, the euro, any claim by the Prime Minister to be at the heart of Europe is a denial of reality. Britain is not alone in being in the outer circle on this issue: Denmark and Sweden are also outside the EMU. To join the inner circle of EMU members, Britain must first satisfy two EU conditions. Meeting macroeconomic criteria for monetary stability is not a problem; Britain has done so longer than the economies of some current EMU members. The British government must also accept the *acquis communitaire*, that is, the rules and regulations already in place in making EMU policy. New members of European institutions cannot negotiate new rules but must accept what has already been established. The use of a French phrase to describe agreed procedures is not an accident, for the *acquis* is not based on Westminster assumptions about how European institutions ought to be run.

The Prime Minister must also be satisfied that domestic political conditions are right. Divisions are already visible within Tony Blair's Cabinet, as Robin Cook and Peter Mandelson make pro-euro noises and Gordon Brown scowls at their attempts to pre-empt the Chancellor's prerogative to decide whether the economic conditions for entry are suitable. A decision by the Prime Minister to hold a referendum on the euro raises one certain problem and an even greater contingent risk. The certain problem is that it would shatter Tony Blair's claim to be leader of all the people. Divisions among MPs cut across party lines. In a referendum campaign the advocates of 'Save the Pound' will argue that the sovereignty of the Mace is endangered by adopting the euro, and doing so will make it impossible to put Britain's interests first at all times, as Blair has promised. The contingent risk is the ultimate disaster of managed populism, the electorate rejecting the Prime Minister's recommendation, as happened in the Danish referendum of 28 September 2000.

As long as anti-euro voters substantially outnumber Yes voters in the opinion polls and anti-euro voters feel more strongly about the issue, the Prime Minister must anticipate a substantial No vote or even defeat. As a private memorandum to Blair from American pollster Stanley Greenberg and Philip Gould emphasizes, 'one will never create anything like a national consensus on the euro'. Few voters are attracted by the argument that joining the euro would give the Prime Minister a big voice in world affairs, and there are many popular political arguments against joining EMU: a loss of British national identity, a loss of national independence, and higher taxes. Blair's pollsters have told him, 'When we marshall the opponents' and proponents' best arguments, the former win.'[17] Given such advice, a prudent Prime Minister would prefer to maintain Hamlet-like indecision indefinitely rather than invite defeat in a popular vote.

In a memorandum on 'Standing up for Britain' Tony Blair declared, 'On the euro, we need to be firmer, more certain, clearer.' However, his statement was not made in a public effort to mobilize a Yes vote for the euro; it was in a private document that only leaked months after it was written. Blair's hesitation is understandable, given the unwelcome prospect of bruising debates and the risk of defeat raised by his pollsters. For the moment, Blair's policy on Europe is like the view of chastity of St Augustine of Hippo: he is in favour of it – but not yet.

Doing nothing is always an option. Old-school prime ministers often pursued this strategy. Since both old-school and new-style prime ministers have stood outside Europe for half a century, Tony Blair and his successors may hesitate for many years to come. But hesitation about Britain's role in a shrinking world prompts the question: whose side is time on?

Appendix A

Prime Ministers since 1945

Clement Attlee, Labour, 26 July 1945–26 October 1951
Born Putney, London, 1883. Educated at Haileybury; Oxford, history, 2nd class. In the First World War in action in France and Gallipoli, retired as major.

Qualified as a barrister, 1905. Joined Fabian Society, 1908. A social worker at Toynbee Hall, in the East End of London, 1910. Lord Mayor of Stepney, 1919–20. Lectured in social administration at the London School of Economics, 1913–23.

MP: Limehouse, Stepney, 1922–50; West Walthamstow, 1950–5. Parliamentary Private Secretary to Leader of the Opposition, Ramsay MacDonald, 1922–4. Under-Secretary of State for War, 1924. Member of the India Statutory Commission, 1927. Chancellor of the Duchy of Lancaster, 1930–1. Postmaster-General, 1931. Deputy Leader of the Opposition, 1931–5.

Elected Leader of the Labour Party on second ballot, defeating Herbert Morrison and Arthur Greenwood, 3 December 1935. In wartime Coalition of Winston Churchill, served as a member of the inner War Cabinet, and Lord Privy Seal, 1940–2, Secretary for Dominions, 1942–5, and Lord President of Council, 1943–5; designated Deputy Prime Minister in 1943. Prime Minister, 1945–51, and served as Minister of Defence, 1945–6. Leader of Opposition, 1951–5.

In four general elections as leader, won two, 1945 and 1950, and lost two. After the 1955 election he retired to the House of Lords as the 1st Earl Attlee. Died 1967.

Autobiography: *As It Happened*, 1954. Francis Williams, *A Prime Minister Remembers*, 1961. Kenneth Harris, *Attlee*, 1982.

Winston Churchill, Conservative, 10 May 1940–26 July 1945; 26 October 1951–5 April 1955

Born Blenheim Palace, Oxfordshire, 1874. Educated at Harrow, Royal Military College, Sandhurst. Army officer, 1895–8, in India and Egypt. Then war correspondent and author, captured in Boer War; army officer in France, 1916.

MP: (Con) Oldham 1900–04; (Lib) NW Manchester, 1906–8, Dundee, 1908–22; (Constitutionalist, then Con), Epping, 1924–45; Woodford, 1945–64. Under-Secretary, Colonial Office, 1905–8; President of Board of Trade, 1908–10; Home Secretary, 1910–11; First Lord of the Admiralty, 1911–15; Chancellor of Duchy of Lancaster, 1915; Minister of Munitions, 1917–19; Secretary for War and Air, 1919–21; Secretary for Air and Colonies, 1921; Colonial Secretary, 1921–2; Chancellor of Exchequer, 1924–9. Breaks with Conservative leadership and out of office until First Lord of Admiralty, 1939–40.

Became Prime Minister as leader of a Coalition government with Labour and Liberal parties, 1940, and also became Minister of Defence. Became Conservative Party leader five months later following resignation of Neville Chamberlain. Wartime Coalition broke up after the end of the war in Europe. Prime Minister of a caretaker Conservative government, May–July 1945. Then leader of Conservative Opposition. Lost two and won one election.

Became Prime Minister a second time in 1951, and served for one year as Minister of Defence too. Suffered stroke and health deteriorated. Resigned at the age of 80 in April 1955. Remained an MP until 1964. Died 1965.

Churchill's writings were very extensive, and often autobiographical; he received the Nobel Prize for Literature. His *War Memoirs* were published 1948–54 in six volumes. The official biography, *Winston S. Churchill*, by his son, Randolph Churchill, succeeded by Martin Gilbert, is in eight volumes, 1966–88. On the wartime Prime Minister, see J. Wheeler-Bennett, ed., *Action This Day: Working with Churchill*, 1968.

Anthony Eden, Conservative, 6 April 1955–9 January 1957

Born Windlestone Hall, Bishop Auckland, 1897. Educated at Eton; Oxford, Oriental languages, 1st class. Served in First World War, 1915–19, as Major, MC.

MP: Warwick and Leamington, 1923–57. Parliamentary Private Secretary to the Foreign Secretary, 1926–9; Under-Secretary,

Foreign Office, 1931–3; Lord Privy Seal, 1933–5; Minister for League of Nations Affairs, 1935. Foreign Secretary, 1935–8; resigned, 20 February 1938, in protest at appeasement. Secretary of State for War, 1939–40; Dominions Secretary, 1939–40; Foreign Secretary, 1940–5. Leader of House of Commons, 1942–5. Foreign Secretary, 1951–5.

On the retirement of Winston Churchill in 1955, the uncontested heir apparent as Prime Minister and Conservative Party leader. Led party to victory in the 1955 general election. Announced Suez War on 29 October 1956 and cessation of hostilities on 6 November. On 9 November forced to go to Jamaica for three weeks to recover health. Resigned in failure on 9 January 1957 and left House of Commons. Created an earl, 1961. Died 1977.

Autobiographical: *Another World, 1897–1917*, 1976; *Facing the Dictators, 1923–38*, 1965; *The Reckoning, 1939–1945*, 1960; *Full Circle, 1951–57*, 1976. D. Carlton, *Anthony Eden: A Biography*, 1981. R. R. James, *Anthony Eden*, 1986.

Harold Macmillan, Conservative, 10 January 1957–18 October 1963
Born, London SW1, 1894. Educated at Eton; Oxford, classics, 1st class. Active service as officer in France, 1914–18, wounded three times. Entered family publishing business in 1920 and remained active in it for most of his time in Parliament.

MP: Stockton-on-Tees, 1924–9, 1931–45; Bromley, 1945–64. A critic of appeasement; first entered government in May 1940 as Parliamentary Secretary, Ministry of Supply, 1940–2; Parliamentary Under-Secretary, Colonies, 1942; Minister Resident, Allied Headquarters North Africa, 1942–5; Minister for Housing and Local Government, 1951–4; Minister of Defence, 1954–5; Foreign Secretary, April-December 1955; Chancellor of the Exchequer, 1955–7.

Unexpectedly emerged as Conservative Prime Minister in 1957 instead of R. A. Butler, on resignation of Anthony Eden. Led party to victory at the 1959 general election. Under pressure from colleagues to resign, and did so when hospitalized during the 1963 Conservative Party conference. Became Earl of Stockton in 1984. Died 1986.

Autobiography: *Winds of Change*, 1966; *The Blast of War*, 1967; *Tides of Fortune*, 1969; *Riding the Storm*, 1971; *Pointing the Way*, 1972; *At the End of the Day*, 1973. A. Horne, *Macmillan: The Official Biography*, 2 vols, 1988, 1989.

Alec Douglas-Home, Conservative, 19 October 1963–16 October 1964

Born Mayfair, London, 1903. Educated at Eton; Oxford, history, 3rd class. As the elder son of 13th Earl of Home, a landowner in Scotland, he was known as Lord Dunglass from 1918 to 1951 and was the 14th Earl of Home from 1951 to 1963. After retiring from the Commons in 1974, he was given a life peerage, Lord Home of the Hirsel.

MP: South Lanark, 1931–45; Lanark, 1950–1; Kinross and W Perthshire, 1963–74. Parliamentary Private Secretary to the Prime Minister, Neville Chamberlain, 1937–40. Diagnosed as having tuberculosis and invalid, 1940–3. Under-Secretary, Foreign Office, 1945. Minister of State, Scottish Office, 1951–5. Secretary, Commonwealth Relations, 1955–60; Deputy Leader of Lords, 1956–7, and Leader, 1957–60; Lord President of Council, 1957, 1959–60. Foreign Secretary, 1960–3, 1970–4.

Unexpectedly and controversially emerged as Conservative Prime Minister on Macmillan's retirement in 1963 and disclaimed peerage. Led party to defeat in the 1964 election and, after introducing rules for the election of party leader by Conservative MPs, resigned as leader in 1965, remaining active in Commons and government until 1974, when he retired to the House of Lords. Died 1995.

Autobiography: *The Way the Wind Blows*, 1978. D. R. Thorpe, *Alec Douglas-Home*, 1996.

Harold Wilson, Labour, 16 October 1964–19 June 1970; 4 March 1974–5 April 1976

Born Huddersfield, 1916. Educated at Wirral Grammar School; Oxford, philosophy, politics and economics, 1st class. Oxford fellow in economics, 1937. Wartime civil servant in War Cabinet secretariat and various ministries, 1940–5.

MP: Ormskirk, 1945–50; Huyton, 1950–83. Parliamentary Secretary, Ministry of Works, 1945–7; Secretary for Overseas Trade, 1947; at age 31, President of Board of Trade, 1947–51; resigned with Aneurin Bevan in 1951.

Stood for Leader of the Labour Party in 1960 against Hugh Gaitskell, and was defeated. Elected Leader of the Labour Party, 1963, on second ballot, defeating George Brown and Jim Callaghan. Prime Minister, 1964–70; and again, 1974–6, when he announced his surprise retirement at age 60. Became a life peer in 1983.

In five general elections as Leader, won four, 1964, 1966, February 1974, and October 1974; and lost one, 1970.

Autobiographical: *The Labour Government, 1964–70: A Personal Record*, 1976; *Final Term: The Labour Government 1974–76*, 1981; *Memoirs: The Making of a Prime Minister, 1916–64*, 1986; *The Governance of Britain*, 1977. Ben Pimlott, *Harold Wilson*, 1992. P. Ziegler, *Wilson: The Authorised Life*, 1993.

Edward Heath, Conservative, 19 June 1970–4 March 1974

Born, St Peters, Kent, 1916. Educated at Chatham House Grammar School, Ramsgate; Oxford, philosophy, politics and economics, 2nd class. Active as an anti-appeasement Conservative at Oxford. Military service in Europe, 1940–6, major, mentioned in despatches and MBE for services in postwar occupation forces. Briefly a civil servant after the war.

MP: Bexley, 1950–74; Sidcup, 1974–83; Old Bexley and Sidcup, 1983–. Whip, 1951–5, Chief Whip, 1955–9; Minister of Labour, 1959–60; Lord Privy Seal and responsible for negotiations on entry to European Community, 1960–3; Secretary for Trade and Industry, 1963–4.

First elected Conservative Party leader in 1965, defeating Reginald Maudling and Enoch Powell. Prime Minister, 1970–4. Conservative Party defeated in 1966 election. Led party to victory in 1970. Called 'Who governs' election for February 1974 in midst of miners' strike. Lost majority in Commons and resigned when unable to secure Liberal Party support. Defeated in October 1974 election. Challenged for the leadership by Margaret Thatcher in February 1975, and withdrew from contest after finishing second to her.

Remained in the Commons for a quarter-century after leaving Downing Street.

Autobiography: *The Course of My Life*, 1998. J. Campbell, *Edward Heath*, 1993.

Jim Callaghan, Labour, 5 April 1976–4 May 1979

Born Portsmouth, 1912. Educated at Portsmouth Northern Secondary School. Took Senior School Leaving Certificate and became a clerk in the Inland Revenue, where he was active in trade union affairs. In 1936 became assistant secretary of the Inland Revenue Staff Federation. Royal Navy, 1940–5.

MP: Cardiff South, 1945–50; Cardiff South-East, 1950–79; Cardiff South and Penarth, 1983–7. Parliamentary Secretary, Ministry of

Transport, 1947–50; Parliamentary Secretary and Financial Secretary, Admiralty, 1950–1. Chancellor of Exchequer, 1964–7; Home Secretary, 1967–70, including responsibility for Northern Ireland; Foreign Secretary, 1974–6.

In 1963 stood for leadership of the Labour Party, and finished third in the initial ballot. In 1976 elected Leader on the third ballot against M. Foot. Labour government defeated at the 1979 general election. Resigned leadership in November 1980. Given a life peerage in 1987.

Autobiography: *Time and Chance*, 1987. See also *A House Divided: The Dilemma of Northern Ireland*, 1975. K. O. Morgan, *Callaghan: A Life*, 1997.

Margaret Thatcher, Conservative, 4 May 1979–28 November 1990
Born Grantham, 1925. Educated at Kesteven and Grantham Girl's School; Oxford, chemistry, 2nd class. Employed as a research chemist, 1947–51. Married Dennis Thatcher, 1951. Qualified as a barrister in 1954.

MP: unsuccessfully contested Dartford at the 1950 and 1951 elections as Margaret Roberts. MP for Finchley, 1959–92. Parliamentary Secretary, Pensions and National Insurance, 1961–4; Secretary for Education and Science, 1970–4.

Elected leader of the Conservative Party against Edward Heath on 11 February 1975. When challenged for the leadership in 1989, won 314 votes against 33 for relatively unknown opponent and 27 abstentions. When Michael Heseltine challenged the leadership in 1990, she won a majority of votes but fell just short of the margin required for victory. Stood down after being told by Cabinet ministers she had lost their support. Given a life peerage in 1992.

Autobiography: *The Downing Street Years*, 1993; *The Path to Power*, 1995. An exceptionally large number of books have been written about Thatcher and Thatcherism, from radically different political positions and knowledge. Serious critical biographies include: Peter Jenkins, *Mrs Thatcher's Revolution*, 1987; Hugo Young, *One of Us*, 1991 edition.

John Major, Conservative, 28 November 1990–2 May 1997
Born Carshalton, Surrey, 1943. Educated at Rutlish Grammar School, Wimbledon. After leaving school in 1959 without any qualifications took a series of labouring jobs and unemployed; then employed in banks until elected MP. Lambeth Councillor, 1968–71.

MP: unsuccessfully contested St Pancras North, both 1974 elections. MP Huntingdonshire, 1979–. Whip, 1983–5; Social Security: Under-Secretary, 1985–6, Minister of State, 1986–7; Chief Whip, 1987–9; Foreign Secretary, 1989; Chancellor of Exchequer, 1989–90.

In 1990 contested the leadership of the Conservative Party on the second ballot, and defeated Michael Heseltine and Douglas Hurd. Resigned and stood for re-election while Prime Minister, defeating John Redwood. Fought two elections as Leader, winning in 1992 and losing in 1997, and resigning as party leader.

Autobiography: *John Major: The Autobiography*, 1999. Anthony Seldon, *Major: A Political Life*, 1997.

Tony Blair, New Labour, 2 May 1997–
Born, Glasgow, 1953. Educated, Fettes College; Oxford, law, 2nd class. Barrister, 1976.

MP: Unsuccessfully contested Beaconsfield by-election, 1982; elected Sedgfield, 1983 by-election. Opposition front bench spokesperson on various topics, 1984–94.

Elected Leader of the Labour Party, 21 July 1994, on first ballot, defeating John Prescott and Margaret Beckett.

Publications about Tony Blair are numerous and increasing; perspectives differ according to the time of publication and the author. For a start, see: Tony Blair, *New Britain: My Vision of a Young Country*, 1996; *The Third Way: New Politics for the New Century*, 1998. P. Mandelson and R. Liddle, *The Blair Revolution: Can New Labour Deliver?*, 1996. D. Draper, *Blair's Hundred Days*, 1997. P. Gould, *The Unfinished Revolution*, 1998. N. Fairclough, *New Labour, New Language?*, 2000. Andrew Rawnsley, *Servants of the People*, 2000.

Appendix B

A Guide to Further Reading

Since footnotes have been kept to a minimum in this book, the following paragraphs highlight book-length studies that offer perspectives on the changing job of the Prime Minister.

ROLES AND STAFF

J. M. Lee, G. W. Jones and June Burnham, *At the Centre of Whitehall*, 1998. Dennis Kavanagh and Anthony Seldon, *The Powers behind the Prime Minister*, 2000. http://www.pm.gov.uk

MEDIA

Michael Cockerell, *Live from Number Ten*, 1988. Jay Blumler and M. Gurevitch, *The Crisis of Public Communication*, 1995. Peter Oborne, *Alastair Campbell: New Labour and the Rise of the Media Class*, 1999. N. Fairclough, *New Labour, New Language?*, 2000.

PARTIES AND ELECTIONS

Alan Watkins, *The Road to Number 10: From Bonar Law to Tony Blair*, 1998. Peter Riddell, *Honest Opportunism*, 1993. Pippa Norris, *Electoral Change in Britain since 1945*, 1997. www.mori.com.

Parliament, Cabinet and Whitehall

S. A. Walkland, ed., *The House of Commons in the Twentieth Century*, 1979. Simon James, *British Cabinet Government*, 2nd edn, 1999. P. Hennessy, *Whitehall*, 1989. Harold Wilson, *The Governance of Britain*, 1976. Richard Rose and P. Davies, *Inheritance in Public Policy: Change without Choice in Britain*, 1994. R. A. W. Rhodes and P. Dunleavy, eds, *Prime Minister, Cabinet and Core Executive*, 1995. M. J. Smith, *The Core Executive in Britain*, 1999. http://www.gov.uk. http://www.parliament.uk/commons.

Comparative analyses

Richard Rose and E. Suleiman, eds, *Presidents and Prime Ministers*, 1980. Richard Rose, *The Postmodern President*, 1991. George W. Jones, ed., *West European Prime Ministers*, 1991. M. Foley, *The Rise of the British Presidency*, 2nd edn, 2000.

Reference

D. Butler and G. Butler, *Twentieth-Century British Political Facts, 1900–2000*, 8th edn, 2000. D. Englefield, J. Seaton and I. White, *Facts about the British Prime Ministers*, 1995. J. Hayward, B. Barry and A. Brown, eds, *The British Study of Politics in the Twentieth Century*, 1999. Charles Arnold-Baker, *The Companion to British History*, 1996.

Notes

Introduction: The Paradox of Power

1 Walter Bagehot, *The English Constitution*. 1st edn, 1867; Tony Blair, an interview with Peter Riddell and Philip Webster, *The Times*, 2 September 1999.
2 Wilson was quoting Lord Rosebery's study of Sir Robert Peel, published in 1899. See Harold Wilson, *The Governance of Britain*. London: Sphere Books, 1977, p. 21.
3 Clement Attlee, *As It Happened*. New York: Viking Press, 1954, p. 20.
4 An interview on BBC TV 1, 20 October 1993.
5 David Smith, 'The Medicine that Never Works', *Sunday Times*, 30 July 2000.
6 Quoted in Paul Mosley, *The Making of Economic Policy*. Brighton: Wheatsheaf, 1984, p. 44.
7 See Norman Fairclough, *New Labour, New Language?*. London: Routledge, 2000, p. 18.

1 Looking after Number One at Number Ten

1 Cf. Walter Bagehot, *The English Constitution*. 1st edn, 1867, and John Morley, *Life of Walpole*. London: Macmillan, 1889.
2 R. H. S. Crossman, 'Introduction'. Bagehot, *The English Constitution*, p. 51.
3 Cf. Michael Foley, *The Rise of the British Presidency*. Manchester: Manchester University Press, 2nd ed., 2000, and chapter 11 below.
4 See Richard Rose, *Understanding the United Kingdom*. London: Longman, 1982, chapter 7, 'The Mace and the Maze'. Those participating in the maze have since been described as the core executive. See R. A. W.

Rhodes and Patrick Dunleavy, eds, *Prime Minister, Cabinet and Core Executive*. London: Macmillan, 1995.
5 Peter Jenkins, *The Battle of Downing Street*. London: Charles Knight, 1970, p. 163.
6 Quoted in Robert T. McKenzie, *British Political Parties*. London: Heinemann, 1955, p. 328.
7 A whip, quoted in Philip Norton, *Conservative Dissidents: Dissent within the Parliamentary Conservative Party 1970–74*. London: Temple Smith, 1978, p. 71.
8 Quoted in Richard Rose, *Do Parties Make a Difference?*. London: Macmillan, 2nd edn, 1984, p. 4.
9 The Earl of Oxford and Asquith, *Fifty Years of Parliament*. London: Cassell, 1926, vol. II, p. 185.
10 Peter Hennessy, 'The Accretion of History'. In P. Day, D. M. Fox, R. Maxwell and E. Scrivens, eds, *The State, Politics and Health: Essays for Rudolf Klein*. Oxford: Blackwell, 1996, pp. 117–21.
11 *Presidential Power*, p. vii.
12 Kirsty Milne, 'The Court of the Sun King', *Sunday Herald* (Glasgow), 7 February 1999.
13 William Armstrong, quoted in Michael Wolff, 'The Power of the Prime Minister: Should He Pick Up the Ball and Run With It?', *The Times*, 24 May 1976.
14 'The Prime Minister's Day, the Daily Diary of Wilson and Callaghan', 1974–7. *Contemporary Record*, 5, 2 (1988), p. 17.
15 For details, see D. E. Butler, *The British General Election of 1951*. London: Macmillan, 1952, pp. 112ff.
16 Cf. Ian Jacobs, quoted in John Wheeler-Bennett, ed., *Action This Day: Working with Churchill*. London: Macmillan, 1968, p. 191, and a story on the Queen's Speech by Robert Peston in the *Financial Times*, 25 November 1998.
17 See David Butler and Gareth Butler, *Twentieth Century British Political Facts, 1900–2000*. London: Macmillan, 8th edn, 2000, pp. 316ff.
18 James Callaghan, *Time and Chance*. London: Collins, 1987, p. 412. It remains to be seen to what extent Tony Blair's mantra, 'Education, education, education', meets a similar fate.
19 Quotes from Tony Blair's memorandum on 'Touchstone Issues', leaked in *The Times*, 17 July 2000, and reproduced at length in box 11.1.

2 Glendower in a Shrinking World

1 Tony Benn, 'The Case for a Constitutional Premiership', *Parliamentary Affairs*, 33, 1 (1980), pp. 7–22; Lord Hailsham, 'Elective Dictatorship: The Richard Dimbleby Lecture', *Listener*, 21 October 1976. Peter Hennessy, *The Prime Minister*. London: Allen Lane/Penguin Press, 2000.

2   Peter Hennessy, *The Blair Cabinet: A Question of Command and Control?*. London: Public Management Foundation Paper No. 2, 1999, p. 10.
3   Douglas Hurd, *An End to Promises*. London: Collins, 1979, p. 32. Hurd adds, 'It is hard to imagine anyone governing anything from Number Ten.'
4   The term 'chocolate soldiers' refers to the fact that the first political advisers were funded by a trust established by Joseph Rowntree, whose money came from making chocolates.
5   K. C. Wheare, *Government by Committee*. Oxford: Clarendon Press, 1955, p. 27. A more direct way of making the point is to say that civil servants in Downing Street are bisexuals posing as asexuals, being ready to serve either party while posing as having no party political involvement.
6   See Bernard Donoughue, *Prime Minister: The Conduct of Policy under Harold Wilson and James Callaghan*. London: Jonathan Cape, 1987; and Dennis Kavanagh and Anthony Seldon, *The Powers Behind the Prime Minister*. London: HarperCollins, 2000.
7   Cf. Robert Peston, 'Prime Minister Gives Cabinet a Corporate Kick', *Financial Times*, 29 July 1998. See also Performance and Innovation Unit, *Wiring It Up: Whitehall's Management of Cross-Cutting Policies and Services*. London: Stationery Office, 2000.
8   Kavanagh and Seldon, *The Powers Behind the Prime Minister*, p. x.
9   Jill Sherman, 'Backbenchers Urge Ministers to Behave', *The Times*, 14 January 1999.
10 Eleanor Mills, 'Smug? Call Her Quietly Triumphal', *Sunday Times*, 24 January 1999. For an example of entourage warfare at work, see Andrew Rawnsley, *Servants of the People*. London: Hamish Hamilton, 2000.
11 James Blitz, 'PM attacks Blair over Scotland', *Financial Times*, 5 April 1997.
12 The title of a book by David Butler, Andrew Adonis and Tony Travers. Oxford: Oxford University Press, 1994.
13 See Richard N. Gardner, *Sterling–Dollar Diplomacy*. New York: McGraw-Hill, 1969 edn, rev. and expanded, p. xvii and 266n. Gardner, an American academic, lawyer and diplomat, noted in his 1969 preface, 'the sense of a virtual Anglo-American monopoly in the shaping of world economic policy is a thing of the past'.
14 House of Commons, *Debates*, 12 November 1956.
15 See the report of John Major's statement to an inquiry team on mad cow disease, reported as 'Food Safety', *Financial Times*, 7 May 1999.
16 Percy Cradock, *In Pursuit of British Interests*. London: John Murray, 1997.

3 WHAT MAKES DOWNING STREET CHANGE?

1 Quoted in the *Guardian*, 21 April 1963.
2 Quoted in David Marquand, *Must Labour Win?*. Swindon: Economic and Social Research Council, 1998, p. 8. Of Blair's neophilia, Marquand, a former Labour and SDP MP, notes, 'Its attractions are obvious. It enables New Labour to airbrush its past.'
3 Donald Shell, 'The Office of Prime Minister'. In D. Shell and R. Hodder-Williams, eds, *From Churchill to Major: The British Prime Ministership since 1945*. London: Hurst, 1995, p. 6.
4 Lord Blake, *The Office of Prime Minister*. London: British Academy and Oxford University Press, 1975, pp. 23, 45ff.
5 Hugh Cecil, *Conservatism*. London: Williams and Norgate, c.1912, p. 243.
6 Roy Jenkins, 'Home Thoughts from Abroad', *Listener*, 29 November 1979.
7 David Butler and Michael Pinto-Duschinsky, *The British General Election of 1970*. London: Macmillan, 1971, p. 62.
8 'Listening Mode in Ulster', *The Economist*, 22 April 2000.
9 See Peter Oborne, *Alastair Campbell: New Labour and the Rise of the Media Class*. London: Aurum Press, 1999, pp. 70, 103.
10 Max Weber, *The Theory of Social and Economic Organization*. Glencoe, Ill: Free Press, 1947, pp. 61ff.
11 John Colville, in J. Wheeler-Bennett, ed., *Action This Day: Working with Churchill*. London: Macmillan, 1968, p. 119.
12 See William Nordhaus, 'The Political Business Cycle', *Review of Economic Studies*, 42 (1975), pp. 169–90.
13 Robert T. McKenzie, *British Political Parties*. London: Heinemann, 1955.
14 For details, see R. B. McCallum and Alison Readman, *The British General Election of 1945*. London: Oxford University Press, 1947, pp. 142ff.
15 J. Patten, *Things to Come: The Tories in the 21st Century*. London: Sinclair-Stevenson, 1995, p. 2.
16 The youthful aspirant succeeded in making the Commons and Cabinet and is now a respected member of the House of Lords.
17 David Butler and Richard Rose, *The British General Election of 1959*. London: Macmillan, 1960, p. 130.
18 Robin Young, 'For the 25th Time, This Is the Worst Week', *The Times*, 8 July 2000. By the end of the month, Blair had at least one more week of leaks so bad that the *Sunday Times* headlined its account of 23 July, 'Drowning Street'.
19 Cited in Antony Jay, *The Oxford Dictionary of Political Quotations*. Oxford: Oxford University Press, 1996, p. 245.
20 A letter of 17 November 1935, quoted in Jay, *The Oxford Dictionary of Political Quotations*, p. 29.

21 For details, see Richard Rose and Philip L. Davies, *Inheritance in Public Policy: Change without Choice in Britain*. London: Yale University Press, 1994, p. 120.

4 Becoming and Remaining Party Leader

1. In a review of a biography of Enoch Powell, captioned, 'Were We Well Rid of Him?', *Sunday Times*, 22 November 1998.
2. For statistical details, see Michael Rush, 'Career Patterns in British Politics', *Parliamentary Affairs*, 47 (1994), pp. 68–84.
3. See Alan Watkins, *The Road to Number 10*. London: Duckworth, 1998, pp. 274–6.
4. Quoted in Peter Riddell, *Honest Opportunism*. London: Hamish Hamilton, 1993, p. 1.
5. Quoted in the *Independent*, 29 July 1988.
6. See Ben Pimlott, *Harold Wilson*. London: HarperCollins, 1992, pp. 674ff.
7. Matthew Parris, 'Sleep on it, Tony', *The Times*, 3 April 1999.
8. Harold Wilson, *The Governance of Britain*. London: Sphere Books, 1977, p. 53.

5 From Private to Public Government

1. Quoted in Michael Cockerell, *Live from Number Ten*. London: Faber and Faber, 1988, p. 23.
2. Martin Gilbert, *Never Despair, 1945–65*, vol. 8 in the *Life* of Churchill, 1988.
3. Sir William Haley, 'Parliamentary Institutions and Broadcasting', *Parliamentary Affairs*, 2, 2 (1949), p. 112.
4. A generation ago a party official who sought to break free of this constraint by publishing a memoir called *Heroes and a Valet* abandoned the project when the party threatened to withdraw his pension.
5. Quoted in Adam Sherwin, 'Death of Robin Day, Courteous Inquisitor', *The Times*, 8 August 2000.
6. Quoted from an interview with Dick Morris by Tim Hames, 'Spin? You Need More, says US King of Strategists', *The Times*, 29 July 2000.
7. While the practices of 'spin doctors' are old, the term is a 1990s import from the United States, and its use is relatively recent there, sometimes in the mock-German form *spinmeister*; it means one who concocts or makes up stories. The term does not appear in William Safire's compendious *Safire's Political Dictionary*. New York: Ballantine Books, 1980.

8 The statement was made during a trial under the Official Secrets Act in 1970. See Anthony Sampson, *The New Anatomy of Britain*. London: Hodder and Stoughton, 1971, p. 369.
9 Peter Hennessy, *Cabinet*. Oxford: Blackwell, 1986, p. 1.
10 Cmnd 4089. London: Her Majesty's Stationery Office, 1969, p. 6.
11 House of Commons, *Hansard*, 31 October 1956, vol. 558, cols 1452–4, and 1 November 1956, cols 1620ff.
12 At trial in Sydney, Australia, 18 November 1986. The phrase can be traced back to Edmund Burke.
13 W. J. M. Mackenzie, 'The Plowden Report: A Translation', initially appearing in the *Guardian*, and reprinted in R. Rose, ed., *Policy-Making in Britain: A Reader in Government*. London: Macmillan, 1969, p. 274.
14 See Diana Farr, *Five at 10*. London: André Deutsch, 1985, pp. 25ff, and Ben Pimlott, *Harold Wilson*. London: HarperCollins, 1992, p. 522f.
15 Tom Burns, 'Public Service and Private World', in *The Sociology of Mass Media Communications*. Keele: Sociological Review Monograph No. 13, 1969, p. 71. On the priestly role, see Jay Blumler and Michael Gurevitch, *The Crisis of Public Communication*. London: Routledge, 1995, p. 50.
16 Blumler and Gurevitch, *The Crisis of Public Communication*, p. 186.
17 H. G. Nicholas, *The British General Election of 1950*. London: Macmillan, 1951, p. 126.
18 Quoted by John Lloyd in 'The Ferret', *New Statesman and Nation*, 30 January 1987, p. 12. See also Robert Harris, *Good and Faithful Servant: The Unauthorized Biography of Bernard Ingham*. London: Faber and Faber, 1990.
19 Trevor Lloyd-Hughes, 'Is Blair the New Wilson?', *The Times*, 23, February 2000.
20 James Margach, *The Abuse of Power*. London: Star Books, 1979, pp. 145ff. See also Pimlott, *Harold Wilson*, pp. 443ff.
21 This anecdote was related to me by Robert T. McKenzie. On Reith, see Cockerell, *Live from Number Ten*, p. 25.
22 See Richard Rose, 'British Government: The Job at the Top'. In R. Rose and E. Suleiman, eds, *Presidents and Prime Ministers*. Washington DC: American Enterprise Institute, 1980, table 1.6.
23 Social democratic critics seized on the comment, and Downing Street issued, on plain paper, a semi-official explanation of what the Prime Minister meant. Cf. Margaret Thatcher, *The Downing Street Years*. London: HarperCollins, 1993, p. 626.
24 Comments by Gillian Shephard, previewing her book, *Shephard's Watch*. London: Politico's, 2000.
25 'The Labour Campaign'. In I. Crewe and M. Harrop, eds, *Political Communications*. Cambridge: Cambridge University Press, 1989, p. 53.

26 See Peter Oborne, *Alastair Campbell: New Labour and the Rise of the Media Class*. London: Aurum Press, 1999, pp. 100ff.
27 Campbell, describing his dual role in Select Committee on Public Administration, *The Government Information and Communication Service: Minutes of Evidence*. London: Stationery Office, HC 770, 1998, p. 58.
28 *The Government Information and Communication Service*. London: Stationery Office, HC 770, 1998, p. 60.
29 Oborne, *Alastair Campbell*, p. 2.
30 A remark made in a BBC television profile of Campbell by Michael Cockerell, screened on 15 July 2000.
31 *The Government Information and Communication Service*, p. 57.
32 A remark in Michael Cockerell's BBC TV profile of Campbell.
33 Quoted in Bill Hagerty, 'More Spinned Against?', *The Times*, 12 June 2000.
34 See Simon Hoggart, 'Blair's Bleepers Keep It Clean', *Guardian*, 7 May 1998.
35 See both Campbell's view and that of victims, expressed in *The Government Information and Communication Service*, and the account of Romola Christopherson, 'Arise Campbell, the Real Deputy Prime Minister', *Sunday Times*, 10 January 1999.
36 Roland Watson, 'Prescott Puts Left-wing Ideals Centre-stage', *The Times*, 31 December 1998. For Campbell's carefully phrased distancing of himself from personal involvement in briefing against ministers, see *Minutes of Evidence*, HC 770, 23 June 1998, p. 56. For Ingham's admission and regret that he had criticized Cabinet ministers, see ibid., p. 3.
37 D. E. Butler and Dennis Kavanagh, *The British General Election of 1997*. London: Macmillan, 1997, pp. 179, 183. The statement shows how the Blair team cultivated the *Sun*, not how voters behaved. Independent research shows that the *Sun* did not make the difference in Labour's victory. See Pippa Norris, J. Curtice, D. Sanders, M. Scammell and H. A. Semetko, *On Message: Communicating the Campaign*. London: Sage, 1999, pp. 183ff.
38 See Jay G. Blumler, M. Gurevitch and T. J. Nossiter, 'Struggles for Meaningful Election Communication'. In I. Crewe and B. Gosschalk, eds, *Political Communications: The General Election Campaign of 1992*. Cambridge: Cambridge University Press, 1995, pp. 65–84.
39 Alastair Campbell, 'A Man More Spinned against than Spinning', *The Times*, 31 January 2000.
40 Christopher Dunkley, 'Which Way to Middle England?', *Financial Times*, 14 June 2000.
41 David Butler, 'Reflections on British Elections and their Study'. In N. W. Polsby, ed., *Annual Review of Political Science*. Palo Alto, CA:

Annual Reviews, vol. 1 (1998), p. 461. See also Norris et al., *On Message: Communicating the Campaign*, table 5.4.
42 Cockerell, *Live from Number Ten*, p. 53.
43 Cf. Blumler et al., 'Struggles for Meaningful Election Communication', p. 77, and Norris et al., *On Message: Communicating the Campaign*, p. 128; William L. Miller, H. D. Clarke, M. Harrop, L. LeDuc and P. F. Whiteley, *How Voters Change*. Oxford: Clarendon Press, 1990, pp. 176, 208.

6 Winning Elections

1 Graham Wallas, *Human Nature in Politics*. London: Constable, 1948 edn, p. 83.
2 D. E. Butler and Richard Rose, *The British General Election of 1959*. London: Macmillan, 1960, pp. 32–3.
3 See David Butler and Donald Stokes, *Political Change in Britain*. London: Macmillan, 2nd edn, 1974, p. 227.
4 See Russell Dalton, *Citizen Politics: Public Opinion and Political Parties in Advanced Western Democracies*. Chatham, NJ: Chatham House, 2nd edn, 1996, pp. 21–7.
5 See Ivor Crewe and Katarina Thomson, 'Party Loyalties: Dealignment or Realignment?'. In G. Evans and P. Norris, eds, *Critical Elections*. London: Sage, 1999, table 4.2.
6 See Pippa Norris, *Electoral Change in Britain since 1945*. Oxford: Blackwell, 1997, table 5.3.
7 See illustrations in Butler and Rose, *The British General Election of 1959*, facing p. 136, and Richard Rose, *Influencing Voters*. London: Faber and Faber, 1967, facing p. 120.
8 See Mark Abrams and Richard Rose, *Must Labour Lose?*. Harmondsworth: Penguin, 1960.
9 Statistically, a least squares regression trend line shows a very poor fit with actual Gallup Poll ratings. See Richard Rose, 'A Crisis of Confidence in British Party Leaders?', *Contemporary Record*, 98, 2 (1995), p. 280.
10 See Ivor Crewe and Anthony King, 'Did Major Win? Did Kinnock Lose?'. In A. Heath, R. Jowell and J. Curtice, eds, *Labour's Last Chance? The 1992 Election and Beyond*. Aldershot: Dartmouth, 1994, table 8.10.
11 See Ivor Crewe and Anthony King, 'Are British Elections Becoming More "Presidential"?'. In M. K. Jennings and T. Mann, eds, *Elections at Home and Abroad*. Ann Arbor: University of Michigan Press, 1994, pp. 181–206; and Richard Rose and Ian McAllister, *The Loyalties of Voters*. London: Sage, 1990, ch. 9.
12 See Rose, 'A Crisis of Confidence in British Party Leaders?', p. 290.

7 Managing Parliament and Party

1. William Armstrong, *The Role and Character of the Civil Service*. London: Oxford University Press and the British Academy, 1970, p. 15.
2. 'Mandarin Power', *Sunday Times*, 10 July 1973.
3. Kingsley Martin, *Harold Laski*. London: Gollancz, 1953, p. 182.
4. J. Martin, contribution to J. Wheeler-Bennett, ed., *Action This Day: Working with Churchill*. London: Macmillan, 1968, p. 152. 'When any really important event took place, he was always insistent that "the Parl" should be told at once.' Lord Bridges, quoted in ibid., p. 229.
5. Marcia Williams, *Inside Number Ten*. London: Weidenfeld and Nicolson, 1972, p. 78.
6. See Ed MacGregor and Richard Cracknell, *MPs' Participation in Commons Divisions 1999–2000*. London: Social and General Statistics Section, House of Commons Library, 7 July 2000, p. 24.
7. See Richard Rose, 'British Government: The Job at the Top'. In R. Rose and E. Suleiman, eds, *Presidents and Prime Ministers*. Washington DC: American Enterprise Institute, 1980, table 1.5.
8. Data from George W. Jones, 'Presidentialization in a Parliamentary System?', table 9, updated by June Burnham and George W. Jones.
9. See Jones, 'Presidentialization in a Parliamentary System?', p. 121.
10. A number of examples in subsequent paragraphs are taken from June Burnham and George W. Jones, 'Accounting to Parliament by British Prime Ministers: Trends and Discontinuities; Illusions and Realities'. London: Political Studies Association Annual Conference, April 2000.
11. Quoted in R. L. Borthwick, 'Prime Minister and Parliament'. In D. Shell and R. Hodder-Williams, eds, *From Churchill to Major: The British Prime Ministership since 1945*. London: Hurst, 1995, pp. 88ff.
12. See Maurice Chittenden, 'Blair Raises Art of Non-answer to New Heights', *Sunday Times*, 1 February 1998.
13. Jill Sherman, 'Labour Spinning Out of Control', *The Times*, 9 April 1998; David Wighton, 'Blair Rebukes Short over "Toadying" Jibe', *Financial Times*, 14 April 1998.
14. Peter Oborne, *Alastair Campbell: New Labour and the Rise of the Media Class*. London: Aurum Press, 1999, p. 159.
15. See *House of Commons Debates*, vol. 558, cols 1452–4 (31 October 1956) and cols 1620ff (1 November 1956).
16. Downing Street told *The Times* that the use of the word 'war' was a slip of the tongue, a locution leaving open whether the word was accurate. The Foreign Office described the term as a mistake: 'We are not at war. In order for us to be at war, it would require a formal declaration by at least one side, and probably both. Legally, there have been no wars since 1945.' See James Landale, 'Blair Lets Slip the Words of War', *The Times*, 20 May 1999.

17 James Landale, 'Speaker Censures Labour's Media Bias', *The Times*, 6 April 2000.
18 Quoted by Peter Riddell, 'Does Anybody Listen to MPs?', *The Times*, 23 March 1998.
19 Richard Rose, 'Still the Era of Party Government', *Parliamentary Affairs*, 36, 3 (1983), pp. 282–99.
20 See Richard Rose, *Do Parties Make a Difference?*. London: Macmillan, 2nd edn, 1984, ch. 5.
21 Rose, 'Still the Era of Party Government', pp. 288ff. Philip Cowley and Mark Stuart, 'The Parliamentary Labour Party: Daleks or Deviants?', *Politics Review*, 9, 4 (2000), pp. 6–9.
22 Jones, 'Presidentialization in a Parliamentary System', p. 125.
23 Quoted in a news story in *The Times*, 5 March 1967.
24 'Blair Stirs Faithful with Past and Future', *The Times*, 28 February 2000.
25 House of Commons *Debates* (3 March 1999), col. 1075.
26 Carefully straddling the dividing line between old and new, Wilson added, 'You don't have to be a fundamentalist in your religious approach to say that Genesis is part of the Bible.' Remarks made in a radio broadcast reprinted in the *Listener*, 29 October 1964.
27 For evidence over the postwar period, see Samuel Brittan, *Left or Right: The Bogus Dilemma*. London: Secker and Warburg, 1968; Elinor Scarbrough, *Political Ideology and Voting*. Oxford: Clarendon Press, 1984; Richard Rose and Ian McAllister, *The Loyalties of Voters*. London: Sage, 1990, p. 22, ch. 5; and John Blundell and Brian Gosschalk, *Beyond Left and Right: The New Politics of Britain*. London: Institute of Economic Affairs Working Paper No. 1, 1997.
28 For detailed evidence, see Rose, *Do Parties Make a Difference?*.
29 The term was coined by the *Economist*, 13 February 1954.
30 Robert Harris, 'The Centre that Blair Cannot Hold', *Sunday Times*, 6 April 1997.
31 Margaret Thatcher, *The Downing Street Years*. London: HarperCollins, 1993, pp. 7, 10.
32 See Philip Gould, *The Unfinished Revolution*. London: Little, Brown, 1998, pp. 161ff.
33 See Robert Taylor, 'Chattering Against Mr Blair', *Spectator*, 19 April 1997.
34 For details of the classification of manifestos, see Ian Budge, 'Party Policy and Ideology: Reversing the 1950s?'. In G. Evans and P. Norris, eds, *Critical Elections*. London: Sage, 1999, pp. 4ff.
35 Derek Draper, *Blair's Hundred Days*. London: Faber and Faber, 1997.
36 Robert Harris, 'Blair's Glory Ride on the Beast He Hates', *Sunday Times*, 15 November 1998. In an appearance before a Commons select committee, Peter Riddell has referred to Blair's supporters as 'a kind of

Leninist vanguard'. *The Government Information and Communication Service*. London: Stationery Office, HC 770, 1998, p. 23.
37 In an interview with Donald Macintyre, 'How We All Fought to End Labour's Political Corruption', *Independent*, 10 September 1998.
38 See Tom Baldwin and Philip Webster, 'Nothing New as Labour Quietly Drops Old Label', *The Times*, 18 May 2000.
39 House of Commons *Debates*, 12 January 2000, col. 273. Although the *Oxford English Dictionary* seeks to keep up to date with new words, its year 2000 edition had no entry for 'Blairism'. When a journalist inquired about this, a spokesman for the *Dictionary* explained that to receive an entry, 'It will first have to pass the test of time.' See 'Observer Column', *Financial Times*, 11 August 2000.

8 Managing Colleagues and Bastards

1 Walter Bagehot, *The English Constitution*. London: Oxford University Press World's Classics edn, 1955, p. 12n.
2 'Mandarin Power', *Sunday Times*, 10 June 1973.
3 Quoted in Douglas Hurd, *An End to Promises*. London: Collins, 1979, p. 148.
4 Cf. John Major, *The Autobiography*. London: HarperCollins, 1999; Norman Lamont, *In Office*. London: HarperCollins, 1999.
5 The statistic on briefs was given by Wilson in his farewell speech as Prime Minister, reported in *The Times*, 17 March 1976.
6 James Callaghan, *Time and Chance*. London: Collins, 1987, p. 403.
7 Edward Heath, *The Course of My Life*. London: Hodder and Stoughton, 1998, pp. 750f.
8 Quoted in Ferdinand Mount, 'Don't Blame Blair, He's Done Nothing', *Sunday Times*, 11 July 1999.
9 David Hunt, *On the Spot: An Ambassador Remembers*. London: Peter Davies, 1975, pp. 52f.
10 Quoted in Colin Campbell and Graham Wilson, *The End of Whitehall*. Oxford: Blackwell, 1995, p. 45.
11 See Michael Rush, 'The Members of Parliament'. In S. A. Walkland, ed., *The House of Commons in the Twentieth Century*. Oxford: Clarendon Press, 1979, p. 92; and 'Career Patterns in British Politics'. In F. F. Ridley and M. Rush, *British Government and Politics since 1945*. Oxford: Oxford University Press, 1995, p. 81.
12 Margaret Thatcher, *The Downing Street Years*. London: HarperCollins, 1993, pp. 150ff.
13 Michael Prescott, 'Goodbye Peter, Hello a Whole New Ball Game', *Sunday Times*, 3 January 1999.

14 Francis Williams, *A Prime Minister Remembers*. London: Heinemann, 1961, p. 81.
15 Thatcher, *The Downing Street Years*, p. 418.
16 Nigel Lawson, speaking in a symposium, 'Cabinet Government in the Thatcher Years', *Contemporary Record*, 8, 3 (1994), p. 440.
17 Patrick Gordon Walker, *The Cabinet: Political Authority in Britain*. New York: Basic Books, 1970, p. 90.
18 Thatcher, *The Downing Street Years*, p. 188.
19 Lawson, 'Cabinet Government', pp. 442f.
20 For details, see Anthony Barker, Iain Byrne and Anjuli Veall, *Ruling by Task Force*. London: Politico's, 2000.
21 Williams, *A Prime Minister Remembers*, p. 81.
22 Peter Hennessy, *Muddling Through*. London: Indigo, 1997, p. 285.
23 Kenneth Harris, 'Interview with Margaret Thatcher', *Observer*, 25 February 1979.
24 Percy Cradock, *In Pursuit of British Interests*. London: John Murray, 1997, p. 23.
25 Published in 'Quote, Unquote', *Sunday Times*, 4 March 1995.
26 Thatcher, *The Downing Street Years*, p. 722.
27 Text of a talk, 'Co-ordinating Government Policy', to the University of Birmingham Conference on Modernising the Policy Process, 16 September 1997, p. 2.
28 See Linda McDougall, 'Blair's Fallen Star', *The Times*, 5 May 2000, and Julia Langdon, *Mo Mowlam: The Biography*, London: Little, Brown, 2000.
29 Peter Oborne, *Alastair Campbell: New Labour and the Rise of the Media Class*. London: Aurum Press, 1999, p. 5.
30 Brian Groom, 'Blair Brokers Euro Truce to Counter Memo Fallout', *Financial Times*, 28 July 2000.

9 Running – and Running After – the Economy

1 Quoted in the *Sunday Times*, 3 May 1981.
2 Quoted in Peter Hennessy, *Muddling Through*. London: Indigo, 1997, p. 282.
3 Quoted in Philip Stephens, 'Unhappy Anniversary', *Financial Times*, 17 September 1997.
4 See Lord McCarthy, 'The Politics of Incomes Policy'. In D. Butler and A. H. Halsey, eds, *Policy and Politics: Essays in Honour of Norman Chester*. London: Macmillan, 1978, pp. 183ff.
5 Text of Blair's Mais Lecture, as printed in the *Financial Times* under the headline, 'Labour's Long Haul to Control Spending', 23 May 1995.
6 *The Government's Annual Report 97/98*. London: Stationery Office, Cm. 3969.

7 Tony Blair and Gerhard Schröder, *Europe: The Third Way/Die Neue Mitte*. London and Bonn: Labour Party/Social Democratic Party, 1998, p. 5.
8 To control for fluctuating exchange rates, all calculations are based on purchasing power parity adjusted figures. See R. Summers and A. Heston, 'A New Set of International Comparisons of Real Product and Price Levels Estimates for 130 Countries, 1950–1985', *Review of Income and Wealth*, 34, 1 (1988), pp. 1–25; OECD, *OECD in Figures*. Paris: supplement to *OECD Observer* No. 217/218, July, 1999, pp. 12–13.
9 Quoted from a speech to the Economics Club of New York, 14 April 1965.
10 Marcia Williams, *Inside Number Ten*. London: Weidenfeld and Nicolson, 1972, p. 144.
11 Quoted from Kathleen Burk and Alec Cairncross, *'Goodbye Great Britain': The 1976 IMF Crisis*. New Haven and London: Yale University Press, 1992, p. 77.
12 Margaret Thatcher, *The Downing Street Years*. London: HarperCollins, 1993, p. 690. See also Philip Stephens, *Politics and the Pound*. London: Macmillan, 1996, pp. 50ff.
13 *Economist*, 25 September 1993.
14 Reported in 'Quotes of the Week', *The Times*, 27 February 1999.
15 BBC Radio 4, 30 September 1998.

10 Managing Decline in a Shrinking World

1 Quoted in Margaret Gowing, *Independence and Deterrence: Britain and Atomic Energy, 1945–52*. London: Macmillan, vol. 1, 1974, p. 229.
2 Clement Attlee, *As It Happened*. New York: Viking Press, 1954.
3 Quoted in Peter Hennessy, *Whitehall*. London: Fontana, 1990, p. 76.
4 Tony Blair, *The Third Way: New Politics for the New Century*. London: Fabian Society Pamphlet No. 588, 1998, p. 18.
5 Anthony King, 'The British Prime Minister in the Age of the Career Politician', *West European Politics*, 24, 2 (1991), p. 37.
6 See John E. Moser, *Twisting the Lion's Tail: Anglophobia in the United States, 1921–48*. London: Macmillan, 2000.
7 Quoted by Richard Crossman, a temporary wartime intelligence official, in 'The Making of Macmillan', *Sunday Telegraph*, 9 February 1964.
8 Margaret Thatcher, *The Downing Street Years*. London: HarperCollins, 1993, pp. 330f.
9 Thatcher, *The Downing Street Years*, p. 792. For an independent view, see one of her advisers, the Hungarian-born George R. Urban, *Diplomacy and Disillusion at the Court of Margaret Thatcher: An Insider's View*. London: I. B. Tauris, 1996, pp. 118ff.

10 Anthony Seldon, *Major: A Political Life*. London: Phoenix, 1998, p. 151. Without irony, Seldon describes Major's ready assent to American policy as making the Prime Minister a 'warlord'.
11 Quoted in Sue Cameron, 'How Well Was Blair Briefed?', *The Times*, 8 April 1999.
12 Mette MacRae, 'London's Standing in International Diplomacy', *International Affairs*, 65, 3 (1989), pp. 508ff.
13 Quoted in Hugo Young, *This Blessed Plot*. London: Macmillan, 1998, p. 13.
14 Quoted in Young, *This Blessed Plot*, p. 64.
15 Compare Dora Gaitskell's comment on the response to her husband's speech by the anti-Gaitskellite left, 'All the wrong people are cheering.' Quoted in Young, *This Blessed Plot*, p. 164.
16 Young, *This Blessed Plot*, p. 114.
17 Quoted in David Butler and Anthony King, *The British General Election of 1964*. London: Macmillan, 1965, p. 17.
18 Edward Heath, *The Course of My Life*. London: Hodder and Stoughton, 1998, chs 3, 13.
19 David Butler and Uwe Kitzinger, *The 1975 Referendum*. London: Macmillan, 1975, p. 176.
20 Thatcher, *The Downing Street Years*, p. 556.
21 Ian Davidson, 'When Blair Said Ghent, Did He Mean Bruges?', *Financial Times*, 18 March 2000.
22 See Arend Lijphart, *Patterns of Democracy*. New Haven: Yale University Press, 1999.
23 For more details and sources for quotations, see Anthony Glees, 'The Diplomacy of Anglo-German Relations: A Study of the ERM Crisis of September, 1992', *German Politics*, 3, 1 (1994), pp. 81ff.
24 Quotations from Charles Bremner, 'How Europe sees Britain', *The Times*, 19 December 1997, and Christopher White, 'Kohl Slaps Down "Lecturer" Blair', *Sunday Times*, 28 December 1997.

11 TONY BLAIR: A POPULIST PRIME MINISTER

1 In an interview with Peter Riddell and Philip Webster, *The Times*, 2 September 1999.
2 In a memorandum to Blair about 'Getting the Right Place in History and Not the Wrong One', leaked to the press in mid-July 2000.
3 Tony Blair, *New Britain: My Vision of a Young Country*. London: Fourth Estate, 1996, p. 54, italics in the original; p. 35.
4 Tony Blair, *The Third Way: New Politics for the New Century*. London: Fabian Society Pamphlet No. 588, 1998, p. 15.
5 'We Work for One Nation, Blair Tells his Party Critics', *Daily Telegraph*, 7 February 2000.

6 Phrases used by the Prime Minister in a confidential memorandum to select Downing Street staff, and quoted in box 11.1.
7 Interviews by Robert Putnam with Labour and Conservative MPs in the 1960s, as quoted in Richard Rose, *Politics in England*. London: Macmillan, 5th edn, 1989, p. 151.
8 For a detailed account of Heath's difficulties in becoming a unifying leader, see David Butler and Dennis Kavanagh, *The British General Election of October, 1974*. London: Macmillan, 1975, p. 257.
9 Mandelson, 'Co-ordinating Government Policy'. Text of speech to the Birmingham University Conference on Modernising the Policy Process, 16 September 1997, p. 2.
10 A comment in Gould's leaked memorandum, 'We Are Too Late on NHS and Soft on Crime', *The Times*, 19 July 2000.
11 Referendums have been held more than once in Scotland, Wales and Northern Ireland, and in Greater London. This does not reflect a commitment to popular sovereignty, for Downing Street has refused to consider an independence referendum for Scotland.
12 Philip Gould, *The Unfinished Revolution*. London: Little, Brown, 1998, p. 326. The book gives a detailed account of the author's motives and methods in developing New Labour focus groups.
13 See e.g. the Gould report leaked and published under the headline, 'We Are Too Late on NHS and Soft on Crime'.
14 See Tom Baldwin, 'No. 10 Censors Website', *The Times*, 18 March 2000; Cathy Newman, 'Online Interview Leaves Blair Off-message', *Financial Times*, 26 October 1999.
15 An unfriendly journalist, Bruce Anderson, claimed that New Labour strategists did not want a television debate because Blair 'was not to be trusted at more than sound bite length'. See Nicholas Jones, *Campaign 1997*. London: Indigo, 1997, p. 176, who gives a detailed account of the breakdown of negotiations.
16 Robert Parker, 'Tuned In to Richard, Judy and Tony', *Financial Times*, 2 February 1999; Nicholas Wood and Carol Midgley, 'Ministers Shun BBC Inquisitors for Chats on Sofa', *The Times*, 27 June 1998.
17 From the Prime Minister's introduction to *The Government's Annual Report 97/98*. London: Stationery Office, 1998, Cm. 3969, p. 6.
18 See information provided by the Prime Minister's Spokesman in the morning Lobby Briefing of 14 July 2000, at www.pm.gov.uk.
19 *The Government's Annual Report, 99/00*. London: Stationery Office, 2000, and www.annualreport.gov.uk.
20 'Vacuous Drivel is Disgrace to Civil Service', *The Times*, 14 July 2000.
21 See Norman Fairclough, *New Labour, New Language?*. London: Routledge, 2000, p. 18. For Fairclough's gloss on the uses of this word, see pp. 35ff.
22 'Blair's Third Way to Elected Dictatorship', *Sunday Times*, 20 September 1998.

23 Graham Wallas, *Human Nature in Politics*. London: Constable, 1908.
24 Peter Oborne, *Alastair Campbell: New Labour and the Rise of the Media Class*. London: Aurum Press, 1999, p. 5.
25 Blair, *The Third Way*, p. 1.
26 Blair uses an old-fashioned English spelling in advocating what the *Oxford English Dictionary* and his American friends would call modernization.
27 The term 'modernising' appears in ten of the first fifteen lines of Blair's foreword to the Prime Minister and Cabinet Office, *Modernising Government*. London: Stationery Office, Cm. 4310, 1999, p. 7.
28 An anonymous academic quoted in Robert Taylor, 'Chattering Against Mr Blair', *Spectator*, 19 April 1997.
29 A leaked memorandum from Philip Gould to Alastair Campbell, reported in *The Times*, 12 June 2000. It was commenting on a draft of Tony Blair's disastrous speech to the annual meeting of the Women's Institute.
30 Anatole Kaletsky, 'Well Done for Making Tony Blair Say Sorry', *The Times*, 28 September 2000.
31 Quoted in Philip Webster and Roland Watson, 'Unions Won't Haunt Me, Says Blair', *The Times*, 29 September 2000.
32 Matthew Parris went on to add, 'But it was the passion of an actor, not so much deceitful as self-induced. Blair's is the best kind of actor, where the performer gets right inside the part, believing in and for a while, becoming the persona he has taken.' 'Prime Minister Works Up a Sweat over Core Values', *The Times*, 27 September 2000.

12   What Comes After Blair?

1 André Siegfried, *England's Crisis*. London: Jonathan Cape, 1931, p. 303.
2 For the most sustained statement of this argument, see Michael Foley, *The Rise of the British Presidency*. Manchester: Manchester University Press, 2nd edn, 2000.
3 Quoted in Richard Rose, *The Post-Modern President*. Chatham, NJ: Chatham House, 2nd edn, 1991.
4 See Richard Rose and Ezra Suleiman, eds, *Presidents and Prime Ministers*. Washington DC: American Enterprise Institute, 1980; George W. Jones, ed., *West European Prime Ministers*. London: Frank Cass, 1991; and articles in Richard Rose, ed., 'Democratic Reform in International Perspective', *Parliamentary Affairs*, 53, 4 (2000).
5 A. V. Dicey, *The Law and the Constitution*. London: Macmillan, 1910 edn, p. 39.
6 See Foley, *The Politics of the British Constitution*, table 2.1.

7 Eric Roll, quoted in Michael Wolff, 'Governing Great Britain Ltd.', *The Times*, 31 May 1976.
8 House of Commons, *Hansard*, 30 October 1990, reporting proposals put by Jacques Delors at a meeting of the European Union Council of Ministers in Rome.
9 'Diary Column', *The Times*, 10 March 2000.
10 Percy Cradock, *In Pursuit of Britain's Interests*. London: John Murray, 1997, p. 206.
11 Bureau of the Census, *Statistical Abstract of the United States 1994*. Washington DC: Government Printing Office, table 18.
12 Quoted in Timothy Garton-Ash, 'Britain? Where's Britain?', *Independent*, 9 June 1994. The words have gained even more immediacy since the capital of Germany has moved from Bonn to Berlin.
13 For a detailed example of the concept of a domestic foreign policy, see Richard Rose, 'The Relation of Socialist Principles to Labour Government Foreign Policy, 1945–51', Oxford, DPhil thesis, 1960.
14 National Opinion Polls survey of 1,921 respondents, 17–23 March 1995.
15 *Gallup Political and Economic Index*, No. 390, February, 1993, p. 42.
16 Robert Peston, 'Blair Pledges Fresh Start in Europe', *Financial Times*, 10 May 1997.
17 See the Prime Minister's leaked memo, 'Standing up for Britain', and the leaked memo attributed to Greenberg and Gould, 'Why Labour is Losing the Euro Argument', both printed in *The Times*, 27 July 2000.

Index

Abrams, Mark 118f
Acheson, Dean 197
acquis communitaire 249
advisors, political 37–42, 138
ambition 14f, 69–85, 152, 157, 166–74
Anglo-Iranian Oil Company 28
Annual Report of the Blair government 223f
apprenticeship 70–85
Armstrong, Robert 90
Armstrong, William 130, 198
Asquith, H. H. 22
Attlee, Clement 1, 15, 19, 28, 36, 53, 62, 69ff, 86f, 90–2, 117f, 131ff, 158, 161ff, 170, 179, 198, 200, 202, 228, 252

Bagehot, Walter 1, 15, 233
Baldwin, Stanley 132
Balfour, A. J. 69ff
Balogh, Thomas 38
Beaverbrook, Lord 84, 87
Benn, Tony 32, 119, 161f, 171
Berlin Wall 204
Bevan, Aneurin 76, 83, 118, 157ff, 165, 179, 202
Bevin, Ernest 141, 161, 170, 198, 206
Birch, Nigel 180

Blair, Tony 1ff, 18, 21ff, 39–42, 51, 63, 68ff, 88, 97, 100ff, 120, 123, 134ff, 143, 148, 151, 156ff, 169–74, 177, 185ff, 198ff, 214–32, 233ff, 239ff, 258
Blairism 151
Blake, Lord 55
Blatcherism 143–51
bleeper 104, 139
Board of Trade, President of 74
Boothroyd, Betty 138f
Braddock, Bessie 1
British Broadcasting Corporation 86–109
Brown, George 76, 165
Brown, Gordon 35, 161, 174, 177, 195, 210, 231
Bush, President George 204
Butler, David 109
Butler, David and Stokes, Donald 113f
Butler, R. A. 75f, 144–7, 180
Butskellism 143–51
by-elections 124f

Cabinet 15, 25, 73–7, 103, 152–74
Callaghan, Jim 5ff, 19f, 29, 47, 57, 71ff, 91, 97, 134ff, 146, 154, 161f, 170f, 176f, 183, 191, 208f, 256

Index

campaigning at elections 116–20
Campbell, Alastair 35, 41, 58, 88, 100–9, 167, 172f, 215, 220, 222f, 226
Castle, Barbara 131, 153
Cecil, Lord Hugh 55
Central Policy Review Staff (CPRS) 38
charismatic leader 60
Charles I, King 85
Chatham, Earl of 147
Chirac, President Jacques 237
Churchill, Winston 1, 16, 26f, 28, 34, 37, 46, 52, 60–2, 69ff, 86, 94, 117, 134ff, 157, 163, 176, 180, 197, 200ff, 253
civil servants 37–42
Clark, David 105
Clarke, Kenneth 77, 79, 165
class 114
Clinton, President Bill 120, 220
collective responsibility 153
Colman, Prentis & Varley (CPV) 118
consensus politics 144, 212–16
constitution 15, 53ff, 240ff
Cook, Robin 161, 174, 250
Cousins, Frank 175
Cripps, Stafford 161, 179
Cromwell, Oliver 12
Crosland, Tony 156, 161, 165
Crossman, R. H. S. 16, 158ff
Crowe, Sir Eyre 197

Dalton, Hugh 161, 179
Day, Robin 88, 208f
de Gaulle, President Charles 207, 237
Delors, Jacques 24
Deutsche Mark 192–6
devaluation 190–6, 246
Diana, Princess 6, 58, 115
Dicey, A. V. 24
Donoughue, Bernard 38

Douglas-Home, Alec 3f, 71ff, 98, 100, 119, 136, 181, 255

Ecclestone, Bernard 58
Eden, Anthony 4, 20, 48, 71ff, 88, 90, 123, 134ff, 180, 202, 206, 253
Eisenhower, Dwight D. 202
elections 24f, 82, 110–29, 239ff
Empire 48, 64, 197ff
Ethelred II, the Unready 57f
euro 33, 190–6, 210–15, 221, 247–51
European Exchange Rate Mechanism (ERM) 193
European Monetary Union (EMU) *see* euro
European Union 7, 21, 34, 49–52, 67, 207ff, 243, 245–9
events 30, 56–9
Exchequer, Chancellor of the 17, 74, 160f, 176ff
expectations 21–3

Falconer, Lord 30, 163, 226
Falkender, Lady *see* Williams, Marcia
Falkland Islands war 58, 129, 203
federalism 213
Field, Frank 105
Foot, Michael 76, 78, 83, 161
Foreign Secretary 74, 161
France 189, 236–43
Freedom of Information Act 104

Gaitskell, Hugh 76, 111, 118, 143–7, 179, 206
Germany 33f, 50, 66, 189, 204
Glendower 32ff, 244
Gorbachev, Mikhail 204
Gordon Walker, Patrick 168
Gould, Philip 6, 25, 100, 148, 217, 220ff, 230, 250
Government of National Unity 219

Greenberg, Stanley 250
Grenada 203
Grimond, Jo 80f

Hague, William 74, 139
Hailsham, Lord 33
Haines, Joe 96, 105
Haley, William 87
Harris, Robert 150, 226
Healey, Denis 161
Heath, Ted 4, 20f, 26, 48, 71ff, 98f, 120f, 134ff, 155, 183, 207, 208, 214, 219, 256
Hennessy, Peter 22
Heseltine, Michael 80, 84, 101, 165
Hewitt, Patricia 101
Heywood, Jeremy 35
Hill, Dr Charles 1
Hong Kong 64, 204
Howard, Anthony 69
Howe, Geoffrey 165, 193
Humphrys, John 223
Hurd, Douglas 35, 38f, 165, 246

incomes policies 182ff
India 200f
inflation 180–8
Ingham, Bernard 88, 94f, 105
intermestic policies 10, 48–52, 211–15
International Monetary Fund 48, 170f, 191
involuntary exits 81–5
Iraq 204
irreversible structural change 63–8
Irvine, Lord 30, 35
Israel 243

Japan 33f, 51, 66, 189
Jay, Lady 163
Jenkins, Roy 80, 99, 156, 161
Johnson, Lyndon 152

Joseph, Keith 162
Jospin, Lionel 239

Kaletsky, Anatole 231
Kaufman, Gerald 38, 83, 96
Kennedy, President John F. 203
Keswick, W. J. 175
Keynes, J. M. 47, 61f, 179, 186
Khrushchev, Nikita 202
Kinnock, Neil 83, 97
Kohl, Chancellor Helmut 214
Kuwait 204

Lamont, Norman 153, 194, 214, 246
Laski, Harold 63, 131
Lawson, Nigel 58, 80, 156, 165, 168f, 193
Levy, Lord 163
Liberal party leader 127f
Liddle, Roger 89
Liverpool, Earl of 239
Livingstone, Ken 45, 151, 234
Lloyd George, David 36, 69
Lloyd-Hughes, Trevor 95f
lobby 92–5
longue durée 63f
Lord President of the Council 161
Lords, House of 163f

Macdonald, Lord 163
MacDonald, Ramsay 158ff
Mace 1
McKenzie, Robert T. 62
Macleod, Iain 76
Macmillan, Harold 4ff, 20, 26, 37, 56ff, 65, 109, 116ff, 134ff, 166, 180f, 198, 200, 202f, 207, 254
Major, John 5ff, 20, 39, 49, 63, 71ff, 81, 86, 97f, 123, 134ff, 152f, 165ff, 176, 185ff, 193ff, 204f, 210, 239, 257

Mandelson, Peter 35, 39, 42, 100f, 139, 148ff, 150, 163, 172, 174, 219f, 222, 250
Margach, James 93
Marshall, General George 201
Marx, Groucho 14, 247
Maudling, Reginald 79
Mayhew, Christopher 56, 119
maze 17
Melbourne, Lord 153, 163
Mellor, David 171
Meyer, Christopher 104
Miliband, David 35, 172f, 227
millennium 57, 128
Mills, Lord 163
ministers 73–5, 103f, 152–74
monarchy 242f
monetarism 185–96
Morgan, Rhodri 45
Morley, John 15
Morris, Dick 88, 220
Morrison, Herbert 76, 130, 179, 206
Mowlam, Mo 105, 173
Murdoch, Rupert 102f

Napoleon 152
Neustadt, Richard 14, 22f
Nixon, President Richard 102
North, Lord 12
North Atlantic Treaty Organization (NATO) 47, 201f
Northern Ireland 33, 43ff, 58f, 234
nuclear deterrent 202f

Official Secrets Act 90f
opinion polls 18, 118f, 121–9
Opposition, Leader of 127f
Owen, David 148, 165

Palestine 201
Parkinson, Cecil 80, 169
patronage 157
Patten, John 63

Paxman, Jeremy 223
Peel, Sir Robert 3, 55
personality 59–61, 112–16, 123f
petrol taxes 188, 213, 230
Pickwick, Mr 110
Plowden, Lord 91
Policy Unit, Downing Street 38f
political business cycle 61f
political capital 14–23
populism 216–32
pound 188–96
Powell, Enoch 180
Powell, Jonathan 35, 41, 69–85
power-sharing 212–15
President, hypothetical British 236–45
President, France 236–42
President, United States 14, 33, 70, 236–42
press secretary 95ff
Prior, Jim 162
privatization 185
Privy Council oath 22
Profumo, John 58

Questions, Parliamentary 136–9

Reagan, President Ronald 203
referendum 221, 249f
Riddell, Peter 224
Rodgers, William 191
Reith, Lord 93–6
reshuffling Cabinet posts 164ff
Robinson, Geoffrey 42
roles of Prime Minister 22–31
Rosebery, Lord 3
Royal Commission 28f

Salisbury, Marquess of 158
Sawyer, Tom 150
Schröder, Gerhard 188
Schuman, Robert 206
Schwarzkopf, General Norman 205

Scotland 33, 43ff, 234
Scottish National Party 248
Scowcroft, Brent 192
Seitz, Raymond 245
selection of party leader 75ff
Short, Clare 42, 138
Siegfried, André 233
Single Europe Market 209f
Smith, John 75, 100
Social Democratic Party 113, 115, 148
Soley, Clive 42
Stalin, Josef 46
subsidiarity 213
Suez Canal 20, 138, 202
Summers, Larry 227
Sun, The 107
Supermac 89

Tebbit, Norman 99, 162
television 6f, 86–109, 223, 236ff
Thatcher, Denis 37
Thatcher, Margaret 4ff, 18, 21ff, 36, 39, 49, 58ff, 67ff, 91, 97f, 120, 123, 134ff, 147–51, 158, 162ff, 176, 185f, 192ff, 198ff, 209, 225, 239, 257
Thatcherism 147–51, 185f, 228
Third Way 228–32
Thorneycroft, Peter 180
Thorpe, Jeremy 166
time constraints 17, 27
Tizard, Henry 197f
Tomlinson, George 163
touchstone issues 226, 229

Treasury 17, 55, 74, 160f, 176ff
trouble, keeping out of 27–9
Truman, President Harry 46, 48, 201, 240

unemployment 180–8
unions 181ff
United States of America 50, 66, 200ff, 236–42

value added tax 186
Varley, Eric 130
Victoria, Queen 2ff, 67
Vinson, Fred 47
voters 112–29

Wales 33, 43ff, 234
Walker, Peter 165
Wallas, Graham 110, 227
Walpole, Sir Robert 3
Walters, Alan 58, 193
Whelan, Charlie 42
whips 139–43
Whitelaw, William 80, 162, 169
wicked issues 31
Williams, Francis 92
Williams, Marcia 38, 132, 196
Wilson, Harold 3ff, 19, 25, 48, 53, 60, 71ff, 95ff, 119ff, 134ff, 142, 154ff, 162ff, 181ff, 202, 208, 228, 245, 255
Wilson, Richard 41f
Women's Institute 108, 218
Wood, David 93
Wyatt, Woodrow 119